The English
Amongst the Persians

Early British envoys to the Qajar Court (supposedly, L. to R., Ouseley, Jones and Malcolm). From a contemporary copy, *circa* 1826, of a large wall painting once in the Negarestan Palace, Tehran. By courtesy of the India Office Library and Records.

DENIS WRIGHT

The English Amongst the Persians

*Imperial Lives
in Nineteenth-Century Iran*

I.B.Tauris *Publishers*
LONDON • NEW YORK

Revised paperback published in 2001 by I.B.Tauris & Co Ltd
6 Salem Road, London W2 4BU
175 Fifth Avenue, New York NY 10010
www.ibtauris.com

In the United States of America and in Canada distributed by
St Martins Press, 175 Fifth Avenue, New York NY 10010

Copyright © Denis Wright, 1977, 2001

All rights reserved. Except for brief quotations in a review, this book, or any part thereof, may not be reproduced, stored in or introduced into a retrieval system, or transmitted, in any form or by any means, electronic, mechanical, photocopying, recording or otherwise, without the prior written permission of the publisher.

ISBN 1 86064 638 7

A full CIP record for this book is available from the British Library
A full CIP record for this book is available from the Library of Congress

Library of Congress catalog card: available

Printed and bound in Great Britain by Mackays of Chatham

CONTENTS

Illustrations	vi
Preface to the 2nd Edition	ix
Preface	xi
Acknowledgements	xiv
Map	xvi
Chapter 1 The British Interest in Persia	1
Chapter 2 The Diplomatic Scene	12
Chapter 3 Formalities and Frictions	32
Chapter 4 Wars and Warriors	49
Chapter 5 Uncrowned King of the Persian Gulf	62
Chapter 6 Consuls, Khans and Communities	75
Chapter 7 The World of Business	94
Chapter 8 Missionaries and Doctors	113
Chapter 9 The Electric Telegraph and other Innovations	128
Chapter 10 Frontier Makers	139
Chapter 11 Some Travellers	149
Chapter 12 World War I and the End of an Era	171
Appendices: I The Qajar Shahs	187
II British Envoys to Persia during the Qajar Period	188
III British Residents at Bushire during the Qajar Period	190
IV British Consular Posts in 1921	192
References	193
Bibliography	201
Index	211

ILLUSTRATIONS

Early British envoys to the Qajar Court   *frontispiece*

Between pages 46 and 47

Major-General Sir John Malcolm
Sir Harford Jones Brydges
Sir Harford Jones Brydges' coat of arms
Major-General Sir Henry Lindesay-Bethune
Mr Charles Alison

Between pages 78 and 79

The British Legation and the Minister's Residence, Tehran; the Minister's summer Residence, Gulhek
The great *bast*, Tehran, 1906
The battle of Khoshab and the bombardment of Mohammerah, 1857
The British Consulate-General, Mashad

Between pages 110 and 111

The Consul's *sowar* escort
Memorials in the old Armenian Church, Tehran
The Imperial Bank of Persia

The English Amongst the Persians

The Telegraph Station at Jask; stamps of the British-Indian post offices in Persia

Between pages 142 and 143

Sir Henry Layard

Bridge on the 'Lynch' road between Ahwaz and Isfahan; road-making near Hamadan; transporting oil pipe line, Khuzistan

The South Persia Rifles; Dunsterforce on the march

Persian levies, 1918

To
my Iranian friends
with the sincere wish that
the progress and prosperity
which have marked
the first half century
of Pahlavi rule
will long continue

PREFACE to the 2nd Edition

Public interest in Anglo-Iranian relations is, I believe, greater today than it ever was in 1977 when this book was first published. I am delighted, therefore, that it should now appear in paperback when travellers to Iran are increasing in numbers and when, after a number of difficult years, full diplomatic relations with Britain have been restored.

Knowledge of past history, especially during the Qajar period (1787-1925) which coincided with the heyday of British imperialism, is essential for an understanding of the complexities that still underlie Anglo-Iranian relations. It is my hope that this book will contribute in a modest way to this understanding.

Until the Qajars came to power at the end of the 18th century Britain's only interest in the country had been trade, then in the exclusive hands of the East India Company operating from their base at Bushire on the Persian Gulf. However, by the turn of the century the Honourable Company's territorial acquisitions in India had added an over-riding political dimension to Britain's interest in Iran, now seen as an outer bastion in the defence of its growing Indian empire. A century later oil – discovered, developed and owned by the British – enhanced Iran's importance for Britain, especially after the Royal Navy changed from coal to oil to fire their ships.

For Britain a Persia (as Iran was known in the West until the 1930's) "friendly to Great Britain and independent of foreign control" (page 10) thus became a fixation in its foreign policy. In order to protect Iran, first from the ambitions of Napoleonic France, then from Tsarist Russia and eventually from the Communist Soviet Union, Britain often rode rough-shod over Iranian sensibilities and interests. In doing so "the English" (as all Britons were known) left on many Iranian minds feelings of awe, *resentment* and distrust rather than affection – *awe* for British power and might together with a wildly exaggerated belief in British cleverness and ingenuity; resentment that the British were all too inclined, as the Iranian Foreign Minister told Lord Curzon in 1919, "not to treat Persians on equal terms"; *distrust* because Britain was seen to have reneged on treaty obligations

Preface

negotiated with Fath Ali Shah, had forced Iran to abandon its historic claims to Herat and had ignored Iran's declared neutrality in World War I. In Iranian eyes Curzon's cherished Anglo-Persian Agreement of 1919 was an unwanted take-over of their country. Worst of all, though, had been the Anglo-Russian Convention of 1907 – a successful attempt by Britain and Russia to settle their worldwide differences – but which, by dividing Iran into spheres of influence, was seen by Iranians as a betrayal. This destroyed at a stroke the immense goodwill created by the great *bast* of July and August 1906 when between twelve and fourteen thousand Iranians – mullahs, merchants, shopkeepers etc – sought asylum in the British Legation's capacious compound and, by paralysing, the life of the capital, forced the Shah to grant Iran its first constitution.

Much has changed since then. During Reza Shah's reign (1925-41) the British lost their privileged position in Iran; India became independent in 1947; Dr Mossadeq nationalised the oil industry in 1951. And of course after the Iranian Revolution Britain's contracts with Iran were severely curtailed. Yet in some Persian minds old feelings about the English still linger. In recording the historical background of Anglo-Iranian relations I aimed to explain the genesis of these feelings to my Persian and English readers. The publication of this paperback edition will, I hope, contribute to this end.

Denis Wright

PREFACE

IT WAS NOT until 1941 in the course of World War II, when I was British Vice-Consul in the Black Sea port of Trebizond, that I met my first Persian. He was Mr A. Riazi, grandly described on his visiting card as '*Ier Secrétaire et Chancelier du Consulat Impérial de l'Iran*'. There, in that beautiful but remote Turkish port, where the Turks themselves were notoriously suspicious of all foreigners and where the minuscule European community consisted solely of our official enemies or timid neutrals, my wife and I, apart from my Maltese clerk who had never set foot outside Turkey, were the only two British subjects. We felt very isolated. Riazi Bey, as we called him, and his plump, cheerful, English-speaking wife, were among our few friends and provided welcome companionship and our first introduction to the Persians.

It was also in Trebizond that, to while away the long, lonely evenings, I explored the old consular files dating back to 1830 when the Foreign Office first appointed a Vice-Consul there with the object of promoting British exports to Persia via the ancient caravan route which led from Trebizond, across what was once known as Armenia, to Tabriz. As a result of my researches I wrote a piece entitled *Trebizond and the Persian Transit Trade* which I asked the Foreign Office to allow me to publish. While agreeing, they stole my clothes by publishing it themselves as 'Foreign Office Print', the first time any effort of mine had achieved this distinction.

I had all but forgotten these tenuous links with Persia when in late 1953 I was unexpectedly called upon to fly from London to Tehran with a small team to re-establish diplomatic relations with Iran, broken for more than a year as a result of our bitter quarrel with Dr Mussadeq over the nationalisation of the Iranian oil industry, then in British hands. It was an exciting assignment and, as it proved, a rewarding one since both the British and Persian peoples, like estranged lovers, knew they could not really live one without the other. It was therefore not difficult to promote a happy reunion and pave the way for the appoint-

The English Amongst the Persians

ment in February 1954 of Sir Roger Stevens as Ambassador to Iran—a post I was lucky enough myself to fill some nine years later. I was lucky, too, in that I remained in Iran from 1963 until my retirement from Her Majesty's Diplomatic Service in 1971.

My experiences in Iran during these years filled me with a great love for the country and her people. They also taught me that Anglo-Iranian relations are infinitely more complex than I had ever imagined from my reading or from my talks with Riazi Bey and his wife in Trebizond. The relationship between our two countries has sometimes been described in psychological terms as one of love-hate. A contemporary American observer claims that 'nowhere in the world is British cleverness so wildly exaggerated as in Iran, and nowhere are the British more hated for it' (1). Be that as it may, I myself soon became aware during my service in Iran that, despite our weakened position in the world, the British did enjoy a special position in the minds of both high and low and that we were often, without any logical reason, given either credit or (more usually) blame for developments and events beyond our ken. The Shah himself has told in his *Mission for my Country* how, when during World War II he invited Dr Mussadeq to become Prime Minister, the latter said that he would first need British approval. 'What about the Russians?' asked the Shah, to which Mussadeq replied 'Oh, they don't count. It is the British who decide everything in this country' (2). That belief still lingers on.

Why so? The answer must be sought in past history or, more precisely, in the Qajar period which covers the nineteenth century and ends for all practical purposes with Reza Khan's 1921 *coup d'état*, although it was not until 1925 that the last of the Qajars was deposed and Reza Khan became Reza Shah Pahlavi, the founder of a new dynasty in Persia's long and chequered history.

This Qajar period was largely dominated by intense Anglo-Russian rivalry for influence in Persia, inspired on the one hand by Russia's steady expansion into the Caucasus and Central Asia and, on the other, by Britain's concern for the defence of India which she believed would be gravely jeopardised should Persia fall under Russian domination. In these circumstances the weakness of the Qajar rulers invited interference from the two rival Powers, both of whom frequently acted with little consideration for Persian feelings or interests. British power and influence, then at its height, was exerted from London and from India. When later, in the face of the growing menace from Germany, we sought to compose our differences with Russia in the Anglo-Russian Convention of 31 August 1907 and agreed, *inter alia*, on the division of Persia into British and Russian spheres of influence, with a neutral

Preface

zone between, Persian indignation and distrust of Britain reached its height. Firuz Kazemzadeh, an Iranian scholar writing in 1968, considers that 'it was in September 1907 that the modern Persian image of England crystallized. . . . Justifiably or not, most Persians would, from then on, be prepared to believe only the worst of England' (3). Indeed, as Sir Percy Loraine later wrote from Tehran, this Russian alliance was 'a millstone hung round our necks' during World War I (4) and—he might have added—would be for years to come. Memories are long in Persia.

In this volume I am not concerned to describe or defend the diplomatic struggle and subsequent accord between Britain and Russia. Both must, however, be borne in mind as background in my attempt to record what I can of the multifarious activities—and their impact on the Persians—of the British in Persia at this time.

My title is part-borrowed from a famous work by the most honoured of all Englishmen amongst the Persians, the late Professor E. G. Browne, a great Persian scholar and champion of Persian causes. I am fully conscious that many of those of whom I write have names—Malcolm, Jones, Lindsay, Sheil, McNeill, Murray and so on—which are anything but English, but the fact remains that in those far off days they were all known as 'the English' and no more resented this than to-day's Iranian resents our obstinate British habit of continuing to call his country by its old European name of Persia.

ACKNOWLEDGEMENTS

BUT FOR THE encouragement of Professor Ann Lambton of the University of London and Professor Rose Greaves of the University of Kansas I should probably never have begun, let alone completed, this book. I also owe them both an immense debt of gratitude for much help and advice.

Others who have been generous with their time and specialist knowledge of the Persian scene are Stephen Bach, Michael Burrell, Gordon Calver, Ronald Ferrier, Edward Fraser-Smith, John Gurney, Donald Hawley, Basil Robinson, Floreeda Safiri, Wilfred Seager, Roger Stevens, Jennifer Scarce, Gordon Waterfield and Robin Waterfield. In its early stages I planned this book with Stephen Bach, the intention being that he would contribute one or two chapters about the Persians in England during the Qajar period. In the end we decided that this fascinating subject, on which Mr Bach spent much time, required separate treatment: nevertheless he continued to take a keen and very helpful interest in my own efforts.

In my quest for information about the British in Qajar Persia I have been helped by a number of their descendants—Mrs Suzanne Addison, Miss Philippa Bateman-Champain, Mr Bernard Bevan, Mrs J. F. Burton, Lord Denman, Lord Garnock, Mrs Raleigh Gilbert, Mr Lionel Harford, Lord Ironside, Mr Peter Johnson, the late Lieutenant-Commander John Lucas-Scudamore, Mr Antony Moore, Lady Morland, Sir Shapur Reporter, Mr Bruno Schroder and Mr Frank Sykes. I am also grateful to Mr Hosein Ali Qaragozlu for information about his father, Nasir ul-Mulk, the first Persian to study at Oxford: and to other Persian friends for their help.

My thanks are due to the following for permission to quote from papers whose copyright they hold:

> The Controller of H.M. Stationery Office from records in the Public Record Office and the India Office Library and Records.

The English Amongst the Persians

The Church Missionary Society from their archives.
The Librarian, the National Library of Wales, from the Kentchurch papers.
Mrs E. Murray from the papers of Sir Charles Murray.
The Lord Ironside from the papers of the 1st Baron Ironside.
Sir Anthony Rumbold from the papers of Sir Horace Rumbold.
The Marquess of Salisbury from the papers of the 3rd Marquess of Salisbury.

My enquiries took me to the Indian Institute, the Bodleian Library and St Antony's Middle East Centre at Oxford: to the Public Record Office, the Foreign and Commonwealth Office Library and Records, the India Office Library and Records, the Imperial War Museum, the National Army Museum and the Church Missionary Society in London: to the National Library of Scotland and the Scottish Record Office in Edinburgh: and to the National Library of Wales in Aberystwyth. I am grateful to the staff at each of these places for help and guidance which made research a pleasure: to Hilary Bullard, Teresa Fitzherbert and Rex Carslake for their researches on my behalf: to Elizabeth Monroe and Gertrude Williams for some invaluable advice about style: to Desmond Harney for the photographs he took at my request: and to Dr A. B. Emden, friend and mentor since my Oxford days, for his eagle-eyed proof-reading.

Nearer home, I am very grateful to two neighbours, Barbara Lumb and Joyce Deacon, for much help, cheerfully given, in typing and re-typing, copying and re-copying my manuscript; and, above all, to my wife, Iona, for her encouragement and patience.

D.A.H.W.
Haddenham, Buckinghamshire.
November 1976.

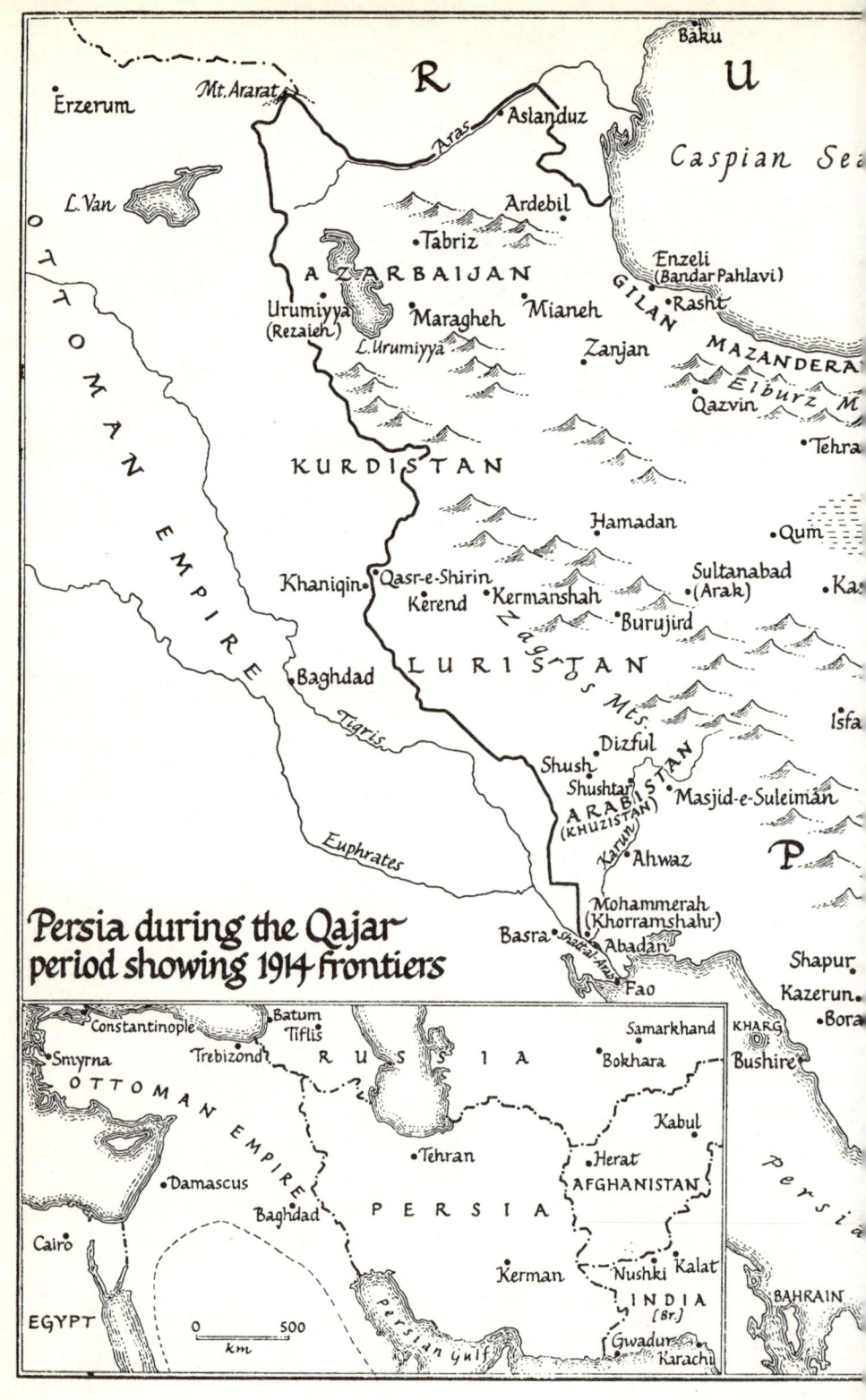

I

The British Interest in Persia

UNTIL THE EARLY nineteenth century Britain's interests in Persia were not considered of sufficient importance to justify the establishment there of a permanent diplomatic mission. Generally speaking, Persia was regarded as a remote, fabulous country, difficult of access, of some commercial but minor political importance.

Little was known of Persia's immense size and her great contrasts of scenery and climate. She lay isolated behind the high walls of the Zagros mountains to the south and west and of the Elburz to the north: to the east desert and stark hills merged with the sands of Afghanistan and Baluchistan. A traveller entering the country by way of Russia and the Caspian Sea would be impressed by the dense jungle and forests that clothed the hills along the Caspian shore: if he first landed in the south at one of the Persian Gulf ports he would note the barrenness and immense heat of the palm-fringed coastal plains. Only after climbing steep mountain passes to the high central plateau would he find himself in the heart of Persia. Here he would discover a great expanse of salt and sandy desert around whose edges lay oasis towns and villages of sun-dried brick and flat roofs, against which the green of slender poplars and tall walnut and plane trees stood in vivid contrast. Water, a perennial problem, was brought to them in long underground conduits or *qanats* whose lines, like a series of giant ant-heaps, ran across the desert from the surrounding hills where the water had accumulated. In summer the heat was great everywhere but on the plateau the air was dry and the nights cool: in winter snow fell and blocked the mountain passes. The sun seemed to shine the year through in a cloudless sky and gave a crystalline quality to the light of the plateau.

Contact between Britain and Persia over the centuries had been intermittent and transitory, decades often passing between one mission or visitor and the next. The earliest recorded visitor from England to

The English Amongst the Persians

Persia was Geoffrey de Langley sent by Edward I in 1290 to seek the Mongol King Arghun's aid against the Turks. A similar, but equally unsuccessful, appeal for assistance against the Turks was made some three hundred years later by the brothers Anthony and Robert Shirley; Robert remained several years at the Persian Court and is entitled to be regarded as the first of a long line of European advisers to a country which to this day makes considerable use of western expertise. Another Elizabethan to visit Safavid Persia was Sir Anthony Jenkinson of the Muscovy Company who saw Shah Tahmasp at his capital, Qazvin, in 1562 but failed to obtain the commercial treaty which was the main object of his journey. He was followed four years later by Arthur Edwards and Richard Watts who succeeded in securing the Shah's permission for British merchants to trade in his territories; but neither these, nor subsequent missions, such as those of Sir Dodmore Cotton in 1628 and Jonas Hanway in 1743, stayed long in the country.

The first British settlements in Persia date from the early seventeenth century when the East India Company, from their base at Surat on the west coast of India, began trading in the Persian Gulf and sent a British vessel, the *James*, in December 1616 to Jask on the Makran coast of Persia. Two years later the Company opened a 'factory' or trading post at this blisteringly hot little port, whence merchandise from England and India was sent overland to Shiraz and Isfahan, the splendid new capital of Shah Abbas I, where they also established factories.

In 1622 the East India Company were constrained to help Shah Abbas expel their commercial rivals, the Portuguese, from the latter's fortified trading station on Hormuz Island, a few miles off the Persian coast opposite the port of Gombroon. The port was renamed Bandar Abbas after the victorious Shah who now allowed the Company to set up their headquarters there. Bandar Abbas remained the East India Company's main centre of activity in the Persian Gulf until 1763 when, because of the disturbed state of the countryside and its increasing isolation from the rest of the country, it was abandoned in favour of Basra, then in Ottoman Turkish territory, at the head of the Gulf. In the same year the Shaikh of Bushire signed an agreement with the Company permitting them to establish a factory at Bushire. This was built at the expense of the Shaikh who also provided the Company with a garden and burial ground. The Persian ruler, Kerim Khan, confirmed the agreement in a royal decree or *farman* which gave the Company a privileged trading position in the Persian Gulf—no customs duties were to be collected on goods imported or exported by them, they alone could import woollen goods, and their employees were not to be taxed or interfered with. In 1778 the Company transferred their headquarters

The British Interest in Persia

from Basra to Bushire which from then on became the principal British centre, both commercial and political, in the Persian Gulf.

In those early days the British had no diplomatic representative in Persia: any official business that might arise was conducted by the East India Company's own agents. These men, representing the Governor-General of India* were received by the Shah and his officials at Isfahan, Shiraz and Tehran, each in turn the Persian capital.†

The East India Company's original interest in Persia had been exclusively commercial. But as their territorial acquisitions and responsibilities in India increased so concern grew about the threat to their possessions from external enemies: Persia, on India's western threshold, assumed a new-found importance in the eyes of those concerned in London and Calcutta with the Company's affairs. Afghanistan, France and Russia in turn appeared to threaten the British hold on India and provoked reactions which, from 1798 onwards, were to involve the British to an ever increasing extent in Persia. Henceforth, though they never lost sight of the trading opportunities, the primary British interest in the country was—and remained so until well into the present century—to maintain its independence and integrity as a vital element in the defence of their Indian Empire.

Although the Afghan and French threats were relatively short-lived they are important as signalling a new era in Anglo-Persian relations. They, rather than incipient fears of Russia, led to the signature of the first treaties between Britain and Persia, the despatch of a fully-fledged military mission to help train the Persian army, and the establishment of permanent diplomatic relations. However, by the early 1830s London and Calcutta had become increasingly concerned with the threat to India from Russia's expansionist policies: henceforth this danger became almost an obsession in British imperial thinking.

The first threat to India came from the Afghan ruler Zeman Shah's Punjab ambitions. In order to divert his attention Lord Wellesley,‡ the

---

* Until the Crown took over after the Indian Mutiny in 1857 day to day responsibility for Indian affairs rested with the E.I.C. acting through the Governor-General in Calcutta. He was appointed by the E.I.C., though, from 1784 onwards, his appointment and policies were subject to the approval of a Board of Control in London. In practice, owing to the slowness of communications, he went very much his own—and the Company's—way.

† Agha Muhammad, the first of the Qajars, made Tehran his capital in 1788. Having killed off the last of the Zand dynasty and defeated the Russians, he had been proclaimed Shah the previous year. The Qajars were a large tribe of Turkish origin inhabiting northeast Persia.

‡ Richard Wellesley, 1st Marquess, Earl of Mornington (1760–1842). Governor-General of India 1798–1805: Foreign Secretary 1809–12: Lord Lieutenant of Ireland 1821–8 and 1833–4. Elder brother of the 1st Duke of Wellington.

The English Amongst the Persians

Governor-General, sent the East India Company's acting Resident at Bushire, Mehdi Ali Khan, to Tehran in 1798 to stir up trouble between the Afghans and the Persians whom he was to encourage to attack Herat, the old Persian city then in Afghan hands. The fact that the Governor-General's envoy to the Shah of Persia was a naturalised British subject of Persian descent probably mattered little in those early days of Anglo-Persian diplomacy but in the coming years the Persian Government would increasingly resent the use the British made of Persians in their employ.

An additional threat now appeared in the shape of Napoleon's eastern ambitions: after his invasion of Egypt in 1798 it seemed possible that he might invade India through Persia. The Government of India therefore decided to follow up Mehdi Ali Khan's mission with an immensely more impressive diplomatic display under one of their ablest young officers, thirty year old Captain John Malcolm. One of seventeen children of a small Eskdale farmer, Malcolm had been commissioned by the East India Company at the early age of thirteen (hence his life-long nickname 'Boy'), spoke Persian, and had already made his mark in India. He and a large entourage arrived by sea from Bombay at Bushire in February 1800. They remained there nearly four months, arguing with the Persians over points of protocol and arranging for the long and arduous 740-mile trek to Tehran by way of Shiraz and Isfahan, then and for some years to come the principal road used by British travellers to the Qajar capital. When Malcolm eventually set off from Bushire his retinue was over five hundred strong: apart from a number of British officers it included a military escort of nearly one hundred Indian cavalry and infantrymen, almost as many Indian servants and well over three hundred Persian attendants and servants. In addition, some 1,200 Persian *charvadars* or muleteers were impressed daily to handle the hundreds of riding and pack animals needed to transport the mission with its tents, provisions and other paraphernalia from the coast to the capital. No European Power had ever sent such a large mission to Persia: both its size and the liberality with which Malcolm dispensed a lavish assortment of gifts made a lasting and, in some ways, unfortunate impression on the Persians, whose expectations of largesse were a frequent cause of embarrassment for future British envoys.

Malcolm was instructed to encourage Persian attacks on Afghanistan, to counteract any possible moves by 'those villainous but active democrats, the French' (1) and to stimulate English and Indian trade. In January 1801 he succeeded in concluding political and commercial treaties with Fath Ali Shah, the first of their kind between the two

The British Interest in Persia

countries. Under the Political Treaty the Shah undertook to attack Afghan territory should that country invade India and to prevent the French from settling or residing in Persia: in return the British were to supply 'as many cannon and warlike stores as possible, with necessary apparatus, attendants and inspectors' should either the Afghans or the French attack Persia and, in the latter event, also to send troops to join Persian forces in securing 'the expulsion and extermination' (2) of the French. By the Commercial Treaty privileges which had been granted to the East India Company in the past were restored and new ones granted.

However, the Shah got no satisfactory response when a few years later he invoked the Political Treaty and appealed to the Government of India for help in repelling Russian attacks on his Caucasian provinces. In ignoring this appeal the British were strictly within their rights since there was no mention of Russia in the Treaty, but in Persian eyes it was a betrayal by their new ally. The Shah, who was already in touch with the French, therefore concluded the Treaty of Finkenstein (4 May 1807) with them and agreed to declare war on Britain, to sever all political and commercial relations with her and to allow French troops the right of passage to India. By the end of the year the French General Gardane had arrived in Tehran at the head of a large diplomatic and military mission whose officers and men were to train the Persian army. This French success caused considerable alarm in London and Calcutta. It also gave rise to an extraordinary diplomatic muddle, comic only in retrospect, whereby envoys were sent to Persia both from England (Sir Harford Jones) and India (John Malcolm of the 1800–1 mission, now raised to the rank of Brigadier-General for the occasion) with the object of persuading the Shah to break with the French and conclude a new treaty with the British.

Harford Jones, who had spent nearly twenty years in Basra and Baghdad in the employ of the East India Company, during which he had paid two visits to Persia and learnt the language, was keen to go there as envoy. It was to him, while the Company's Resident in Baghdad, that the Shah had addressed his first appeal for help from the Government of India. While in London in 1806–7 Jones found supporters among the Company's directors, a number of whom were very critical of Malcolm's extravagance during his first mission. Jones, having successfully argued that the Shah could not be expected to treat with an emissary appointed only by the Company, was duly appointed the Crown's envoy to Persia and created a baronet. At the same time Malcolm, who was very keen to return to Persia, intrigued to this end in Calcutta. He had the advantage of being well known in Persia and

The English Amongst the Persians

of having powerful support in the person of Arthur Wellesley* at home and Lord Minto,† the new Governor-General, in Calcutta. In addition rivalry between London and India for control over policy towards Persia—a rivalry that was to persist for many years—contributed to the appointment of both men, though the authorities in London and Calcutta recognised that this might cause misunderstanding and trouble. Fearing perhaps that it might be too late to foil French activities to await Jones' arrival from England Minto sent Malcolm ahead. Almost inevitably there was soon an undignified clash, of major proportions, between the Governor-General and Malcolm on one side and Harford Jones on the other, the former doing their best to undermine Jones' position and humiliate him in the eyes of the Persians. Yet, although Jones was a less gifted man than Malcolm, it was he who succeeded and Malcolm who failed.

While Harford Jones was still at sea on his long voyage out from Portsmouth via the Cape of Good Hope Malcolm sailed from Bombay for Bushire on 17 April 1808 with a small suite of European officers and a contingent of about five hundred Indian marines and soldiers. On arrival at Bushire he threatened dreadful consequences unless the Shah expelled Gardane and all Frenchmen; without this he refused to proceed to Tehran to discuss a new treaty with the Shah who, not surprisingly, rejected the demand. Malcolm, furious at his failure, left for India in July without having set foot outside Bushire. Harford Jones, who missed Malcolm at Bombay by only nine days and had agreed to remain there pending the outcome of Malcolm's mission, sailed in September for Bushire whence on 17 December 1808, despite instructions from Minto which reached him on arrival there ordering his return to India, he set out for Tehran. He would have left Bushire sooner but for problems of protocol and precedence which, as on Malcolm's first mission, were the cause of some friction with the Persian authorities.

Harford Jones' party consisted of eleven Europeans, some of whom had joined him in Bombay while others, including James Morier his Private Secretary, an English groom and two Swiss servants, had travelled from home with him. Jones brought an array of gifts rivalling in variety and value those of Malcolm in 1800. Luck was also on his side. The Treaty of Tilsit, signed in July 1807 by Napoleon and the Czar, as well as difficulties in Spain inhibited the French from helping

---

* Arthur Wellesley, 1st Duke of Wellington (1769–1852) and brother of Richard (q.v.). Military service in India 1797–1805 where he first met Malcolm. Victor of Waterloo, 1815: Prime Minister 1828–30: Foreign Secretary 1834–5.

† Gilbert Minto, 1st Earl (1751–1814). Governor-General of India 1807–13.

The British Interest in Persia

repel Russian attacks on Persian territory. The French thus proved themselves worthless allies when it came to the point and Fath Ali Shah now needed little persuasion to agree to expel them and turn once more to the English; the more so as Jones, unlike Malcolm, had come with full powers from the King of England and was not slow to make capital of his superior position.

Harford Jones reached Tehran early in mid-February 1809 and within a few days—negotiations having begun at Shiraz while he was *en route* for the capital—achieved his objective of a Preliminary Treaty of Friendship and Alliance which was, under Article 1, 'to become a basis for establishing a sincere and everlasting definitive Treaty of strict friendship and union' between the two countries. The Shah declared previous treaties with any European Power to be 'null and void', undertook not to allow passage of any European forces towards India nor to 'enter into any engagements inimical to His Britannic Majesty or pregnant with injury or disadvantage to the British territories in India', and to provide military assistance should the Afghans or any other power attack India. In return he was promised the help of British forces or, in lieu, 'a subsidy with warlike ammunition, such as guns, muskets, etc. and officers' necessary for the expulsion of any invading European forces even should Britain herself have concluded peace with the invader. Additionally the British undertook not to intervene in any hostilities between Persia and Afghanistan unless requested by both parties to mediate. The tables had thus been turned on the French; and the Government of India, who would have to bear the cost, had little alternative other than grudgingly to accept the terms negotiated by an envoy they had tried to disown and discredit. They would have preferred to bring the Shah to heel by allowing Malcolm to pursue his cherished plan of seizing Kharg Island off the Persian coast with a force of 6,000 men whom they were ready to provide.

There being no telegraph in those days Jones sent Morier to London with the text of the Preliminary Treaty so that it could be amplified into a 'definitive Treaty'. Morier was accompanied by *Mirza** Abul Hasan, the first Qajar envoy to London, whose main task was to assist in drawing up the new treaty: he also provided Morier with his hero for *Hajji Baba of Isfahan* and made a big hit with London Society.† While these negotiations were proceeding in London the Government of India, smarting under Malcolm's failure and Jones' success, decided to despatch

---

* *Mirza* as a prefix signifies Secretary or Scribe: as a suffix Prince.

† Morier reported to Jones that the *mirza* was 'the principal feature' of every party and that 'the women particularly are quite mad after him' (4). On his return to Persia the E.I.C. paid him a generous pension for life.

The English Amongst the Persians

Malcolm once more to Persia despite the awkwardness created by Jones' continued presence there. Their purpose was to replace Jones by Malcolm and, in so doing, to reassert Calcutta's responsibility for Persian affairs and at the same time restore the East India Company's prestige, allegedly undermined by what the Governor-General described as Jones' 'injudicious and unwarrantable proceedings' (5). A secondary purpose was to collect all possible information about the country, the recent invasion scare having brought home to the Government of India how little they knew about Persia.

So anxious were they to clip Jones' wings that they sent Dr Andrew Jukes from the Residency in Bushire to prepare for Malcolm's arrival and, pending this, to take charge of British interests: but Jones stood his ground and refused to acknowledge the Governor-General's authority to displace him. Malcolm, accompanied by a talented team of officers* from the Company's Indian establishment, reached Bushire for the third time in February 1810 and took the usual road to Tehran. Inevitably there were problems and frictions arising from Jones' presence at the Persian Court and their past differences, but an open clash was avoided when the Foreign Office informed Jones (who had asked to return home) of the Government's decision to replace him by Sir Gore Ouseley. Malcolm, realising that there was no hope of becoming resident envoy in Persia, decided to return to India by way of Baghdad. At Jones' request he left some of his officers behind to help train the Persian army while he himself went to Bombay and London where he spent time writing his monumental two-volume *History of Persia* before undertaking other duties.

Harford Jones, now aged forty-eight, left Persia a year after Malcolm in June 1811, travelling home through Constantinople where the Sultan presented him with a diamond-encrusted snuff box for the help he had given the Turks in Persia. He all but lost his life when ship-wrecked on the Needles off the Isle of Wight on the last lap of his journey. Both the Government and the directors of the East India Company in London applauded his Persian success. The Foreign Secretary wrote to inform him that the King approved of his having induced 'the King of Persia to reject the insidious offers of the French Government . . . and the Moderation and Temper which you have manifested under the embarrassing Circumstances which arose from the Conduct of the Government of India' (6). Yet, to his regret, he was rewarded neither with honours† nor with further employment. Jones had hoped for the Bombay Governorship: instead he retired, somewhat embittered, to the life of a

---
* See pp. 149-50.
† Eventually he was made a Privy Counsellor in 1835.

country gentleman and writer at the modest country seat built for him by Robert Smirke, a well-known architect of the day, at Boultibrooke outside Presteigne in Radnorshire where he had been born. There he rejoined his wife Sarah who, during his absence abroad, had, in addition to her own children, nobly cared for the two daughters and a son he had fathered during his Basra days. In 1833 Jones Brydges'* translation of a Persian work, *The Dynasty of the Kajars*, was published: a year later there followed a detailed account of his own mission to Persia,† a fascinating story enhanced by the author's egoistic account of his own achievements and the bitterness with which he describes his harassment by Malcolm and the Governor-General. He died at Boultibrooke in 1847: a simple tablet to his memory in the village church makes no mention of the years he spent abroad nor of his Persian achievements, which were considerable.

Malcolm had died in 1833. He had been knighted in 1815 and from 1827 until he retired three years later had been Governor of Bombay, the post Jones coveted. His friends and admirers made sure that his achievements would not be forgotten by erecting a life-size marble statue to his memory in Westminster Abbey, that shrine of the nation's heroes, fulsomely inscribed as follows:

IN MEMORY OF
MAJOR-GENERAL SIR JOHN MALCOLM, G.C.B.,&C
BORN AT BURNFOOT OF ESK, DUMFRIESHIRE MDCCLXIX
DIED IN LONDON MDCCCXXXIII
EMPLOYED CONFIDENTIALLY IN THOSE WARS AND
NEGOTIATIONS WHICH ESTABLISHED BRITISH SUPREMACY IN
INDIA, BY THE INDEFATIGABLE AND WELL-DIRECTED EXERTION
OF THOSE EXTRAORDINARY MENTAL AND PHYSICAL POWERS
WITH WHICH PROVIDENCE HAD ENDOWED HIM, HE BECAME ALIKE
DISTINGUISHED AS A STATESMAN, A WARRIOR, AND A MAN OF
LETTERS.
DISINTERESTED, LIBERAL, AND HOSPITABLE, WARM IN HIS
AFFECTIONS AND FRANK IN HIS MANNERS, THE ADMIRER AND
PATRON OF MERIT, NO LESS ZEALOUS, DURING THE WHOLE OF
HIS ARDUOUS AND EVENTFUL CAREER, FOR THE WELFARE OF
THE NATIVES OF THE EAST THAN FOR THE SERVICE OF HIS
OWN COUNTRY, HIS MEMORY IS CHERISHED BY GRATEFUL

---

* In 1826, having inherited property from his maternal grandmother, he assumed the additional name of Brydges.

† *An Account of the transactions of His Majesty's Mission to the Court of Persia in the years 1807–11.*

The English Amongst the Persians

MILLIONS, HIS FAME LIVES IN THE HISTORY OF NATIONS. THIS STATUE HAS BEEN ERECTED BY THE FRIENDS WHOM HE ACQUIRED BY HIS SPLENDID TALENTS, EMINENT PUBLIC SERVICES AND PRIVATE VIRTUES.

The activities and achievements of Malcolm and Harford Jones mark a turning point in Anglo-Persian relations. Though the attention of London and Calcutta might flag from time to time there was, from their day onwards, to be a continuous British interest and official presence in the country. What was to become an enduring political interest had been defined by Malcolm in 1806 when he had written that 'the English have an obvious and great interest in maintaining and improving the strength of Persia as a barrier to India' (7). Over thirty years later the British Government reminded the Russian Government that 'Great Britain has regarded Persia as a barrier for the security of British India against attack from any European power. With this defensive view Great Britain has contracted an alliance with Persia and the object of that alliance has been, that Persia should be friendly to Great Britain, independent of foreign control, and at peace with all her neighbours' (8). That was, and remained throughout the Qajar period, the essence of the British interest in Persia.

However, as the nineteenth century progressed other, more material, interests developed. The maintenance and operation of the telegraph line which the British had built across Persia and down the Persian Gulf to link London with India after the Mutiny in 1857 became a major British interest. Increasing attention was paid to Persia as an outlet for the products of Britain's industrial revolution. A handful of British trading firms established themselves in Tabriz, Bushire and elsewhere: one of them was officially subsidised so that it might develop trade with the interior of the country. Seekers of concessions for mines, railways, tobacco and banking descended on Tehran from London as well as Paris and Moscow, and the British-owned Imperial Bank of Persia, founded in 1889, soon became a powerful institution. The discovery of oil in commercial quantities at Masjid-e-Suleiman in 1908 and the rapid development, entirely through British enterprise and capital, of the Persian oil industry led in the course of time to the Anglo-Persian Oil Company becoming Britain's major commercial interest and the cause, long after the end of the Qajar period, of a bitter quarrel between the two countries. The decision to use oil instead of coal to fire the ships of the Royal Navy and the British Government's majority shareholding in the Anglo-Persian Oil Company added a new dimension to Britain's interest in Persian oil on the eve of World War I.

The British Interest in Persia

A confidential *Handbook on Persia* prepared by the Foreign Office for the use of the British Delegation to the Paris Peace Conference in 1919 listed British commercial interests in the following order:

(a) The Indo-European Telegraph Department and the Indo-European Telegraph Co. Ltd.
(b) The Imperial Bank of Persia.
(c) The Maritime trade of the Persian Gulf.
(d) The Anglo-Persian Oil Co.
(e) Messrs Lynch Bros.' concession on the Karun River and the Lynch Road from Ahwaz to Isfahan.
(f) The Persian Railway Syndicate's concession.
(g) Various British and Indian trading firms.

In the same year Lord Curzon,* the then Secretary of State for Foreign Affairs, circulated a memorandum to his Cabinet colleagues in explanation and justification of a new Anglo-Persian Agreement of which he was the architect. It was impossible, he argued, to allow Persia to 'rot in picturesque decay . . . her geographical position, the magnitude of our interests in the country, and the future safety of our Eastern Empire render it impossible for us now—just as it would have been for us at any time during the past 50 years—to disinterest ourselves from what happens in Persia. . . . Furthermore if Persia were to be left alone there is every reason to fear that she would be over-run by Bolshevik influences from the north' (9). Thus at the very end of the Qajar period, as at the beginning, Britain regarded her paramount interest in Persia to be the maintenance of that country's independence and territorial integrity as a safeguard for her Indian Empire: additionally she now had large commercial interests within the country to protect. But Curzon's ideas for preserving that independence and territorial integrity did not commend themselves to the Persians who were tired of foreign tutelage, whether British or Russian, and rejected his proposed treaty.

---

* George Nathaniel Curzon, 1st Marquess Curzon of Kedleston, K.G. (1859–1925). Author of *Persia and the Persian Question*, etc. M.P. (C) for Southport 1886–96: Viceroy and Governor-General of India 1898–1905: Foreign Secretary 1919–24.

2

The Diplomatic Scene

LONDON'S DECISION TO replace Harford Jones with Gore Ouseley at the Qajar Court was not only a slap in the face for the East India Company: it was also an indication that the British Government recognised the need for permanent diplomatic representation in Tehran now that political power was effectively concentrated in the hands of Fath Ali Shah, the second of the Qajars.*

Unlike Jones, who had been accredited as 'Envoy' to the Persian Court, Ouseley was designated 'Ambassador Extraordinary and Plenipotentiary'—a clear sign of the increased importance attached to the post. In their instructions to Ouseley the Foreign Office stated that he would be under their sole authority though he was 'to pay the most vigilant and constant attention to the interests of the East India Company' (1). The Shah was also assured that the Ambassador would be immediately responsible to the King and that the Governor-General would 'possess no power to interfere with this Royal Mission' (2).

Though neither a nominee of the Company nor one of their officers, Ouseley, who quickly adopted an anti-Jones line, was well-known and acceptable to them, having spent many years in India as a successful trader.† When Morier and *Mirza* Abul Hasan returned to London from Tehran with the draft of Jones' treaty Ouseley had been attached to the Persian envoy as escort and interpreter. He was therefore an obvious choice to succeed Jones and conclude the treaty negotiations.

The British Government's new interest in Persia was clearly set out

---

* He succeeded his uncle, Agha Muhammad Shah, in 1798 and reigned until 1834; renowned for his long black beard and his several hundred concubines and children.

† Sir Gore Ouseley, 1st Baronet (1770–1844). In India from 1787–1806: attached to the Court of Oudh at Lucknow, 1800–4. A considerable Persian scholar. Author of *Biographical Notes on Persian Poets*. One of the founders of the Royal Asiatic Society.

The Diplomatic Scene

in the instructions they issued to Ouseley on the eve of his departure from London. He was to employ every means in his power 'to obtain an accurate knowledge of the military and financial resources of the Kingdom of Persia . . . the principal productions of the Empire . . . the State of Agriculture, Trade, and the mechanical arts' as well as 'every attainable information respecting the manners, customs, revenues, commerce, history and antiquities of Persia'. He was authorised to recruit staff for this purpose and to spend up to £600 annually on the purchase of 'any Persian or Arabic manuscripts at moderate prices' for the British Museum (3). He was also instructed to collect 'any rare plants, seeds or roots' for the King's Gardens at Kew (4). More important still as a manifestation of the British Government's decision to maintain a permanent mission in the Persian capital was the instruction it gave him to obtain a grant of land from the Shah and permission to erect on it a 'Palace' whose cost, including furniture, was not to exceed £8,000. Credit for this decision must be given to Ouseley himself who earlier in the year had suggested to the Foreign Office that a residence should be built in Tehran for the Ambassador so as 'to impress the Nation at large with the permanence of our connexion' (5).

A further indication that this mission was to be of a more permanent nature than earlier ones was that the Ambassador was accompanied by his young wife and three-year-old child, Janie, as well as three British men-servants and two maids.

Sir Gore and Lady Ouseley and their party sailed from Spithead for Persia in two naval vessels, H.M.S. *Lion* and *Chichester*, on 18 July 1810: during the course of their long and tedious journey they touched at Madeira, Rio de Janeiro, Ceylon, Cochin and Bombay before reaching Bushire in March 1811. On board the *Lion* with Ouseley and his family were his elder brother William who shared the Ambassador's scholarly interest in Persian literature and history and came as his private secretary: James Morier, Secretary to the Embassy: the Hon. Robert Gordon, attaché: two clerks: the five servants: and a cow to provide milk. Also travelling in the *Lion* was the returning Persian envoy, Mirza Abul Hasan, with eight Persian servants. On board the store-carrying *Chichester* were two British officers, Majors D'Arcy and Stone with twelve sergeants and privates who were to help train the Persian army: their ship also carried a cargo of guns, muskets and ammunition for the Persians and a number of bulky gifts for presentation to the Shah and other Persian dignitaries as well as furniture and fittings for the envoy's new residence.

Despite the seven months' voyage to Bushire Ouseley showed little inclination to hurry on to Tehran. He eventually reached the capital

The English Amongst the Persians

in November 1811, nearly sixteen months after leaving England and over eight months after landing on Persian soil! Some excuse for his dilatory progress lies in the fact that his wife was already well gone in pregnancy when they landed at Bushire: although she was carried in a palankeen or covered litter by relays of Indian porters brought especially from Bombay, she must have suffered terribly on the long journey to Shiraz across one of the roughest caravan tracks and some of the most precipitous mountain passes in Persia. The two maids travelled, even more uncomfortably, on seats slung on either side of a mule, a contraption known as a *kajavah*. Understandably Ouseley decided that his wife should rest and have her child in Shiraz where a daughter was born on 17 June 1811,* almost certainly the first all-British child to be born in Persia. She was christened Eliza Shirin by the Rev. Henry Martyn,† a missionary recently arrived in Shiraz from India. Another three months' delay followed in Isfahan due in part to serious illness which struck most of the Ambassador's party including his English coachman, who died there.

Ouseley's first task was to secure the Shah's agreement to the Definitive Treaty he had brought from London. This was duly agreed and signed in March 1812. It confirmed and amplified the terms of Jones' Preliminary Treaty. The British Government undertook, *inter alia*, to provide an annual subsidy of 200,000 tomans (£150,000) if the Government of India were unable to send troops in response to an appeal for help against any European nation invading Persia: the subsidy was to be paid so long as Persia was at war with the invader and used solely for the purpose of raising and training an army. Additionally the British undertook, if so required, to help the Shah establish a naval force on the shores of the Caspian and to assist him with ships of war and troops if needed in the Persian Gulf. The British Government were to pay the officers and men sent to train the Persian army but the Shah was to provide extra allowances which were set out in detail, from colonels down to corporals. The British also reaffirmed their undertaking not to interfere in any hostilities between Persia and Afghanistan unless requested by both parties to mediate. The Persian Government, for their part, reaffirmed their various commitments in the Preliminary Treaty.

Soon after Ouseley's arrival hostilities had again broken out between Russia and Persia. A number of officers and men from the British Military Mission fought with the Persians—a matter of some embarrassment to the British Government who were now allied with the Russians

---

* She died in Tehran some months later. A son, christened Wellesley Abbas, was born in Tabriz in 1813.
† See pp. 113–14.

14

The Diplomatic Scene

against Napoleon. Because of this Ouseley, who saw that continued fighting would only mean worse terms for the Persians, acceded to a Russian request to act as peace-maker. The resultant Treaty of Gulestan of 12 October 1813 was a bitter blow for the Persians who were obliged to surrender virtually all their territory north of the river Aras, which became, as it has since remained, the country's north-western boundary. Ouseley has been blamed by the Persians for this humiliation and accused of placing British above Persian interests in his anxiety to stop the fighting.

Britain's new-found friendship with Russia also meant second thoughts in London about the Definitive Treaty. Much to the annoyance of the Persians the British Government insisted on revising the new treaty barely before the ink of Ouseley's signature on it was dry. Their main concern—for fear of upsetting the Russians—was to remove those clauses which committed them to help train the Persian armed forces. A new and watered-down treaty had, in consequence, to be drawn up. By the time it was ready Ouseley was about to return to London and a Mr Henry Ellis* was sent to Tehran to finalise the new draft. Both Ellis and Morier, who had been left in charge of the mission on Ouseley's departure, signed the new Treaty on behalf of the British Government in November 1814.

For the Persians this second edition of the Definitive Treaty, known as the Treaty of Tehran, was less satisfactory than the 1812 version. Nevertheless, given the circumstances in which they found themselves after the Treaty of Gulestan, they could scarcely afford to be choosers and almost any treaty was better than no treaty with Britain, then the only European power capable of affording them protection against the Russians. At least, if invaded, they were promised military assistance or, alternatively, an annual subsidy and a supply of arms and ammunition. But Britain's decision, soon after the signing of the Treaty, to withdraw most of her military mission coupled with disputes about payment of the subsidy and delays in delivery of arms soon caused serious differences between the two allies. A virtual break in diplomatic relations occurred in 1822 when Captain Henry Willock, then in charge of the British Mission, precipitately departed for London in fear of his life when an emissary from the Shah informed him that his head would be cut off if a bill drawn on him by the monarch was not honoured. It seems that the Shah, having lost a large sum gambling with one of his ministers, decided to kill two birds with one stone by discharging his debt with a

* Sir Henry Ellis, K.C.B. (1777–1855). On the civilian establishment of the E.I.C. Accompanied Malcolm on his third mission to Persia and Lord Amherst on his mission to China, 1816.

The English Amongst the Persians

bill on the British envoy for the arrears of subsidy! The Shah sent an emissary to London in Willock's wake and in due course got his subsidy.

In 1826 when hostilities with Russia were resumed the Shah appealed for help under Article 4 of the Treaty but this, as well as payment of the subsidy, was refused on the grounds that the Persians were the aggressors—this was untrue and, in Persian eyes, merely an excuse to escape a treaty commitment. Following Russian victories the British once again became involved in peace-making. Macdonald, the British Minister in Tabriz,* and his assistant McNeill played important roles in securing a cease-fire and the withdrawal of Russian forces. But the Treaty of Turkmanchai of 21 February 1828 between Russia and Persia was as humiliating for the latter as the imprecise Treaty of Gulestan. Apart from the loss of his remaining territories north of the Aras the Shah was obliged to pay a heavy war indemnity: being almost bankrupt he accepted Macdonald's offer of 250,000 tomans towards this, in return for which the British Government exacted the cancellation of the all-important Clauses 3 and 4 of the Tehran Treaty, under which they undertook to pay an annual subsidy and come to Persia's aid if she were attacked.

The Persians bitterly resented this emasculation of the treaty by their ally, the more so when the British Government arbitrarily reduced their payment by 50,000 tomans. At home, too, there were a number of critics of the shabby treatment meted out to Persia at this time. The fact was that some years earlier the British Government had concluded that it was hopeless to try to intervene between Persia and Russia. They were determined therefore to be rid of their embarrassing obligations under the 1814 Treaty. They no longer saw any need for a high-powered Ambassador in Tehran: all they wanted was someone 'to watch the intrigues and encroachments of Russia' (6). Morier, who took over the Mission briefly on Ouseley's departure, was given the lower rank of Minister Plenipotentiary while his successor, Captain Henry Willock, was never more than a Chargé d'Affaires though he remained in charge of the Mission for eleven years.

Those who manned the Tehran Mission in its early days became diplomats more by accident than design. Morier and Willock, who had both come to Persia with Harford Jones in 1808, were cases in point.

---

* Tabriz was the capital of the important province of Azerbaijan of which Abbas *Mirza*, the Crown Prince, was Governor-General. He also commanded the Persian armed forces and in 1810 had been placed in charge of foreign affairs by his father. Tabriz thus became a second capital where the British Minister spent much of his time and maintained a residence.

The Diplomatic Scene

Morier was born in Turkey in 1782 of a Swiss father and Dutch mother, his father having migrated to Smyrna (now Izmir) as a young man and become a naturalised British subject. After school in England the young Morier returned to Turkey where his father had become one of the Levant Company's consuls. The young Morier met Harford Jones when the latter was passing through Constantinople in 1806 and accepted an offer of a seat in his carriage to London. When, some months later, Jones was appointed envoy to Persia, Morier was happy to accept his invitation to join the mission as its secretary. Later, when he returned to London with the text of the Preliminary Treaty, Morier persuaded the Foreign Office to engage him on a regular basis—much to the annoyance of Jones who only held a temporary appointment. Apart from a brief mission to Mexico Morier's diplomatic career came to an end after he left Tehran in 1815. Thereafter he devoted himself to writing, achieving fame with his amusing satire of the Persians in *Hajji Baba of Isfahan*—a book which caused considerable offence to many Persians when they learnt that the author was an Englishman.

Henry Willock* came of a large family which had made money in the West Indies. He and his younger brother had entered the service of the East India Company at an early age as cornets in the 6th Madras Cavalry which in 1808 provided the escort for Harford Jones' mission. Henry travelled to Persia from Bombay with Jones as commandant of the escort and interpreter to the mission. His brother George followed in 1811, commanding Ouseley's escort. Apart from short visits to England both brothers remained in Persia until 1830, mixing soldiering with diplomacy. They assisted in the training of the Persian army with which they fought against the Russians and Kurds, both being decorated with the Order of the Lion and Sun by the Shah for their services. When Henry was placed in charge of the diplomatic mission on Morier's departure he nominated George as his assistant and left him in charge of the mission in 1822-3 when he himself went to London.

The Willocks set a pattern, soon to become familiar, of soldiers from India turning diplomat and taking charge of the Mission in Persia. That this should happen was largely due to India's greater interest in and proximity to Persia than London's and the availability of young men in the East India Company's employ who were either, like the Willocks, in Persia when needed or already knew the country. Also, Persian then being the official language of much of India, most of the

---

* Lieutenant-Colonel Sir Henry Willock (1788–1858). Knighted in 1827: served in Persia 1808–30, then retired to England; director of the E.I.C. 1838–58 and chairman in 1845. Married Eliza Davis in 1827: their first three children were born in Persia.

The English Amongst the Persians

Company's ambitious men learnt it at an early stage in their careers.*

However, though the small Mission staff was largely recruited from India until the latter half of the century, its control fluctuated between the Foreign Office in London and the Government of India at Fort William in Calcutta. From the time of Jones' appointment in 1808 until 1823 responsibility lay with the Foreign Office when, because 'the objects of the intercourse with Persia are principally, if not purely, Asiatick' (7) Canning, the Foreign Secretary, decided to transfer responsibility for the Mission to the Government of India.

The East India Company nominated Colonel John Macdonald† of the 24th Madras Native Infantry as their envoy in March 1824 but the Shah regarded it as 'derogatory to his dignity to recognise an envoy from a body of merchants' (8), particularly as his neighbour the Sultan of Turkey was honoured with an envoy from the Crown. At first the Shah refused to accept Macdonald unless appointed by the King of England, whom he considered more likely to help him against Russia than the Company: later, thanks to Henry Willock's efforts, he agreed to compromise by accepting notice of Macdonald's appointment from the Crown. However by this time the Government of India were riding their own high horse and insisting on a formal invitation to their envoy and the despatch of a high-ranking Persian nobleman to Bombay to accompany him on his journey to Persia. The Persians gave in and in due course Macdonald reached Tehran over two years after his appointment had first been announced. He was soon playing an important role as peace-maker between the Persians and the Russians and was rewarded for his services with a knighthood and the Order of the Lion and Sun as well as presents from the Shah and Czar of Russia. Although he had the invidious task of securing Persian acquiescence in the abrogation of Articles 3 and 4 of the Treaty of Tehran, he managed, according to a contemporary observer, to win the respect of the Crown Prince and other important Persians by his 'quiet and unobtrusive, yet firm and discriminating' manner (9). He died in June 1830 at Tabriz where, after being accorded full military honours and a 49-gun salute to mark his age, his body was carried for burial in the precincts of the Armenian Cathedral at Etzmiadizin.

On the Minister's death Captain John Campbell of the Madras Cavalry, who had joined Macdonald's Mission in 1826, assumed charge

---

* Persian was taught at the E.I.C.'s two educational establishments, Fort William College, Calcutta (founded 1800) and East India College, Haileybury (1806).

† Sir John Kinneir Macdonald (1782–1830). Accompanied Malcolm's second and third Persian missions. Sometimes used his mother's surname Kinneir. His and Malcolm's wife were sisters. See p. 151.

18

The Diplomatic Scene

and immediately began active lobbying for substantive appointment as his successor. In this he eventually succeeded, despite competition from Henry Willock, then in London. In 1834 Campbell was nominated 'Consul General and Plenipotentiary' by the British Government: he was also knighted. His preferment probably owed much to the influence of his father who was Chairman of the East India Company's Court of Directors in London. Contemporary accounts of Campbell leave little doubt that, despite good looks, he was a most unattractive, quarrelsome and unreliable character. John McNeill, who was his principal assistant, described him as 'a man for whose mental qualifications one could feel no deference . . . for his moral character no respect . . . too devoid of discretion to be entrusted with a secret and too devoid of truth to be implicitly believed' (10). The Persians also had no regard for him and protested formally in November 1834 in the strongest terms to the Foreign Office about his behaviour. He has, however, been given credit by historians for the effective part he played at a critical moment—by advancing some £20,000 to pay the Persian forces—in securing the throne for Muhammad *Mirza*, on the death of his grandfather Fath Ali Shah in 1834.

About this time the authorities in London were again becoming uneasy about the Russian threat to India: they were also aware that Russian influence in Tehran had greatly increased at Britain's expense. By 1832 the Foreign Office were sufficiently worried to seek advice from their former Ambassador to Persia, Gore Ouseley, who in a long memorandum attributed the extinction of British influence to a Persian 'feeling of being abandoned by England' following the substitution of an envoy from the Government of India for one from the Crown and 'the annulment of the defensive and subsidiary articles' (11) in the Treaty of Tehran. To regain lost influence Ouseley recommended the appointment of a Minister by the Crown and the reinstatement in the Treaty of the abrogated Articles 3 and 4 which were crucial for the defence of Persia. The British Government, who received similar advice from others, while unwilling to reinstate the Articles, decided in 1834 that charge of the Persian Mission should revert to the Foreign Office. The East India Company agreed, as they considered the Foreign Office the more appropriate body to handle relations with Persia now that Russia had become so important in the Persian context. As, in the words of Ouseley, 'the principal object of a Mission to Persia is the preservation of our Eastern Empire' the Government of India were persuaded to contribute to the expenses of the Mission. This, after some haggling, was fixed at £12,000 a year; in addition they continued to bear the full cost of the Residency at Bushire.

The English Amongst the Persians

After the Indian Mutiny and the transfer of responsibility for Indian affairs from the Company to the Crown it was decided that Persian affairs should also be handled by the newly-created India Office. However, the decision was reversed in a matter of months on the grounds that the Foreign Office was better suited to handle diplomatic relations with a country in which other foreign powers, notably Russia, France and Turkey, were increasingly interested. Since that time Persian affairs have remained the responsibility of the Foreign Office despite the recommendation of a House of Commons Committee in 1870 that the Persian Mission should be placed under the authority of the Secretary of State for India—the Committee also recommended that, in the event of this not proving acceptable, the mission staff should be drawn from India. This recommendation was also largely ignored though certain consulates were staffed from India, while the Military Attaché, first appointed in 1877, was invariably drawn from the Indian Army; also the Political Residency at Bushire continued to be staffed exclusively by officials from India.

The Government of India, however, were never happy with an arrangement which saddled them with most of the financial load* but left the making and conduct of policy mainly in the hands of what one of their elder statesmen contemptuously called 'home-bred secretaries of the European Legations' (12): Indian interests would, it was believed, be best served by officials trained in oriental ways by Indian experience. This was a view shared neither by the Foreign Office nor by the Persians who resented what they felt to be the arrogant and overbearing attitude of the British in general but of those from India in particular. This feeling was never eradicated and as late as 1919 when the Persian Foreign Minister was in London begging his opposite number, Lord Curzon, to speed up the despatch of British experts to Persia he insisted that 'none of them should be Indian officers or Indian officials: not so much because he distrusted individuals with that experience, as because there was a popular impression in his country that they did not treat Persians on equal terms' (13).

To mark the resumption of Foreign Office control of the Persian Mission the same Henry Ellis who had signed the Treaty of Tehran in 1814 was sent from London in 1835 as Ambassador on a special mission to convey to the new Shah the King of England's condolences on the death of Fath Ali Shah and congratulations on his own succession; he was also required to negotiate a commercial treaty but in this he failed

* By 1899 the Foreign Office was contributing only £15,000 annually against the Government of India's £61,000 to the cost of running the various official British establishments in Persia.

The Diplomatic Scene

and left for London after less than a year in Persia. On his departure Dr John McNeill was appointed Minister Plenipotentiary by the Crown.

McNeill was perhaps the most able and influential of all the British envoys to Persia in the nineteenth century, yet he had begun as a doctor, not as a diplomat or administrator. Having completed his medical studies at Edinburgh he joined the East India Company in 1816; after he had taken part in an expedition against pirates in the Persian Gulf the Company sent him to Persia in 1821 as Assistant Surgeon to the British Mission. Except for brief intervals at home he remained in Persia until 1842 when he returned to his native Scotland to embark on a new but equally distinguished career.*

In Persia, owing to the small size of the Mission's staff, McNeill was soon involved in political work. When Henry Willock, the chargé d'affaires, left hurriedly for London in 1822 he insisted on McNeill travelling with him. While home McNeill re-married (his first wife had died in 1816) and towards the end of 1823 returned to Tabriz with his bride: of the five children she bore only one, a daughter, survived infancy. McNeill served as assistant, sometimes in Tabriz, sometimes in Tehran, to three successive envoys—Willock, Macdonald and Campbell. He played an important role in the negotiations which resulted in the Treaty of Turkmanchai and the withdrawal of Russian troops from Azarbaijan. For his services on this occasion the Shah rewarded him with a portrait of himself set in diamonds—a tribute perhaps also to the increasing confidence the royal family placed in him as their doctor. His good looks and thoughtful, reserved manner appealed to the Persians, who held him in high esteem even though they blamed him for their failure to seize Herat.†

In December 1831 McNeill, who had long hankered after a political post, set off with his wife from Tabriz for Bushire, where he understood he was to become Resident. Near Basra, after a difficult journey, they were told that the appointment had been cancelled. Greatly disappointed they had to retrace their steps under terrible winter conditions. Mrs McNeill, over seven months gone with child, recorded in a letter home how the horse litter in which she was travelling 'fell from twelve to twenty times daily. I had often to walk from five to seven miles knee-deep in snow or mud' (14). A daughter was born at Hamadan at the end of March after which the McNeills continued their journey to Tabriz where he returned to his old job as Medical Officer and Assistant

---

* Sir John McNeill, G.C.B. (1795–1883). Chairman of the Board of Supervision of the Scottish Poor Law Act, 1845–68: Report on the State of the Highlands and Islands of Scotland, 1851: Commission of enquiry to the Crimea, 1855.

† See pp. 58–59.

The English Amongst the Persians

to the envoy. Eventually, on returning to London in 1834 after eleven years away from home, he was appointed Minister Plenipotentiary to Tehran—a post he occupied from 1836 until 1842 apart from the period when diplomatic relations were ruptured over the Herat dispute. McNeill was a strong believer in the importance for Britain of maintaining the independence and territorial integrity of Persia in the face of Russian expansion. He voiced his views, which carried considerable weight in London and Calcutta, in a 150-page book entitled *Progress and Present Position of Russia in the East* published in 1836.

After McNeill's departure in 1842 the Mission was left in the hands of his assistant, Lieutenant-Colonel Justin Sheil, who was appointed Minister Plenipotentiary in 1844. Like his four predecessors Sheil had originally come to Persia under the aegis of the East India Company, as a Captain in the Bengal Native Infantry and second-in-command of a detachment of officers and men sent from India in 1833 to help train the Persian army. In 1836 he was attached to the British Legation as secretary, being joined later by another member of the military mission, Lieutenant Francis Farrant of the Bombay Light Cavalry. The pair, though soon on notoriously bad terms with each other, were to run the Legation together until 1852 when Farrant resigned, allegedly owing to his differences with Sheil; Sheil himself followed a year later.

Sheil was a good Persian and Turkish scholar: notoriously frugal in his habits, he possessed a very quiet and retiring disposition—by contrast to Farrant who was said to be a typical Indian cavalryman and 'a merry fellow, full of fun and anecdote and never looks at books' (15). Sheil's own reports and despatches show him to have been an able diplomat who travelled widely and was ever ready to protect British interests without being insensitive to Persian feelings. In 1849 he returned to Tehran from home leave with his newly wedded wife who was later to write an engaging account of her life and travels in Persia, the first such book by a woman. By the time the Sheils left Tehran in 1853 she had produced three young children, all of whom survived the overland journey to Trebizond where they took ship for Constantinople and home.

At first it seemed likely that Sheil would be succeeded in Tehran by yet another member of the 1833 Military Mission to Persia, Colonel Henry Rawlinson,* who was British Resident in Baghdad at the time and was an old friend of the Sheils. However in the event the Foreign

---

* Major-General Sir Henry Rawlinson, G.C.B. (1810–95). Joined E.I.C.'s army 1827: served in Persia 1833–8, Afghanistan and India 1839–43: Consul-General and Resident, Baghdad 1843–55. M.P. (C) for Reigate 1858 and Frome 1865–8: Minister, Tehran 1859–60. Member of India Council 1858 and 1868–95: Trustee, British Museum 1876–95.

The Diplomatic Scene

Office chose the Hon. Charles Murray,* the second son of the Earl of Dunmore.

If Rawlinson, with his keen intelligence and interest in Persia, instead of Murray had succeeded Sheil at a time when Anglo-Persian relations were at a very low ebb it is possible their disastrous deterioration into actual war might have been avoided. Murray, despite his linguistic and literary abilities, was probably the clumsiest and most inept envoy ever appointed by the British Government to the Persian Court. He was not without diplomatic experience, having served in Naples, Cairo (from where he sent the Zoological Society the first hippopotamus to be seen in England) and Berne but, as the pro-Indian school were only too apt to point out, he was, with the exception of James Morier, the only envoy without Indian experience to have been appointed to Persia.

Through no fault of his own Murray started off badly. The Shah was unhappy to learn that he was on friendly terms with his old enemies the rulers of Egypt and Muscat. *The Times* had not helped with an article predicting that Murray would soon bring the Shah's nose to the grindstone, while Murray's arrival with neither an expected loan nor a draft defensive treaty nor presents caused disappointment. His own behaviour soon made matters worse. Within days of his arrival in Tehran in April 1855 he dismissed the Legation's senior *mirza* or Persian secretary and sought Foreign Office permission to reinstate another whom Sheil had dismissed some years earlier—his motive apparently being to spite Sheil, who was now in London advising the Foreign Office on Persian affairs. Even more foolishly he defied the Persian Prime Minister, known as the *Sadr Azam*, and incurred his bitter enmity by appointing a certain *Mirza* Hashem Khan as British Agent in Shiraz. Murray knew full well that this man was anathema to the Prime Minister who only the previous year had intervened to prevent his appointment to the Legation staff on the alleged grounds that he was not yet formally discharged from the Shah's employ and was connected by marriage with the royal family. The Prime Minister quickly retaliated by arresting the *mirza*'s wife, who was living in the Legation precincts at Gulhek, and accusing—almost certainly falsely—Murray and his senior assistant Taylour Thomson of having an *affaire* with her. There followed an exchange of notes between Murray, who demanded the lady's release, and the Prime Minister, which must be among the most offensive ever to have been exchanged between a British diplomat and the head of a foreign government. The Shah joined the fray and in a rescript to the

---

* Sir Charles Murray K.C.B. (1806–95). Fellow of All Souls', Oxford: Diplomatic Service 1844–74. After Tehran he served successively as Minister in Saxony, Denmark and Portugal.

The English Amongst the Persians

Sadr Azam, of which he ordered copies to be sent to the Russian, Turkish and French Ministers, protested at 'the rude, unmeaning and insolent tone' of Murray's note to his Prime Minister and his conviction 'that this man, Mr Murray, is stupid, ignorant and insane' (16).

Though several members of Palmerston's Government considered Murray's behaviour unwise and offensive he was authorised to break off relations with Persia if unable to obtain satisfaction over his quarrel about the *mirza* and his wife. Murray therefore hauled down his flag in November 1855 and, when he realised that the Persians were not to be intimidated, moved with his staff to Baghdad where he remained for the better part of two years. In the meantime negotiations in Constantinople, designed to agree terms which would allow Murray to return to Tehran without loss of face, broke down owing to the unacceptability of the British conditions which included the dismissal of the *Sadr Azam*.

Murray's troubles were one of the causes of the war against the Persians on which the British Government embarked the following year.* Only after their defeat in battle were the Persians prepared to accept the stiff conditions which were to mark the return of Murray to Tehran. These terms were set out in humiliating detail in an annexe to the main Treaty of Paris and stipulated that the Prime Minister was to write a letter to Murray in the Shah's name regretting 'the offensive imputations upon the honour of Her Majesty's Minister'. Copies were to be sent to the other foreign envoys and the original delivered to Murray in Baghdad by a high ranking Persian who was to invite him, on the Shah's behalf, to return with his staff to Tehran where 'Mr Murray, on approaching the capital, shall be received by persons of high rank deputed to escort him to his residence in the town. Immediately on his arrival there the *Sadr Azam* shall go in state to the British Mission and renew friendly relations with Mr Murray, leaving the Secretary of State for Foreign Affairs to accompany him to the royal palace, the *Sadr Azam* receiving Mr Murray, and conducting him to the presence of the Shah. The *Sadr Azam* shall visit the Mission at noon on the following day, which visit Mr Murray will return, at latest, on the following day, before noon' (17).

Murray, who had returned to Tehran from Baghdad in August 1857 and been received with the agreed ceremonial, stayed on for nearly two years before returning to London on sick leave. Shortly afterwards, when the newly created India Office assumed responsibility for Persian affairs, he agreed to resign but had to wait until 1866 for the knighthood for which he now asked.

* See pp. 59-61.

The Diplomatic Scene

The India Office chose Rawlinson to replace Murray. He seemed an admirable choice, having served in Persia from 1833 to 1838, first with the Military Mission, then under McNeill at the Legation. He liked the Persians. He was deeply interested in their history and had already made a name for himself with his decipherment of the rock inscriptions at Bisitun near Kermanshah.* However his appointment was not the success it should have been: after only a few months in Tehran he resigned on learning that the India Office had surrendered control of the Tehran Legation to the Foreign Office. Rawlinson, having spent all his life in the service of the Government of India, was not prepared to serve under the Foreign Office. From now on it would be the exception rather than the rule for the envoy to have any Indian experience, Sir Mortimer Durand (1894-1900) and Sir Percy Cox (1918-20) being the two exceptions.

There followed a long spell when the Foreign Office seemed almost to have forgotten the existence of the Tehran Legation, being content to leave its incumbent undisturbed until he died or was ready for retirement.

Charles Alison was appointed to succeed Rawlinson in 1860 and remained *en poste* until he died there twelve years later. His successors were in turn William Taylour Thomson and Ronald Thomson, two bachelor brothers who had already spent many years in Tehran on the Legation staff, and were to end their careers there after serving seven and eight years respectively as Ministers Plenipotentiary for which they duly received the customary reward of a knighthood—an honour denied, however, to Alison. With the exception of the present writer nearly a century later no subsequent envoy to the Court of Persia was to serve so long as these men who, in Curzon's view, 'had lived so long in Persia as to yield somewhat to the pressure of their environment, and to lack the initiative that comes from change of atmosphere and scene' (18). Those who criticise the too-rapid transfer of diplomats from one part of the world to another would do well to remember Curzon's strictures.

Alison was a curious choice for the Tehran post as he was without any experience either of Persia or India, having spent all his official career as a dragoman or interpreter in the Constantinople Embassy: there he had been the protégé of Sir Stratford Canning, the 'Great Elchi', and close friend of Henry Layard, the discoverer of Nineveh. Alison was always reticent about his origins, one story being that he was born in Malta, the son of an English regimental paymaster. Layard described him as being without formal education, an excellent linguist and musician, and a brilliant eccentric whose fine features were dis-

* See pp. 155-7.

figured by an untidy head of hair and a bushy beard which he had the habit of pushing upwards to conceal his face. He married late in life the rich widow of a Greek banker: she died before being able to join him in Tehran, where he soon acquired an Armenian mistress by whom he had a daughter, patriotically christened Victoria. Alison's behaviour and eccentricities in Tehran caused Edward Eastwick,* a scholarly member of his staff, to risk his career by writing formally, in August 1862, to the Foreign Secretary accusing his chief of a variety of sins including gross intemperance, fiddling the Legation accounts, uttering 'abominable obscenities and blasphemies' and 'surrounding himself with infamous characters, pimps and prostitutes' (19). In the same letter Eastwick claimed that Alison often received his visitors in a state of semi-nudity and walked about in 'a Turkish dress with a Muhammedan rosary in his hands'. The Foreign Secretary called for a full enquiry as a result of which Eastwick was informed that there was not sufficient 'unimpeachable' evidence to support his charges and that it was no part of a Foreign Secretary's duty 'to scrutinise closely the conduct of Her Majesty's diplomatic servants in their private life: or to sift and weigh imputations upon their moral conduct, except in so far as the public service may be thereby affected' (20). So Alison survived while Eastwick was quietly removed from the diplomatic service. Alison died in Tehran in 1872 and was buried in the Armenian Church there.

Alison deserves to be remembered as the envoy who persuaded the authorities in London to build a new Legation in place of the porticoed, and once impressive, Mission House erected by Gore Ouseley in the southern part of the town.† Alison skilfully argued that the old Paladian-style house, badly damaged by earthquake in 1830, was rapidly falling apart—'as fast as one room or wall is patched up another crumbles down' (21); it would be better, he wrote, that 'the mission should be transferred to a more salubrious site in the new suburb which has during the last few years been formed to the north of the City immediately beyond the town wall' (22). He reinforced his case by mentioning that the Russians were erecting 'a large new Palace' and that Persian Ministers and high officials were also building themselves bigger and better houses. It was necessary for the British to keep their end up and Alison was duly authorised to spend £32,000 on the project, including

---

* Edward B. Eastwick (1814-83). On the civilian establishment of the E.I.C. Professor of Hindustani, East India College, Haileybury 1845-58: Tehran Legation 1860-3. Author of *Three Years' Residence in Persia*: translator of Saadi's *Gulestan*: M.P. (C) for Penryn and Falmouth 1868-74.

† Nothing today remains of the old Mission House, although the quarter where it stood is still known as the *Bagh-e-Elchi*, or Ambassador's Garden.

The Diplomatic Scene

£8,000 on the fifteen acre site. A spacious new residence and offices, with separate houses for the secretaries and doctor and stabling for fifty-one horses was built in the desert on what was then the northern fringe of Tehran. Other foreign Missions followed in due course and the broad avenue along which they built became known to the Europeans and their Persian imitators as the *Avenue des Ambassadeurs*: it was the first street in Tehran to be lit by gas-light.

Captain William Pierson of the Royal Engineers, then serving in Tehran with the Indo-European Telegraph Department, was appointed to superintend the erection of the new buildings. They were designed, under his direction, along Anglo-Indian lines by Mr J. W. Wild of the South Kensington Museum who had helped design the great Hyde Park Exhibition in 1851. In Tehran Pierson was assisted by one of his telegraph sergeants and a clerk of works from England, all the others on the job being Persians. In addition he employed a German gardener to plant the barren site with fifteen hundred plane saplings which were nurtured by runnels of water from the Legation's copious *qanat*. By the time of Curzon's visit nearly twenty years later they had become a dense grove of trees.* The buildings, completed shortly after Alison's death, won high praise from the fastidious Curzon and were the envy of other foreign Missions in Tehran. An English visitor in 1890 proudly recorded that 'the finest of all the Legation enclosures is that of England, which is beautifully wooded and watered. The reception-rooms and hall of the Minister's residence are very handsome, and a Byzantine clock tower gives the building a striking air of distinction' (23). As a special favour the British Minister was allowed by the Shah to keep peacocks, a royal bird, to adorn his spacious garden.

Alison was also responsible for the erection of the first houses on the Legation's property at Gulhek, then a small village in the hills about seven miles above Tehran. In 1835 Muhammad Shah had granted the British Minister extensive rights† over the village where for some years past the Mission had been in the habit of camping during the hot

---

* Some survive to-day and, with their slender stems, tower high above surrounding buildings to provide a magnificent oasis in what is now the heart of the city. Water from the Legation's *qanat* was for many years considered the best drinking water in Tehran.

† Persian officials were forbidden to interfere with the villagers who thus enjoyed British protection. They were exempt from military service and paid their annual tax to the British Minister who appointed their headman. None but British and Persians might own property in Gulhek: foreigners residing there had to obtain British permission before flying their national flags. The Russians enjoyed similar privileges at nearby Zargandeh. They surrendered these in 1921: the British, reluctantly, followed in 1928.

The English Amongst the Persians

summer months. But it was not until 1862 that the Legation acquired ownership of any land at Gulhek through a gift from the Shah. Alison then persuaded the Foreign Office that it would in the long run be cheaper to build small houses there for the Minister and his staff than to continue providing and repairing tents. Posthumously, however, Alison was to cause a problem in Gulhek as he had himself bought land there adjoining the Legation's: he left this to his Armenian mistress who in turn transferred it to her illegitimate daughter Victoria, by then a Russian subject through marriage. Backed by the Russian Legation Victoria held out until 1906 before agreeing to sell the plot to the British who were anxious to expand and consolidate their property which eventually extended to about forty-five acres of beautiful parkland, well-watered by *qanats* from the nearby mountains. There the Legation moved *en bloc* to spend the summer in cool offices and verandahed houses with thick walls and high ceilings, more reminiscent of India than of England or Persia. Each May or June a long procession of sturdy servants would carry furniture, bedding, crockery and other household goods from Tehran to Gulhek and down again in October when the nights became too cold for comfort.

The Thomson brothers, who, one after the other, succeeded Alison, were the sons of a well-to-do Edinburgh Writer to the Signet. The elder, William Taylour, came to Persia by chance: after completing his education at Edinburgh University he had, in 1835 at the age of twenty-two, joined Chesney's Euphrates expedition* as assistant astronomer. He had been lucky to survive the wreck of one of the expedition's two paddle-steamers in a storm the following year. Without it there was no room for him with the expedition but, as a reward for his services, he was appointed Military Secretary, though a civilian, to the British Mission in Tehran. On reaching Tehran in September 1837 Thomson found that his new chief, McNeill, was encamped in the Lar valley some miles outside Tehran under the shadow of Mount Demavend. Thither he rode to pay his respects and to climb the 18,600 ft. mountain—the first European to do so. Having mastered Persian the young Thomson was duly promoted First Paid Attaché and remained with the Legation until Murray, who greatly disliked him,

* The development of steam navigation stimulated British interest in two possible routes to India—the 'overland' route via Egypt and the Red Sea and the 'direct' route via Syria, the Euphrates valley and the Persian Gulf. In 1834 a House of Commons Select Committee on Steam Navigation voted £20,000 to finance a fifty-man expedition under Colonel Francis Chesney to test the possibilities of the Euphrates route. Two flat-bottomed paddle steamers were shipped in sections to the Syrian coast whence, with enormous difficulty, they were transported overland for assembly on the banks of the Euphrates.

The Diplomatic Scene

withdrew with his staff to Baghdad in 1855: then Murray managed to arrange for him to be posted to Chile where he remained nearly thirteen years before being appointed Minister in Tehran on Alison's death in 1872. When Thomson retired seven years later he had spent over a quarter of a century in the Tehran Legation—a record only to be surpassed by his younger brother Ronald who succeeded him in 1879, and had first joined the Legation in 1848 at the age of eighteen as the Third Paid Attaché. Except for a short break in Europe Ronald Thomson spent his entire working life with the Persian Mission, from which he eventually retired in 1887. A confirmed bachelor, tall and handsome, with a soft, low voice, he was said to be deeply interested in Persian literature and on excellent terms with the Persians.

Though both the Thomsons acquitted themselves reasonably well in Tehran there was a feeling in London that, unless Britain's political and growing commercial interests were to be submerged by Russian influence, more dynamic, professional representation was needed at the Legation. So it was that future Ministers were men of a very different background and training from their predecessors: for the most part they were up-and-coming career diplomats of the traditional Eton and Oxford mould who stayed only a few years in Tehran before moving on to higher things, among them being Frank Lascelles, Arthur Hardinge and Cecil Spring-Rice. Their secretaries, too, were often bright young diplomats with a big future ahead of them, and included Charles Hardinge (a future Permanent Under-Secretary and Viceroy of India), Horace Rumbold, Ronald Graham and two other future Permanent Under-Secretaries at the Foreign Office, Arthur Nicolson and Robert Vansittart.

The first of the new school, Sir Henry Drummond Wolff,* was the most dynamic and active of them all. He was the son of the Rev. Joseph Wolff,† a German Jew who had emigrated to England. After some years as a diplomat Henry Drummond Wolff became active in international finance; he sat in Parliament as a Conservative for ten years and moved in high political and City circles. When he went to Tehran in 1887 he could therefore count on powerful backing at home. He considered his main task was to attract British commerce and capital to Persia as a means of making the country less vulnerable to Russian penetration. Bored stiff by 'the dreadful and monotonous life' of Tehran (24) he devoted himself to promoting British commercial

---

* Sir Henry Drummond Wolff, G.C.B., etc. (1829–1908). Diplomatic Service 1852–64; M.P. (C) 1874–85; Minister, Tehran 1887–90 and Bucharest 1891; Ambassador, Madrid 1892–1900.

† See pp. 116–17.

interests and bombarding London with what must then have seemed wild schemes for railway construction, exploitation of oil and reviving the lost prosperity of Khuzistan by dam building. Largely through his efforts the Karun river was opened to foreign shipping and a valuable banking concession obtained for British interests.

Drummond Wolff was also an early champion of the idea of an Anglo-Russian accord over Persia. Some years later, in 1907, his ideas bore fruit in the Anglo-Russian Convention which divided Persia into British and Russian zones of influence with a neutral zone between. The Persians, who had come increasingly to look upon Britain as their protector against Russia and the champion of liberal ideas, were shocked beyond measure by this alliance with the devil. So was Cecil Spring-Rice, the British Minister in Tehran, who wrote to his old Oxford friend, Edward Grey, the Foreign Secretary, that 'we are regarded as having betrayed the Persian people' (25). The British, thinking about India* and little about Persia, hoped, by securing Russia's formal recognition in the Convention of Persia's independence, to check her advance towards India and the Gulf: in the wider context they sought an accommodation with Russia as an insurance against the growing menace of Germany in the west. For the Persians, however, the Anglo-Russian Convention appeared as the first step in the partition of their country and to this day they have neither forgotten nor quite forgiven what for them was a great betrayal.

Sir Frank Lascelles, Drummond Wolff's successor, was a polished and experienced diplomat described by his German colleague in Tehran as 'the perfect representative' who 'rode his Legation, so to say, with loose reins, but he rode it well' (26). His successor, Sir Mortimer Durand, had a much harder time with the Persians, who did not take to him at all. They realised, it was said, that he saw through their flattery and lies. He knew the East well, having served all his life in India where he negotiated the Durand Line separating Afghanistan from India and had finished as Foreign Secretary there. The Persians were put off by his dry manner and soon sensed that both his and his wife's hearts were in India. Charles Hardinge, a member of his staff, considered 'his appointment as Minister in Tehran was a mistake as the Persians particularly dislike Anglo-Indian officials' (27). Horace Rumbold, another talented member of his staff, recorded in his diary that Durand 'had a good deal of contempt for the Persians and the impression got around that he wished to treat them as if he had been a Resident in India in a Native State' (28).

* The Government of India, however, did not favour the Convention; nor did Curzon who criticised it in Parliament.

The Diplomatic Scene

The only other envoy with an Indian background to be appointed to Tehran was Sir Percy Cox at the end of the Great War. Chosen as a strong man with long experience of the Persian Gulf his appointment was also an unhappy one. Cox's Indian and Gulf background made him unwelcome to the Persians and was not calculated to help him sympathise with or understand the post-war wave of nationalism then abroad. Had he done so, he might possibly have deflected rather than encouraged Curzon's ill-fated Anglo-Persian Agreement which some, including the authorities in India, correctly feared would prove offensive to Persian opinion. It was left to Cox's successor, Herman Norman,* a rather fussy bachelor endowed with intelligence and vision, to warn Curzon in a series of courageous reports that he was putting his money (almost literally) on the wrong Persian horses and that his proposed agreement was unlikely to succeed. This was not what Curzon wished to hear or was prepared to believe: in consequence Norman, whom events were to prove right, was recalled to London and never again employed by the Foreign Office.

---

* Herman Norman, C.B. etc. (1872–1955). Career diplomat who served in many of the world's capitals. Minister in Tehran for little more than a year, 1920–1.

3

Formalities and Frictions

ON HIS FIRST mission to Persia in 1800 John Malcolm, drawing on his Indian experience, set a precedent in his approach to the Persian authorities. Today the punctilious insistence on form and ceremony, the expensive gifts and the hard cash may seem incongruous but in those early Qajar days there was no recognised procedure for the reception of foreign envoys and Malcolm did what he considered best for his country. On his return to India he argued in justification of his alleged extravagance that 'in all Asiatic Courts but particularly one constituted like that of Persia, it is necessary for an Envoy of a foreign Nation to assume a style that shall appear magnificent to the Court to which he is despatched not only with a view of supporting the honour and dignity of the Country he represents, but in order that he may have a chance of accomplishing the object of his mission' (1).

Some years later a member of Henry Ellis' 1835 Mission explained that 'a great deal really depends on the first impression made upon the Persian authorities by an ambassador's firmness in matter of etiquette; and in a barbarous country, where the eyes must be spoken to, England will be considered powerful by the ignorant multitude very much in proportion to the outward marks of respect bestowed by the Shah upon the representative of her king' (2).

Malcolm's first consideration had been to impress the Persians with respect for the power and wealth of the country he represented. The large escort of Indian cavalry and infantry he brought with him helped to serve this purpose as well as to provide protection during the long march to Tehran, but it was the Persians' own pretensions which also needed tempering, for they seemed only too anxious to score points designed to humiliate the foreign visitor. On disembarking at Bushire Malcolm waited nearly four months in uncomfortable camp there

Formalities and Frictions

before receiving what he considered a sufficiently respectful letter from the Prince-Governor of Shiraz, a brother of the Shah, whose first letter he had rejected. In Shiraz there was trouble over his first meeting with the same Governor, Malcolm insisting that he and all members of his suite should be seated. By the time he reached Isfahan the Persians realised that Malcolm was not to be trifled with and about ten thousand horsemen were waiting to greet him: at Tehran over a thousand of the Shah's cavalry escorted him into the city. When, eight years later, Harford Jones reached Bushire he also objected to the terms in which he was addressed by the Prince-Governor; he also delayed his entry into Shiraz until the Governor there conceded that at the *esteqbal*, the traditional welcoming ceremony for important personages on the outskirts of town or village, all the Persian dignitaries riding out to meet him should dismount before presenting their greetings while he, the British envoy, remained mounted.

When Gore Ouseley was sent in 1811 to Tehran as full Ambassador he was instructed by the Foreign Office to ensure that his reception should be commensurate with the fact that he enjoyed a rank superior to that of any recent European envoy to Persia. With these instructions in mind Ouseley proved a stickler for form. He objected to the *mehmandar*, or official host, whom it was at first proposed should accompany him from Bushire to Tehran on the grounds that the man was in the employ of the Prince-Governor not of the Shah. At Shiraz he insisted on seeing the Governor without the 'humiliating delay' which was customary: on his arrival in Tehran there were tedious negotiations about the ceremonial with which he was to be received by the Shah, as a result of which Ouseley scored what he considered to be two important points, namely that the Shah would receive him one day earlier than was customary and that his chair would be placed five or six yards nearer the throne than that of any previous envoy. But his request that the Persian Prime Minister should pay a first call on him was refused. Ouseley and his suite, in full-dress uniform, were escorted to the Palace by their 'sepoy dragoons, having their swords drawn, the Royal standard of England flying, and trumpets sounding' (3). They must have been a startling sight for the inhabitants of Tehran. Ouseley was also permitted to hand personally to the Shah, in a second audience, a letter and diamond ring from George III: he had refused to accept the recognised procedure of transmitting the letter through a Persian Minister or placing the ring on a silver tray because this would, he argued, look like paying tribute to the Shah.

Questions of protocol continued throughout most of the Qajar period to cause friction between the British and Persians. On John Macdonald's arrival in Isfahan on his way to Tehran in 1826 there was trouble and delay over his call on the Prince-Governor since the British considered it 'excessively degrading' for their envoy and his suite to be placed in one room and allowed to communicate with the Governor only through a window giving into the separate room in which he was seated (4). In 1835 Henry Ellis, though welcomed outside Tehran with the traditional *esteqbal* headed by one of the Shah's highest ranking grandees, refused to enter the capital until the Foreign Minister had himself ridden four miles out to greet him. When Charles Murray was appointed to Tehran twenty years later he was warned by Lord Clarendon, the Foreign Secretary, that the Persian Government would be 'disposed to take advantage of your presumed ignorance of the forms of Persian etiquette to withhold from you those attentions to which you are entitled'. Clarendon instructed Murray to resist such stratagems since 'you will not win esteem or acquire influence by neglecting to exact the respect due to your position according to Persian notions' (5). It is tempting to speculate whether, without such instructions, Murray's behaviour in Tehran might have been less provocative. Consuls were sometimes in dispute with provincial governors, often proud men of considerable local importance, about the call which the Governor was expected to make first. Even Boundary Commissioners, camping close to each other in the remote deserts of Baluchistan, argued about the all-important first call. When in 1903 Curzon sailed on a viceregal progress round the Persian Gulf he refused to land at Bushire, despite the lavish preparations there for his reception, because the Shah's representative would not agree to make the first call.

Another cause of misunderstanding and friction was the custom of present-giving which John McNeill, writing from Tehran in the 1830s, described as 'one of the greatest annoyances to be encountered by a new Envoy' (6). An Ambassador's position and influence tended in those days to depend on the value of the presents he brought to Court. Malcolm had set the standard and spoilt the market for those who followed—including the Russians, who complained that the British had 'introduced a system of prodigality with which the Persians have for some time been accustomed to be treated by foreigners' (7). Yet if his Mission was to cut any ice, Malcolm cannot altogether be blamed for following an established oriental custom. India had, however, given him big ideas and he spared no expense in his choice of gifts. These included a large diamond for the Shah, jewelled watches, enamelled golden caskets, glass lustreware, guns, pistols and such European novelties as 'airguns and electrifying machines'. He did not, it seems, distribute any cash and later was highly critical of Harford Jones for doing so—Jones however

Formalities and Frictions

took the realistic view, based on his earlier experiences in Persia and Basra, that 'presents in money are always the most acceptable, because neither the presenter nor the presented, could possibly estimate their value differently' (8). The crude fact was that the Persians had an unpleasant habit of asking the value of the presents they were receiving and did not hesitate, if disappointed, to express their dissatisfaction and ask for more.

In addition to cash Harford Jones brought an array of expensive presents for the Shah and his Ministers. Having, during his service with the East India Company, become something of an expert on precious stones he congratulated himself on presenting the Shah with a fine sixty-one carat diamond which had only cost the Company £10,000 but which he had valued to the Persians at £25,000. Malcolm, too, had gloated that Persian ignorance of the value of many of his gifts made them estimate them at double the real amount. Amongst Jones' other gifts for the Shah was an enamelled gold snuff box with a miniature portrait of George III surrounded in diamonds on the lid.

The heavy cost of these presents was borne by the East India Company, which had already called Malcolm severely to account for his extravagance in 1800. Gore Ouseley, who succeeded Jones, was therefore asked before he left London 'not to exceed the most economical limits' (9) when purchasing his presents. He duly reported to the Foreign Office that he had only spent £20,000 on presents which included a diamond ring for the Shah, a portrait of the Queen set in diamonds for the Shah's favourite wife, a landaulet, china and glassware, guns and telescopes.

Understandably Ouseley was somewhat put out when a Court official complained that the diamond ring only weighed eighteen carats and that, unlike Malcolm and Jones, he had failed to give the Shah £5,000 worth of pearls and £5,000 in cash. Whether they had in fact done so seems improbable, it being more likely that the Court official used this ploy in an attempt to feather his own nest. Many of the gifts, especially the bulkier ones, suffered great damage on the long and rough journey from Bushire to Tehran. Over a third of Ouseley's large mirrors were smashed but the specially made carriage with silver fittings, though damaged, was fit to present to the Shah. It was, however, put away and never used—the fate of many such royal gifts, not only in Qajar times.

Jones' practice of making large gifts in cash, abandoned by Ouseley, was revived by Macdonald, the Government of India's envoy to Persia in 1826. He arrived loaded with cash as well as the by now customary gifts of European manufacture such as chandeliers, cut-glass lustreware and a sporting gun inlaid with gold: in addition there was a Wedgwood breakfast set, various fabrics and 'a very considerable quantity of Hodgson's ale' for the Shah's principal consort. Some of the cash and presents were distributed at Shiraz and Isfahan on the journey to Tehran but the lion's share was reserved for the Shah, including twelve scarlet bags each containing 1,000 tomans in hard cash (10).

Macdonald's successor, Campbell, was the unfortunate victim of an economy drive by the East India Company which severely cut his pay and allowances. The presents he had to offer, including only 2,000 tomans in cash, compared very poorly with Macdonald's and caused much offence to the Shah who thought, not incorrectly, that this was a reflection of his diminished importance in British eyes. To mollify him the Shah's ministers recommended that the cash payment should be increased but, as this was not possible, Campbell eventually agreed to add a gun and a glass lustre to the gifts already presented. Needless to say this gesture scarcely sufficed to obliterate the first bad impression and one of the reasons given later by Campbell for the loss of British influence in Tehran during his tenure of office was the diminished value of his royal gifts. Over twenty years later Charles Murray attributed the disastrous failure of his own mission to his arrival in Tehran without the customary presents for the Shah and the Prime Minister—'when it became known that I had brought nothing but my own private baggage and supplies the indignation of the Court knew no bounds', he sadly recorded after leaving Persia (11).

With the transfer of responsibility for Persian affairs to the Foreign Office steps were taken to curb a practice which was both expensive and embarrassing. McNeill in 1836 was authorised to spend £1,000 on presents for Persian ministers but only when the treaties he had been instructed to negotiate were concluded: as the negotiations were interrupted by the Herat dispute the money was probably not all spent by the careful Scot. In 1847 Palmerston informed Sheil that none of his staff was in future to accept the shawls traditionally presented by the Shah at *Nau Ruz*, the Persian New Year's Day, since 'it is a general rule that Her Majesty's Diplomatic servants are not to accept Presents from any Government, and there seems to be no good reason why this Rule should not be observed in Persia as elsewhere' (12). Presumably the refusal of Persian gifts was to balance the stoppage from the British side. When Charles Murray was appointed to Tehran in 1854 he lamented that the post was no longer under the Government of India which would, he believed, have allowed him to bring suitable presents. His successor, Rawlinson, who was appointed by the newly created India Office, was permitted to spend £1,000 on presents, a paltry sum compared with past expenditure but more than was ever to be allowed again. Although the custom of present-giving on arrival was never entirely eliminated during the Qajar period (Sir Percy Loraine in 1921 was allowed £200 for the purpose) Rawlinson was the last British envoy to arrive with the traditional array of gifts for the Shah personally. It is, therefore, of interest to record that they consisted of a jewelled watch forming the clasp of an embroidered waist-belt: a Copeland porcelain dinner service: a pair of double-barrelled Purdey guns with gold mountings: a double-barrelled Purdey rifle: a pair of Purdey duelling pistols: a ruby glass chandelier: twelve pieces of rich flowered silk: a large Negretti and Zamba stereoscope with slides: and an embroidered hawking glove. In addition there were watches and guns for the *mehmandar* and others who had assisted with the envoy's arrival.

When, shortly after reaching Tehran, Rawlinson was informed that the Foreign Office had resumed responsibility for Persian affairs and were not prepared to enter into a competition with other Powers in the distribution of presents he resigned. Rawlinson subscribed to Charles Murray's view that there were only two ways of securing attention in Persia, the purse and the sword, and pointed out to the Foreign Office that the Persian system of offering presents to the Shah and his Ministers was a national institution dating from the time of Cyrus the Great. He feared that if England now discontinued the practice she would suffer to the advantage of the other European powers represented in Tehran, who were less squeamish on such matters. But the Foreign Office stuck to their guns and informed Alison, Rawlinson's successor, that the Government were not prepared 'to conciliate the favour of foreign Potentates or their Ministers by making presents to them' (13). In practice the exchange of gifts, being part of the Persian way of life, continued though on a much smaller scale. 'Presents', wrote Lady Durand after her 1899 tour of Western Persia with her husband, 'are very necessary in Persia ... the custom adds considerably to the cost of travelling' (14).

On the Persian side it was customary during the Qajar period for the Shah to present the new envoy, either during the *esteqbal* on the outskirts of the capital or shortly after his arrival, with a white stallion from the royal stables. In the early days, too, the envoy and each of his suite would be given a *khel'at*, or embroidered robe of honour, and shawl which they would be expected to don and wear at least once in the Shah's presence. Also, when departing envoys took final leave of the Shah, they were, in the early days, handsomely rewarded—Harford Jones, who had indicated that as he was not rich he would prefer cash to kind, was given a thousand tomans in addition to a jewelled aigrette which he valued at between £200 and £300. Gore Ouseley was given a valuable sword and an emerald-studded belt in addition to £2,400 which the Shah remitted to London for the purchase of gold plate to be engraved with the royal arms of Persia.

The bestowal of decorations then, as to-day, was part of the royal ritual. The principal Order of the Qajar kings was that of the Lion and Sun which was given in 1810 to Malcolm who claimed that it had been specially created for him. There was some truth in this. A year earlier, at the annual *Nau Ruz* ceremony, Harford Jones had refused the Order of the Sun because of its close association with the French and, as he explained to the Foreign Office, 'of all the circumstances which had given rise to the creation of the Order and the persons on whom it had been bestowed' (15).* The Shah, though hurt by Jones' refusal, seems to have accepted his explanation and instead issued a *farman* authorising him to incorporate the royal arms of Persia into his own arms, a unique distinction. No more was heard of the Order of the Sun which now became the Order of the Lion and Sun. Many British and other foreigners received this decoration during the Qajar period. Among the last to do so was the late Lord Ironside,† then commanding British troops in north Persia, on whom it was unexpectedly conferred by Ahmad Shah a few days before the *coup d'état* that was to sweep away the dynasty.

Decorations, being essentially personal awards bestowed by the sovereign, formed no part of the stock in trade of the early British envoys. However, with the consolidation of British power in India Persians were sometimes rewarded, in return for services rendered or expected, with the Most Exalted Order of the Star of India, which had been created in 1861 and was in the gift of the Viceroy. Masud *Mirza*, Zill ul-Sultan, Nasir ed-din Shah's eldest son and the all-powerful governor of most of southern Persia, greatly coveted the Grand Cross of the Order and let it be known that the grant of navigation rights on the Karun river and a railway concession for the British were linked with it. Contrary to the advice of the British Minister, Ronald Thomson, who correctly feared that it would upset other members of the royal family, the Viceroy decided in 1887 that the Grand Cross should be conferred on Zill ul-Sultan. A few months later the Shah, who had not been consulted, stripped his son of most of his powers

---

* The Order of the Sun, modelled on the *Légion d'Honneur*, had been instituted in 1807 and awarded to General Gardane and some members of his mission. Before paying his farewell call on the Shah in July 1810 Malcolm asked for the same honours as had been conferred on the French General *viz*, the Order, and the titles of Khan and Sardar. The Shah granted him all three.

† See p. 180 *et seq*,

Formalities and Frictions

and thus gave a warning that such honours could be the kiss of death for Britain's friends. But the irrepressible Drummond Wolff, who succeeded Thomson, was a great believer in presents and decorations to help oil the wheels of diplomacy: apparently with Foreign Office permission, he created his own 'Wolff Medal' of which there were three classes, gold, silver and bronze, each with the head of the Queen on one side and a pretty red and blue riband. Wolff himself awarded the medal to all and sundry, whether Qajar princes, high officials or Legation servants.

Ever since the days of Cyrus the Great the Persians have celebrated their New Year's Day at the Spring equinox. In Qajar times, as to-day, it was an occasion for popular rejoicing when the foreign envoys as well as Persians offered the Shah their congratulations and good wishes. At least until the middle of the nineteenth century it was customary, either on the eve or morning of *Nau Ruz*, for the Shah to send to the British and other Missions gifts of robes of honour, shawls, sweetmeats and small silken purses of newly minted gold and silver coins: they were borne through the streets on immense trays on the heads of twenty or more royal *farashes*. Later in the morning the envoy with his staff, in full-dress uniform, would ride to the palace, escorted by their own bodyguard: as they neared the palace ten or twelve royal footmen in long scarlet tunics preceded by silver mace-bearers would join the cavalcade which would slow down to walking pace. By the turn of the century the Minister had abandoned his horse for a carriage and, shortly before World War I, for a motor-car.

On these occasions footwear was a matter of considerable importance. It then was—and still is in some parts of Persia—a normal custom to remove one's dusty shoes before crossing the threshold of a house. It would have been unthinkable for anyone to enter the Shah's or a Prince-Governor's presence in ordinary footwear: Court etiquette required that all entering a royal presence should wear long scarlet stockings or cloth boots held by garters at the knee and, over them, high-heeled green slippers which, on approaching the audience chamber, were removed at stated distances according to one's rank. The Europeans regarded the gear as ridiculous: after 1828, under the terms of an Annexe to the Treaty of Turkmanchai the red stockings were abolished in favour of galoshes which diplomats had to don before entering the Palace precincts and then discard on the threshold of the audience chamber.* Unusual also for Europeans was the custom of keeping the head covered throughout the audience and on other formal occasions such as banquets.

* This procedure ended with Nasir ed-Din Shah's death in 1896.

39

The English Amongst the Persians

The mounted escorts of the British and Russian Ministers and their Consuls were a feature of the later Qajar period which aroused considerable ill-feeling: most Persians resented this flaunting of power by these foreign envoys as they rode through narrow streets flanked by Indian *sowars* or Russian cossacks.

Malcolm, Harford Jones and Ouseley, when they arrived at Bushire, had been accompanied by bodyguards of Indian cavalry and infantry under British officers: they escorted the envoys on their journeys to Tehran and Tabriz and then remained as part of the Mission's complement. When, in 1814, it was decided to run down the Military Mission an escort of some thirty sepoys was left behind for the Legation's protection and probably remained at this strength until the break in relations in 1839 when all military personnel were withdrawn. For some years afterwards the British were apt to complain that their Minister cut a forlorn figure by comparison with his Russian and Turkish colleagues, both of whom could boast impressive mounted escorts. With their star in the ascendant the Russians later employed their own cossacks as escort for their Minister and Consuls while, in order not to be placed entirely in the shade, the British decked out the Legation's twelve *gholams* (mounted messengers) in scarlet tunics for ceremonial occasions. In the struggle for influence, where appearances mattered much, the British Minister, Arthur Hardinge, eventually persuaded London and Calcutta in 1901 that, in order to keep his end up, he must have an escort of Indian *sowars* who, with their turbans and pennoned lances, could be expected to impress the Persians 'with the might and majesty of the British Empire' (16).

The consulates, too, which were sprouting up all over Persia were provided with impressive *sowar* guards—indeed Mashad could boast such a guard from its opening in 1889: by 1901 the Sistan Consulate had fifteen *sowars* on its strength. Three years later, mainly as a riposte to a large increase in the number of Russian cossacks, over a hundred additional *sowars* were brought in from India—despite Persian objections —and distributed among the various consulates.

Other injury to Persian feelings was caused less by Anglo-Russian rivalry than by an almost total breakdown of law and order in southern Persia, considered by the British as their sphere of influence. Although the threat to British lives and property was a real one this made British action, usually taken without a by-your-leave, no less unpalatable to the Persians. In 1898 a small naval party was landed at Bushire to protect the Indo-European Telegraph Station and European colony there against invading Tangistani tribesmen and remained ashore until twenty-five sepoys arrived from Bombay as additional guards for the

Formalities and Frictions

Residency. A year later another naval party was put ashore at Lingeh to guard the British Agency there when fighting broke out between Persians and Arabs. In 1907 twenty *sowars* of the 18th Bengal Lancers under Captain A. T. Wilson* were sent to Ahwaz ostensibly to reinforce the existing twelve-man Consular guard, but in reality to protect the British drillers then searching for oil in Khuzistan. In 1909, at the behest of the British Political Resident, a naval force was landed at Bushire to protect the foreign communities there: in 1912 and 1913 naval parties went ashore at Lingeh and Bandar Abbas for the same purpose. But most humiliating of all was the landing in October 1911 of four squadrons of the Central Indian Horse at Bushire where one squadron remained while the other three marched up country to reinforce the consular guard at Shiraz and Isfahan: they remained there over a year before being withdrawn. On the march up there was a skirmish with tribesmen in which Walter Smart, the British Vice-Consul at Shiraz, was wounded and six sepoys killed. As retribution a force of two hundred and fifty Indian sepoys was sent from Bombay: they, too, marched to Shiraz to swell the large guard already there and to embarrass Frederick O'Connor, the Consul, in his dealings with the Persians who, he recorded, regarded them as 'an insult and a threat to their independence' (17). In addition, detachments of Indian troops, each forty-five or so strong, were stationed at Bushire, Jask and Chahbahar to protect the Indo-European Telegraph Department's installations.

Two other tiresome causes of friction, involving prestige on both sides, were the protection afforded by the British to certain Persians and the sanctuary or *bast* given by the Legation and Consulates to Persians seeking refuge within their walls.

The Treaty of Turkmanchai gave the Russians extra-territorial rights for their subjects and any others, including Persians, under their protection. Similar rights were duly conceded to Britain and other countries enjoying 'most favoured nation' treatment. These capitulatory rights, as they were known, entitled those under British protection to be tried in special courts and to enlist diplomatic and consular support in case of need. Additionally it was officially recognised in a *farman* issued by the Shah in 1840 that 'all the servants and dependants of the English

---

* Sir Arnold Wilson, K.C.I.E. (1884-1940). A man of many parts and great energy. From the Indian Army he transferred to the Indian Political Service. Served in Persia 1907-14 and in Mesopotamia, 1915-20: Resident Director in Persia of the A.P.O.C. 1921-6: M.P.(Nat.C) for Hitchin, 1933-40. Author of books on Persia and the Persian Gulf, including an invaluable *Bibliography of Persia*. Killed in 1940 as a rear-gunner with the RAF during a raid over Germany.

Mission, whether these be Persians or natives of other countries' would enjoy safety and protection and not be punished without the knowledge of the English Minister (18). The Persian authorities not unnaturally resented the privileged position thus acquired by many of their own subjects. In particular there were the *mirzas* employed by the British and other Legations as interpreters and intermediaries who, being human, often made the most of their position in their own and their families' interests. In 1854 the Persian Prime Minister formally requested the British Chargé d'Affaires not to employ *mirzas* to transact business with himself or the Foreign Minister; he stated that he had no confidence in these people though they were natives of Persia. Understandably Persian ministers felt slighted in having to deal with Persian employees rather than with the British diplomats themselves, though the system cut both ways as these same employees must in many cases have proved an invaluable source of information about British activities.*

Charles Murray's bitter quarrel with the Persians stemmed mainly from his ill-judged championship of *Mirza* Hashem Khan and his wife. However the fault was not all Murray's as the couple had been taken under British protection before his arrival in Tehran at the time when an unsuccessful attempt had been made to appoint the *Mirza* to the Legation staff. Murray felt obliged to continue this protection although the Persians argued that there were no grounds for it.

Inevitably in the David and Goliath situation that then existed between the two countries the British tended to read more into the 1840 *farman* than had been intended. In addition to protecting the often large families of the many Persians, including domestic staff, in their employ, the British Legation were also ready to recognise as Protected Persons other Persians to whom they felt, for one reason or another, under an obligation. One such was Mir Ali Naqi Khan, for long a trusted confidant and protégé of the Legation, who alleged that some £50,000 worth of property had been stolen from his Tehran house at the time of the Anglo-Persian War of 1856. The Legation, though doubtful of their right to intervene, felt honour bound to continue their protection of this Persian subject. Their demand for compensation was disputed and resented by the Persian Government. The case dragged on for six years and was only settled by a personal appeal to the Shah by Eastwick, the Chargé d'Affaires. Eastwick sensed Persian feelings

---

* Surprisingly, despite the resentments and risks, the British continued to employ *mirzas* on confidential business until long after the end of the Qajar period. They were important members of the Legation's Oriental Secretariat, which acquired a reputation in Persian eyes for interference in their affairs.

Formalities and Frictions

when he asked 'What Government in the world would like redress of a wrong to be exacted for one of its own quondam subjects by a foreign Power?' (19). Count de Gobineau, the French diplomat who took charge of British interests during the Anglo-Persian War, complained bitterly about the problems caused for him by the dozen or so Persian-born British protégés, many of whom he considered to be *'les plus fameux coquins qu'il y ait de Trébizonde à la frontière de Chine'* (20).

With the extension of their sovereignty in India the British felt obliged to offer their protection to a number of Indian merchants, many of them long resident in Persia and hitherto without any such advantage in their dealings with the rapacious Persian authorities. There were also men of Persian origin who claimed British protection on the score that they were born in India on what was now British territory. The Persians resented, and often queried, the British claim to protect these people. A particularly acrimonious *cause célèbre* was that of *Hajji* Abd al-Karim who had acquired immense wealth since settling in Persia in the early days of the century and been given British protection in 1849 on the grounds that he was born in British India. The Persian authorities disputed this and claimed that the *Hajji* was a native of Kandahar; they much resented British support for an individual who was linked by marriage with the Shah and was claiming large sums of money from the Persian Government. Differences over this case reached such a pitch that Taylour Thomson, the British Chargé d'Affaires, in November 1853 hauled down his flag and suspended diplomatic relations with the Persian Government until they capitulated after three weeks and agreed to settle with the *Hajji*.

Under the terms of the Treaty of Paris of 1857 the British Government renounced its right to protect any Persian subject not actually in the employ of the British Mission or Consulates. However, this did not prevent a few important Persians from making embarrassing demands which were sometimes difficult to refuse, given their past services or the importance of securing their goodwill. Without such assurances, in the Persia of those days, their lives might well have been at risk. Among those who sought and secured limited assurances of protection, qualified by such a phrase as 'so long as Your Excellency continues to act in a loyal manner towards H.I.M. the Shah' were Zill ul-Sultan, the leading Bakhtiari khans and, most embarrassing of all, the Shaikh of Mohammerah whose ultimate fate exposed the emptiness of such assurances in a rapidly changing world. There were others who, by maintaining close contact with individuals in the Legation or Consulates, sometimes considered themselves under British protection and almost made a profession of their links with the British. They were the 'professional anglophils' who have incurred much odium in their own country but who, because of their touching faith in Britain, deserve an honourable mention, embarrassing though they often were to the cause of Anglo-Persian relations. One such was Bahram, Christopher Sykes' hero in his *Four Studies in Loyalty*.

There was another class of British protégés, created by Anglo-Russian rivalry and both countries' efforts, when they considered their interests threatened, to make sure that provincial governorships were in friendly hands. To this end the British, like the Russians, did not hesitate to bring pressure on the Persian authorities, though such interference in internal affairs was greatly resented. In 1899 Durand was able to report to the Foreign Office that 'in the south we have greatly strengthened our position by insisting upon, and obtaining, the removal of an obnoxious Governor of Bushire' (21). In 1903 the British Minister protested against the threatened removal from office of the Governor of Sistan in whose support the Government of India were even prepared to occupy Nusratabad (now Zabol). As a result of a secret agreement made with the Bakhtiari khans before World War I the British Government undertook to help secure the appointment of Bakhtiari candidates to certain governorships. In Persian eyes such governors were little more than British puppets.

From time to time the oppressed and persecuted religious minorities —Zoroastrians, Jews, Nestorians, Armenians and Bahais—would seek the protection of the British Legation or Consulates. Sometimes the British, who in those days were inclined to regard themselves as the keepers of the world's conscience, would take up the cudgels, embarrassing though it was to intervene on behalf of Persian subjects.

The Zoroastrians, or *guebres* as the Persians called them, were concentrated in and around the desert towns of Kerman and Yazd but some were also settled in Tehran where they provided the Legation's gardeners. Their co-religionists, the Parsees of India, were much exercised by the harsh conditions under which their Persian kinsmen were forced to live and in 1854, with funds raised by the rich Parsee community in Bombay, sent an agent to reside in Persia and do what he could to ameliorate their lot. From then on the Persian Zoroastrian Amelioration Society of Bombay was able to maintain a permanent representative in Persia who, being a British subject, enjoyed the full support of the British Legation. When Nasir ed-Din Shah paid his first State Visit to London in 1873 the British Government arranged for him to receive a four-man delegation of Bombay Parsees who urged him to improve the position of the *guebres*. The support of the British Legation in Tehran was largely responsible for the abolition in 1882 of a discriminatory poll tax on them. In 1908 the British Minister reminded the Persian authorities that his Government took 'a very warm interest in the welfare of the Zoroastrians' (22) and called for the punishment of those implicated in the murder of a prominent member of their community. At that time the agent of the Bombay Parsees was a Mr Ardeshir Reporter, who had been sent to Tehran from Bombay in 1893 at the age of twenty-seven and died there in 1933. He, too, kept in close touch with the British Legation and counted many influential Persians among his friends, by whom he was known as Ardeshirjee.

It was less easy for the British to assist the Jews but they did what they could. In 1850 a Jewish traveller from Germany found that the position of the seventy-odd Jewish families in Bushire was less oppressive than elsewhere in Persia due to the presence there of a British representative. The interest and activities of the London Society for the Promotion of Christianity among the Jews also provided Persian Jews with some moral support. In London the leader of British Jewry, Sir Moses Montefiore, armed with a Legation report on the Jews in Urumiyah, also spelt Urmia (now Rezaieh), in western Azarbaijan, persuaded the Foreign Office to instruct the British Minister to protest to the Persian Government about their situation. On the occasion of the Shah's visit to London in 1873 the Foreign Office arranged for him to receive Sir Moses and a deputation from the Jewish Board of Deputies, to whom he promised better treatment for Persian Jews. In 1896, on instructions from the Foreign Office, the British Minister intervened successfully on behalf of some three hundred Jews, living in Fars, who were threatened with forcible conversion to Islam. A few years previously the British Minister, alone among the foreign envoys, had protested to the Shah about the massacre of over twenty Jews in the Caspian town of Barfurush (now Babol). Such interventions were never welcomed and in 1905 when the British Consul at Shiraz sent his *sowars* to protect Jewish women and children from anti-Jewish rioters the Persian Government lodged an official complaint against him.

A little known facet of Anglo-Persian history is the protection at one time afforded by the British, at Persian request, to the large Christian Armenian population of Azarbaijan. This happened shortly after the signature of the Treaty of Turkmanchai in 1828 when the Armenians showed signs of emigrating to Russia. The British Minister, having pointed out to the Crown Prince what a loss this industrious people would be for the country, was asked to use his good offices in persuading them to remain in Persia. This he successfully did and, as a result, the Crown Prince issued a *farman* placing the Armenians under Macdonald's protection. On Macdonald's death this responsibility passed first to

The English Amongst the Persians

Major Hart and then to Dr Cormick, the senior British residents in Tabriz. After Cormick's death in 1833 British responsibility for the Armenians lapsed until 1848. In that year, following strong British complaints about the treatment of the Armenians, the newly crowned Shah issued a *farman* placing them under the protection of Stevens, the British Consul in Tabriz. But this authority was withdrawn a few months later, almost certainly on the insistence of the Russians who now regarded the Armenians as their protégés. However this did not deter the British from protesting from time to time to the Persians about their treatment of the Armenians.

The British were also interested in another large Christian minority, the Nestorians, or Assyrians as they came to be called. Most of them lived under Ottoman rule but perhaps as many as 30,000 inhabited scattered villages around Lake Urumiyah on Persian territory and were from time to time the victims of persecution and ill treatment by Persians and Kurds alike. A succession of British Ministers in Tehran remonstrated, on instructions from the Foreign Office, against their treatment: they also sent members of their staff to Urumiyah to demonstrate British concern for these people. 'You must', wrote Palmerston to Alison, 'impress on His Majesty that Persia will never be able to take a place among civilised nations as long as one class of His Majesty's people are permitted, on account of their creed, to oppress with impunity another class' (23). In 1898 the British Minister insisted on the dismissal of the Governor of Urumiyah for allowing the execution of a Nestorian without trial or investigation. Though resented, these interventions could not be ignored and did usually lead to a temporary improvement in the plight of the Nestorians.

The right of sanctuary or *bast* at certain places such as mosques, shrines and the royal stables was an old Persian tradition. In the course of the nineteenth century foreign Legations and Consulates were also recognised as places where Persians, whether or not officially under foreign protection, could take refuge without fear of molestation; in due course the Indo-European Telegraph Department's stations also acquired *bast* status.

The Persians complained that Sheil was the first British envoy to make the Mission 'a sanctuary and house of refuge for discontented persons and mischief makers and dangerous characters' (24). There had, in fact, been differences as early as 1827 between the two countries over Persian subjects who had taken refuge in the Residency at Bushire during disturbances there. It then seems to have been decided by the British that it would be bad for their good name to violate local custom by refusing to harbour refugees, though this was to be done with discretion

Major-General Sir John Malcolm by Samuel Lane. By courtesy of the Committee of Management of the Oriental Club, London.

Sir Harford Jones Brydges by Sir Thomas Lawrence. By courtesy of the late Lt. Commander J. H. S. Lucas-Scudamore.

Sir Harford Jones Brydges' coat of arms, showing the Qajar crown, the Lion and Sun, and the motto 'By Royal Favour' in Persian.

Major-General Sir Henry Lindesay-Bethune by Sir Francis Grant.
By courtesy of David Lindesay-Bethune, Viscount Garnock.

Mr Charles Alison by Capt. W. H. Pierson, 1865. By courtesy of Miss Philippa Bateman-Champain.

so as to minimise difficulties with the Persian authorities. Difficulties were, of course, unavoidable as, more often than not, the *bastis* were seeking to escape from the Persian authorities. Neither the Foreign Office in London nor the Legation in Tehran liked the practice, which they did their best to discourage. Stevens, the Tabriz Consul, had greatly annoyed the authorities there by his willingness to grant asylum to all and sundry. Sheil therefore wrote to tell him in 1852 that 'as a general rule it is only in cases of real danger of life or person from unjust accusation that the privilege of sanctuary ought to be accorded: for as I have before stated to you, every instance of this kind is an encroachment on the independence of Persia' (25). A year later the Foreign Office informed Sheil that they would gladly prohibit Consuls from granting asylum provided the Russians would do the same—but took a different line three months later when they said they would not give up the right of affording sanctuary until a better system of government was established in Persia. As the Russians were not willing to move and the system of government got worse the British did not give up the privilege; to have done so unilaterally would only have damaged their prestige among the Persians despite the embarrassment it caused in official relations.

From Sheil's time the Legation grounds at both Tehran and Gulhek frequently provided sanctuary for *bastis* who made their own eating and sleeping arrangements. Some stayed only a few days, others months. Later in Qum, Yazd, Kerman and elsewhere *bastis* resorted to the British-run telegraph stations, sometimes because of religious persecution, sometimes because they wished to stage a protest against what they considered unjust official action, sometimes as fugitives from justice. The bigger *basts* which took place in Tabriz and Tehran in the early years of the twentieth century were connected with the constitutional movement whose leaders looked to Britain for inspiration and support. In 1905 about three hundred 'Constitutionalists' sought sanctuary in the gardens of the British Consulate in Tabriz where they camped for over a week. A year later the most celebrated of all *basts*, lasting three weeks from mid-July until 5 August, took place when between 12,000 and 16,000 Tehranis of all classes found sanctuary in the gardens of the Tehran Legation. As a result the bazaars were closed and life in Tehran was virtually paralysed so that the Shah was forced to give in and issue his famous *farman* of 5 August 1906—a day still celebrated in Persia as Constitution Day—granting the people a constitution and National Assembly or Majles.

The British acquired much credit for this successful 'sit-in' though they had only reluctantly allowed it to take place at all. But much of

The English Amongst the Persians

the goodwill thus created, particularly among the nationalists and liberals, was dissipated the following year by the signature of the Anglo-Russian Convention. Nevertheless when, in 1908, the reactionary new Shah, Mohammad Ali, sought to turn back the clock, between thirty and forty of them, including their famous leader Taqizadeh, took refuge in the Legation. The Shah's Cossack Brigade,* under their Russian commander, not only bombarded the Majles buildings but, in an effort to intimidate intending *bastis*, surrounded the British Legation which they also threatened to bombard.

The Legation, Consulates and telegraph stations continued to provide sanctuary, despite all attempts by the British and the Persians to discourage the practice, almost to the end of the Qajar period for those who sought it and were able to gain admittance.

* Modelled on the Czar's Cossack Regiment, the Persian Cossack Brigade, composed of Persian soldiers trained and manned by Russian officers and N.C.O.s, was started in 1879. Although it also included Persian officers and N.C.O.s, it was, until 1920, always commanded by a Russian. The Brigade thus served as an instrument of Russian policy.

4

Wars and Warriors

THE FAILURE OF the French to honour their 1807 Treaty with Fath Ali Shah had opened the way for Harford Jones' successful negotiations. A key issue was the training, already begun by the French, of Abbas *Mirza*'s new army. The Crown Prince was convinced that this must be along European lines if his country was to have any chance of withstanding Russian attacks. The British realised that if they were to displace the French they must be prepared themselves to train and equip this force. Accordingly when Malcolm arrived at Bushire on his second, and abortive, mission he sent his relation, Captain Charles Pasley, ahead to inform the Shah 'that the English are ready to supply the place of every French Officer and Artificer that he orders out of the country'. He was also to offer the Shah a 'voluntary gift' of twenty pieces of cannon, 5,000 stand of small arms, 2,500 carbines and 2,500 pairs of pistols (1).

Pasley got no further than Shiraz but in the course of his discussions there the Persians seem to have recognised the makings of a good bargain. By the time Harford Jones arrived on the scene, hot on Malcolm's heels, he was told that the Shah insisted on the fulfilment of Malcolm's alleged promises, now grown in size, before he would agree to expel the French or receive the new envoy. Jones, determined to succeed where Malcolm had failed, took it upon himself to promise an annual subsidy of 160,000 tomans, then equivalent to £120,000, so long as Russia was at war with Britain, to cover the cost of military stores, equipment and instructors from Britain as well as the pay of 16,000 Persian soldiers. This was the price, somewhat increased in subsequent negotiations, paid for the Preliminary Treaty and the expulsion of the French.

When Malcolm returned to Persia in 1810 on his third mission he brought ten cannon specially cast in India and decorated with the Shah's name and arms. On leaving Persia a few months later he agreed to Jones' request that various members of his suite, including Captain Charles Christie of the Bombay Regiment, Lieutenant Henry Lindsay of the Madras Regiment, Ensign William Monteith of the Madras Engineers and Surgeon John Cormick, should remain behind to form the nucleus of the Military Mission provided for in Jones' Preliminary Treaty. Henry and George Willock of the Madras Cavalry, who were already in Persia, joined the Mission which was further increased with the arrival in Tabriz in early 1812 of Majors Joseph D'Arcy and Stone with two NCOs and ten privates of the Royal Artillery and Engineers; they had travelled from England with Ouseley, since gunners and engineers could not be spared from India. A number of drill sergeants recruited from the 47th Regiment in India joined the Ouseley party in Bombay. By the time they all reached Tabriz, which was to be their headquarters, the Military Mission numbered over thirty British officers and men together with a French soldier of fortune, Major Gaspard Drouville, who had been recruited by the Crown Prince and foisted on the British, of whom, with the exception of Christie, he had little good to say. D'Arcy commanded the Mission and under him Stone, Christie and Lindsay were respectively in charge of arsenal and ordnance, infantry, and horse artillery: Drouville, assisted by Henry Willock, was responsible for training the cavalry and Monteith the engineers.

Later in the year a party of twenty-five British officers, sergeants and privates under the command of Lieutenant G. Forster Sadleir of the 47th Regiment sailed from India, ultimately reaching Tabriz in early 1813 when they brought the British contingent up to over fifty. In addition, native Indian troops, or sepoys, who had travelled to Persia either as escort to Jones or Ouseley or with the British contingent from India, were attached to the Military Mission to help with the training of the Persians. They must have suffered terribly from the bitter cold winters of north-western Persia.

Military stores and equipment were shipped from England and India. Even before Ouseley left London for Persia in 1810 Wellesley, the Foreign Secretary, had written to inform the Persian envoy there that the new Ambassador would be authorised to provide an annual subsidy of 200,000 tomans from 1 January 1810 'to be expended solely on such part of the Military Establishment of Persia as may be agreed'; that facilities would be available for the conveyance to Persia of 'British Officers, Artillerymen, Artizans and Manufacturers' in numbers to be agreed between the Shah and the Ambassador: that the East India Company had issued orders 'for the supply of 16,000 Musquets, and twenty pieces of Horse Artillery . . . and in addition to that number,

4,000 Musquets will be sent later from Europe and India' (2). Ouseley himself brought a quantity of military stores including guns and muskets from England. The British seemed determined to do all they could to help modernise the Persian army.

The armed forces were mostly concentrated in Azerbaijan province which bordered on Russia. Members of the Military Mission were responsible to the Crown Prince who commanded the army and had his headquarters in Tabriz: in the last resort, however, the Mission were under the orders of the British envoy. When in Tabriz the officers, who were unaccompanied by wives in the early days, took it in turns to dine in each other's houses and relieved the monotony of their lives —for they rarely, if ever, entered the houses of the local Moslem inhabitants then, as now, very shy of foreigners—by hunting, making music, entertaining the occasional European traveller and exchanging visits with the Russian Mission. The sergeants and privates cultivated potatoes* and other little known European vegetables, made their own wine and flirted with girls from the large Christian Armenian population, a number of whom they married. When the time came for their return to India or England they were not allowed to take their brides with them and D'Arcy, their sympathetic Commanding Officer, proposed to the British envoy in Tehran that the Catholicos, or Head of the Armenian Church, in Etchmiadzin should be asked to take a leaf from the Pope's book by annulling the marriages so that both parties might be free to marry again if they wished. History does not record what answer, if any, he received but at least one British sergeant, Dawson by name, is known to have purchased his discharge from the Army on his arrival in England and, perhaps to rejoin the girl he left behind, returned to enter the Crown Prince's army.

The British quickly established an arsenal with foundry in the *Arg* or Citadel at Tabriz under the supervision of Robert Armstrong, who had started life as a coach-builder in Calcutta and come to Persia with Malcolm. He was a highly skilled Master Artificer and with his 'boring machine' was soon turning out thirty good cannon a year in addition to shot, cartridges and gun-carriages. An Ordnance Department was opened under a Mr Clarke, known officially as Deputy Commissioner for Stores, who, like Armstrong, was an employee of the East India Company. Difficulties sometimes arose over conflicting orders given to these men by the Crown Prince and the British officers. Barracks were built near Maragheh, which the Crown Prince planned to make 'the Woolwich of Azarbaijan' (3). A drum and fife band which greeted

---

* In his account of his mission to Persia Harford Jones pours cold water on Malcolm's claim to have introduced the potato to Persia.

visiting dignitaries with gay British airs was started. Muskets, sabres and cloth, all of English make, replaced equipment supplied earlier by the French: the uniforms of the Persian troops—blue or red jackets, wide white or blue trousers—took on a distinctly British appearance though the pointed Persian lambskin hat continued to be worn. Men who had never before shaved became clean-shaven in conformity with British army regulations—all this being made possible by the strong support of Abbas *Mirza*, who was remarkable among his generation in Persia for his determination, despite opposition, to introduce western ways into his country.*

Officers and men were at first fully occupied in recruiting, equipping and training their new charges: recruits came forward without trouble now that they were paid regularly. Commands were at first given in English but, if Drouville is to be believed, were through his efforts later given in Azeri Turkish, the language of most of the Azerbaijanis.

When the Russians renewed their attacks on the Caucasian provinces in 1812 four of the British officers—D'Arcy, Lindsay, Christie and George Willock—together with twelve sergeants of the Artillery and 47th Regiment, accompanied the Persian soldiers into battle. They were delighted when, after a series of defeats, the Persians, albeit numerically greatly superior, routed a small Russian force after a four-and-a-half-hour encounter at Sultanabad near the river Aras on 13 February 1812: about 500 Russians were killed or wounded for the loss of only 100 Persians and one British sergeant whose headless body was found the next morning. The Crown Prince, though barely recovered from treatment for venereal disease at the hands of the Mission's doctor, had insisted on leading his troops. He generously gave full credit for the victory to the British officers who had directed the operations. He also took the trouble to write to his old friend Harford Jones, recently arrived back home, to tell him that '*your* artillery was the sole cause of the victory' (4). Nor were the British slow to claim credit for themselves. Robert Gordon, of Ouseley's staff, wrote from Tehran to his brother, the twenty-eight-year-old Lord Aberdeen and future Prime Minister, that the victory 'has elated us all beyond measure—the fact is that the Persians have hitherto fled from the Russians, 500 of whom have been known to keep a whole Persian army at bay! The merit if there be any is entirely due to ourselves, and the English officers have only now prevailed upon them to face the enemy,

* He sent the first Persian students to England, to study medicine, engineering, etc.: two went in 1811 with Harford Jones and were placed in the care of Major James Sutherland who had been surveyor to Jones' mission: five more followed in 1815 in the care of Major D'Arcy. The Crown Prince also imported Persia's first printing press.

Wars and Warriors

after long drilling and teaching them to use the Artillery we have given' (5).

By now news that England and Russia had settled their differences and were at peace had filtered through to Persia, causing misgivings among both Russians and British about the role of the British Military Mission. The commander of Russian naval vessels in the Caspian wrote to D'Arcy after the capture of the coastal town of Lenkoran to complain that D'Arcy and other members of the British Mission had been fighting there against the Russians whom the British were now helping in Europe. Earlier in the year Robert Gordon had written to his brother to voice his own doubts about the wisdom of placing weapons 'in the hands of these barbarous Mussulmans and even fighting their battles against our brothers in Christianity' (6). It was hardly surprising therefore that the British Ambassador should now forbid members of the Military Mission to take part in any further action against the Russians though, under strong pressure from the Crown Prince and the officers themselves, he agreed exceptionally that Christie, Lindsay and Monteith with some thirteen sergeants might continue to do so. Monteith remained with the Persian frontier forces near Erivan, in charge of six guns and some cavalry, while Christie and Lindsay took part in the disastrous battle of Aslanduz on the north bank of the Aras on 31 October 1812 when the Persians were routed. Christie, a paragon of a man to judge by contemporary reports, was killed and twelve of Lindsay's fourteen precious guns lost. Dr Cormick, who was also present at the battle, found his friend Christie's body on the battlefield next morning. Earlier in the year another of the British officers, Major Stone, had died at Ardebil.

This was the end of British campaigning with the Persians against the Russians. Peace between England and Russia, followed by peace between Persia and Russia in 1813, caused the British Government to order the running down of the Military Mission, to quibble over the subsidy and to pay less attention to deliveries of military supplies. Napoleon's defeat at Waterloo in 1815 only served further to divert London's attention from Persia, much to the disappointment of the Shah and Crown Prince who had put their faith in British assistance and been impressed by the high calibre of many of the British Mission and their readiness to fight and die alongside the soldiers they had trained. A suggestion at this time by the Crown Prince that Persian officers should be sent to India for training was turned down by Lord Moira,* the new Governor-General, on the grounds that they 'would

---

* Francis Rawdon-Hastings, 1st Marquis of Hastings and 2nd Earl of Moira (1754–1826). Governor-General of India 1813–23.

The English Amongst the Persians

afford to the Native Corps an example of arrogance, licentiousness and depravity which might produce a baneful influence on the discipline and moral character of these Corps' (7).

By the end of 1815 most of the Military Mission, British and Indian, had been withdrawn though, on the entreaties of the Crown Prince, a small group of officers and seven or eight sergeants were allowed to remain, on condition that they took no part in operations against countries with whom Britain was at peace. Among them were Lindsay (now known as Lindesay-Bethune); Isaac Hart of the 65th Regiment, who had first come to Persia in 1812 and been put in charge of the infantry shortly after Christie's death at Aslanduz; Monteith; the brothers Willock who, after campaigning with Persian forces against the Kurds, turned to political work at the Legation; Dr Cormick and his assistant Campbell. Robert Armstrong, who had returned to India in 1815 and become an overseer in the East India Company's gun-carriage factory at Bombay, returned to Persia the following year at the urgent request of the Crown Prince and was again put in charge of the arsenal. He remained another five years in Persia: years later, when eighty years old and retired at home, he petitioned the Foreign Secretary to help obtain arrears of pay which, he claimed, the Persian Government still owed him.

Lindesay-Bethune retained charge of the horse artillery and Hart of the infantry: both men were held in high regard by the Shah and Crown Prince as well as by their own compatriots. Lindesay-Bethune, a giant of a man, six foot eight inches tall and looking every inch a soldier, had greatly impressed the Shah who likened him when they first met in 1810 to the Persian national hero Rustam: he infused an *esprit de corps* into the men he trained—no mean feat for a foreigner—and performed bravely in action, for which the Shah awarded him the Order of the Lion and Sun in 1816. He left Persia in 1821 to retire on pension to the estate he had inherited at Kilconquhar, Fife, but returned to Persia thirteen years later at the request of the British Government, then desperately trying to recover lost influence in Tehran. Lindesay-Bethune thereupon played an important role, commanding Persian troops which accompanied the newly proclaimed Shah from Tabriz to Tehran in 1834. In Tehran he and his soldiers secured the *Arg* and Royal Palace for the new Shah, then marched on to Isfahan and Shiraz to defeat and capture the Shah's two uncles who were disputing the succession. Three of the pretenders' sons fled the country and soon became the cause of some embarrassment to the British.* Muhammad Shah thus largely

* The three young princes went to London from Beirut on a British naval vessel in 1836. Later they settled in Baghdad with the help of a small pension from the British

Wars and Warriors

owed his throne to British support and in particular to Lindesay-Bethune who, though given the rank of General in the Shah's army, soon found that without the backing of his old friend Abbas *Mirza* he no longer commanded the same authority as of old. He returned to England in 1835 but was back in Persia a year later with a baronetcy and financial backing from the British Government to start an iron mine and foundry in Azerbaijan in addition to his military duties. The mining venture failed and he, with all other members of the Military Mission, left the country in early 1839 following the dispute over Herat. Lindesay-Bethune returned to Persia once again, in 1850, in search of health and a better climate than his native Scotland could offer. But he died in Tehran in February 1851, aged sixty-six, and was buried in the Armenian Church, near the British Legation.

Hart, who enjoyed the same excellent relations with the Crown Prince as Lindesay-Bethune, acquired a high reputation among the Persians as a disciplinarian; he died of cholera in Tabriz in 1830. It is on record that over thirty years later both these two British officers were still spoken of with admiration and affection by many Persians.

Among the members of the Mission who remained behind, Monteith left a memorial to himself in the fortress he built at Ardebil. He served with the Persian forces in their campaign against the Turks in 1821 and the Russians in 1826 and assisted with the delimitation of the frontier between Persia and Russia after the Treaties of Gulestan and Turkmanchai. He was also employed by the Government of India to map and collect topographical information about north-western Persia before leaving the country in 1829 after nineteen years' service there.

Of the two doctors, John Cormick married an Armenian lady and settled down in Tabriz as the Crown Prince's physician, accompanying him almost everywhere. He died at Nishapur in 1833 when hurrying to join Abbas *Mirza*, then on his way to Herat. James Campbell, who had also attended the Crown Prince in Tabriz, moved to Tehran to become the Legation doctor but died there in 1818, aged thirty-one.

Little is known about the activities of the sergeants other than that, under the command of Captain Benjamin Shee,* five of them took part in a two-year campaign against the Turkomans and other turbulent

---

Government who refused to hand them over to Muhammad Shah though the 1814 Treaty provided for the surrender of political refugees 'showing signs of hostility and rebellion'. The Shah suspected British intentions in harbouring them.

* Captain B. Shee of the Madras Regt. had joined the Mission in 1826 and been placed in temporary charge on Hart's death in 1830. In 1826 he climbed one of Persia's highest mountains, Mt. Savalan. He married a Georgian lady and in 1835-6 campaigned (and commanded) Persian troops in Fars.

elements in central and north-eastern Persia. They first marched from Tabriz to Yazd and Kerman, the old desert cities in the heart of the country over 1,000 miles away. They then went by way of Isfahan and Kashan along the northern fringe of the *Dasht-e-Kavir*, the Great Salt Desert, to Mashad, the capital of Khorasan. Finally, in December 1832, without Sergeant William Hammond who had died of wounds near Nishapur, they left Khorasan for their base at Tabriz which they reached in March 1833. They had covered little short of 4,000 miles on foot or mule, mostly across the inhospitable deserts of the high Iranian plateau, swelteringly hot in summer and bitterly cold in winter, through towns and villages where civil war, plague and famine were rampant. They certainly earned the gold medals awarded them by the Crown Prince on their return, yet Sergeant Richard Gibbons, who wrote a paper for the Royal Geographical Society about the routes traversed on this long march, records nothing of the hardships he and his fellow sergeants must have suffered.

At this time growing alarm in London and Calcutta over the Russian threat to India and the loss of influence in Tehran galvanised the British Government into recovering lost ground by responding to a renewed appeal from the Crown Prince for military assistance. The modified 1814 Treaty was still valid and although, following the run-down of the Military Mission, Abbas *Mirza* had been obliged to recruit officers from France and Italy he still preferred the British: on Hart's death in 1830 he pressed the British envoy to find a new commandant for his forces, together with an adjutant and four subalterns 'whose duties, when they are not required at Headquarters, will be to proceed to the chief places of the Districts and drill the troops' (8).

The new Military Mission was recruited in India from all branches of the military service but only reached Bushire in December 1833: also military stores were shipped to Persia from India and London. This Mission consisted of eight officers, fourteen sergeants and an assistant apothecary under the command of Colonel Passmore of the Bengal Native Infantry. Passmore was accompanied by two officers from his own regiment, Captain Justin Sheil as second-in-command and Ensign Henry Rawlinson: also Lieutenants Francis Farrant, Charles Stoddart and D'Arcy Todd—all in time to become familiar names to students of Persian and Central Asian history.

The Mission had barely reached their headquarters in Tabriz when, with the death of Fath Ali Shah, they had to turn round and march back to Tehran under Lindesay-Bethune's command as part of the force supporting Abbas *Mirza*'s son, Muhammad *Mirza*.* A number of the

---
* Abbas *Mirza* had died in 1833 leaving the succession in doubt.

Wars and Warriors

British officers attended Muhammad *Mirza*'s coronation in January 1835: they were then posted to out-lying districts to raise and train troops—Passmore to Sultanabad (Arak), Sheil to Sarab between Tabriz and Ardebil among the Azeri-speaking Shaqagis, Rawlinson to Kermanshah among the Kurds, and Farrant to train cavalry at Zanjan, halfway between Tehran and Tabriz. D'Arcy Todd ran the Headquarters in Tabriz,* while Stoddart remained in Tehran to instil elements of western military science into the sons of twelve noblemen chosen by the Shah. Rawlinson, who was given wide powers by the Governor of Kurdistan, had to quell a mutiny among the Kurds he was training. He also had to march his men through unexplored Luristan and Khuzistan to Dizful, Shustar and Shush to suppress trouble among the powerful Bakhtiari tribe who were thus for the first, but by no means last, time brought into contact with the British. After this, in February 1836, Rawlinson marched his men across Persia to join the Shah's forces at Astarabad in the north-east where Turkoman tribesmen were causing trouble.

Relations between the British and Persians were far less harmonious than in the days of Abbas *Mirza*: there was constant friction over the functions and responsibilities of the British officers who were now regarded essentially as instructors: they were not permitted to have a say in the running of the regiments they were training nor, as previously, to take over command from Persian officers who resented being ordered about by young foreign officers, even though they all held brevet rank of Lieutenant Colonel or Major. Passmore, the Mission's commandant, wrote in despair to the British Minister in September 1835 calling for a clear definition of his officers' duties without which 'the Detachment is useless with the Persian Army, and its presence with it can only give rise to bickerings and bad feelings' (9). A year later Muhammad Shah, who favoured the Russians, unceremoniously dismissed all the British officers from his summer camp.

Despite these difficulties it was decided—largely under pressure from McNeill and Lindesay-Bethune, who had returned temporarily to London—to strengthen the Mission by the despatch of eight sergeants of the Rifle Corps under a Captain Richard Wilbraham to instruct the Persians in the use of the rifle. They reached Persia from England in mid-1836, having travelled from Constantinople to Trebizond on the S.S. *Essex*, one of the first steamships to start a regular service in the Black Sea. Two thousand muskets, sections of howitzers and half-a-

---

* The military stores and arsenal were under the care of Alexander Nisbet who had served under Hart; he lived in the *Arg* with his English wife; known as 'the commisary' he also acted as paymaster and Tabriz agent for the Legation. See p. 115 n.

The English Amongst the Persians

million flints had been shipped ahead of the Mission as a present for the new Shah, while Lindesay-Bethune brought for the Persian army two sets of regimental band instruments on which he had spent £400 in Vienna: ten years later they were found by Sheil, unpacked, in the old Mission House in Tabriz.

However, any hopes of displacing Russian influence were to founder on the question of Herat, the city which at various times had been part of the Persian domain and was regarded by the Persians as theirs to be re-taken. In British eyes, now clouded by growing alarm at Russian ambitions, Herat was the gateway to India, whose safety would be endangered should the city ever fall into Persian hands and become accessible to Russian influence. It thus became a cardinal principle of Anglo-Indian policy to prevent Persian occupation of Herat, though less than forty years previously, in order to divert an Afghan ruler's attention from India, envoys had been sent from India to encourage the Shah to attack Afghanistan and seize Herat. But in 1833 the British had tried to restrain the Persians from laying siege to Herat: and in 1837 when the Shah led his army into Khorasan with the intention of attacking the Afghans the British Minister, McNeill, had forbidden members of the Military Mission to accompany him.

In March 1838 McNeill himself hastened from Tehran to the Shah's camp outside Herat in an unsuccessful effort to persuade him to raise the siege and make suitable amends to the British for the arrest of one of their confidential couriers. McNeill argued that Persian activities in Afghanistan were a flagrant violation of the spirit of the 1814 Treaty, whose purpose was to give security to India. The Persian view, not surprisingly, was quite different, being founded on the letter of the Treaty which stated in categoric terms, as the two earlier treaties on which it was based had done, that the British Government undertook not to intervene in any hostilities between Persia and Afghanistan unless requested by both parties to mediate. The Persians considered this gave them a free hand as far as Herat was concerned and greatly resented the fact that a British officer, Lieutenant Eldred Pottinger, should now be leading the Afghans in their defence of the city: they were also probably aware that McNeill, from the Shah's camp outside Herat, had secretly sent Pottinger funds. The Shah, who had at one point accepted the stiff demands put to him by McNeill, went back on his word—to the disgust of the British envoy who, in June 1838, broke off relations with the Persian Government and left for Tabriz. Then early in 1839 he withdrew with his staff to Erzerum in Turkey: at the same time he ordered members of the Military Mission to make for Baghdad. In the meantime a British force of nearly 400 men from India had occupied Kharg Island

Wars and Warriors

in the Persian Gulf and threatened to invade the mainland. Faced with this the Shah decided to abandon Herat and withdrew his forces. The Persians, with reason, placed their failure fair and square on the British. Nor were they alone in doing so. Henry Willock, now a Director of the East India Company in London, protested to Lord Palmerston about the Government's behaviour over Herat and the 'unjustifiable' occupation of Kharg Island. 'We have', he wrote, 'professed to be her [Persia's] protector . . . we have now become aggressors upon a more slight pretext than ever Russian encroachment was founded on' (10). British forces remained on Kharg Island until March 1842, McNeill having by then returned to Tehran and re-established full diplomatic relations. But no Military Mission was to return until the very last days of the Qajar period, nearly eighty years later, despite a number of appeals from the Persian Government for assistance with the training of both the army and navy.

The Herat question was, however, to bedevil Anglo-Persian relations for many years to come, eventually leading to war between the two countries. In 1852, thinking perhaps that the British attitude had softened, Nasir ed-Din Shah, who had succeeded to the throne in 1848, launched his forces against Herat, which was occupied and formally annexed by royal decree as Persian territory. The British reacted strongly and the Shah, threatened with another break in diplomatic relations and the re-occupation of Kharg Island, reluctantly withdrew his troops and undertook, in a written agreement with Sheil, the British Minister, not to send troops to Herat unless it was attacked 'from the direction of Cabool or from Candahar or from other foreign territory' (11). Once again British pressure had forced the Persians to surrender their cherished national aspiration. Yet only three years later Persian forces once more moved against Herat, which fell to them in October 1856: even before this news reached London the Government of India, acting under instructions from London, had issued a Proclamation to the effect that Britain was at war with Persia because of her breach of the Herat Agreement negotiated with Sheil. In British eyes the Persians had broken a solemn undertaking: as the Persians saw it, however, they were justified in responding to an appeal for help from the ruler of Herat who saw his territory threatened by Dost Muhammad of Kabul. The Shah was also, perhaps, encouraged to defy the British by knowledge of the difficulties they were encountering in the Crimea and rumours of trouble in India.

Although the Persian move against Herat—the fourth in less than a quarter of a century—was the immediate cause of the British Government's decision to go to war, the possibility of such action had been

The English Amongst the Persians

contemplated for some time as a means of securing redress for the insulting treatment of Murray, the British Minister, who, after his withdrawal from Tehran in December 1855, had bombarded Clarendon, the Foreign Secretary, with proposals for a punitive expedition against Persia. Partly with this in mind an expeditionary force had been assembled in Bombay and was ready to sail for the Persian Gulf when orders to this effect were sent from London in September 1856. No formal declaration of war was issued by Palmerston's Government as this would have meant recalling Parliament, then in recess, and possibly facing public criticism: the Cabinet was itself divided on the issue: hence the Proclamation of a State of War by the Government of India. In England, news of the war, in the words of its most recent historian, was greeted 'with a mixture of derision and disgust' (12).

Predictably the better armed and better disciplined British and Indian forces had little difficulty in defeating the Persians. The campaign was over in less than six months, beginning in December 1856 with the unopposed occupation of Kharg Island and the bombardment and capture, after hard fighting, of Reshahr and nearby Bushire where the British established their base. After a lull and the arrival of strong reinforcements from India (including three officers, James Outram, Henry Havelock and John Jacob, all to become legendary Anglo-Indian figures) Outram, who was in overall command, marched his troops in appalling weather on 3 February 1857 to Borazjan, some forty-six miles inland from Bushire. There he found that the enemy had abandoned their camp, leaving much impedimenta behind: battle was joined the next day at Khoshab where the Persians were routed, some 700 being killed against one British officer and nine men killed and sixty-two wounded. Back in Bushire there followed two extraordinary tragedies in the British camp where on 14 March General Stalker, in command there, shot himself as, two days later, did Commodore Ethersley, the commander of the naval forces. No explanation has ever been found for this double tragedy other than that both men had cracked under the strain of their responsibilities. In the meantime the bulk of the expeditionary force—4,800 men and twelve guns—re-embarked in four armed steamers and two war sloops. They sailed, under Outram's command, up the Persian Gulf to the mouth of the Shatt al-Arab which they reached on 8 March, then moved up river with their guns and horses and trans-shipped into vessels of lighter draught before storming the defences of Mohammerah (now Khoramshahr) where about 200 Persians were killed and many more butchered by the local Arab population. British losses amounted to five killed and eighteen wounded. From Mohammerah Outram sailed with his men in pursuit of the

Wars and Warriors

retreating enemy in two steamers, each towing a second vessel, to Ahwaz seventy-five miles away which was captured without resistance: the Persian forces and garrison there, about ten thousand strong, had, according to British sources, fled in confusion at the sight of the enemy. News now reached Outram in early April that peace had been signed in Paris with the Persian Government a month earlier. He therefore led his troops back to Mohammerah and left for Bushire in mid-May, sailing a month later for India on hearing of the outbreak of the Mutiny there. But because of Persian evasiveness in fulfilling the terms of the Treaty of Paris the last British troops were not withdrawn from Kharg Island until February 1858.

Under the terms of the Treaty the Persian Government relinquished 'all claims to sovereignty over the territory and city of Herat and the countries of Afghanistan'. By and large this undertaking was honoured. Herat never again caused a rupture in relations with Britain though it left a legacy of resentment and bitterness which lingered on even after the British Government, in a sudden reversal of policy in 1879, offered the guardianship of the city to the Persian Government. But Russian pressure and the strings attached to the offer were too much for the Persians, who rejected the offer.

5

Uncrowned King of the Persian Gulf

A CURIOUS FEATURE of the British position in Persia during the Qajar period was the presence there alongside the Minister Plenipotentiary of a proconsular figure, known at first simply as the Resident and, later, as the Political Resident for the Persian Gulf. He was appointed by the Government of India and had his headquarters at Bushire. Almost invariably selected from army or naval officers in the employ of the East India Company and, later, the Indian Political Service, the Residents retained their military titles and looked to the Governor-General in India as their immediate chief. Their duties were primarily concerned with upholding the *Pax Britannica* in the Persian Gulf by ensuring that the independent and turbulent shaikhs on the Arabian shore honoured the various arrangements and treaties they had, since 1820, entered into with the British Government. In this capacity the Resident operated more like a Colonial Governor than a diplomat, often with scant regard for the feelings of the Persians who, in the words of a traveller in the 1870s, 'regarded the Residency at Bushire with great and not altogether unnatural jealousy . . . our presence at Bushire and our undefined position in the Gulf trouble the repose of the politicians of Tehran' (1).

What, in the course of time, became the important post of Political Resident in the Persian Gulf grew directly from the appointment by the East India Company of a Factor or Resident in Bushire, the Company's headquarters in the Gulf after 1778. At first the Resident's functions were essentially those of a trader, acting both on the Company's and his own account. He was also expected to keep the Government of Bombay* informed of political developments in the area. In

* Until 1873 the Governor of Bombay was responsible, under the overall control of the Governor-General in Calcutta, for British relations with the Persian Gulf.

Uncrowned King of the Persian Gulf

addition, until a permanent diplomatic Mission was established in Tehran, the Resident would from time to time be entrusted with diplomatic missions. In 1798 he was sent to Tehran to persuade the Shah to divert the Afghan ruler's attention away from the Indian frontier. In 1804 Samuel Manesty, self-appointed Resident at Bushire, took it upon himself to go as 'Ambassador' to the Persian Court to express, on behalf of the Governor-General, condolences on the killing in a brawl of the Persian envoy in India. In 1810 Surgeon Jukes was sent from Bushire to prepare the way for Malcolm's third mission; and in 1822, though there was by then a permanent diplomatic Mission in Tehran, the Prince-Governor of Shiraz, with whom it was customary for the Resident to conduct business, invited him to Shiraz to settle outstanding Anglo-Persian differences over the Gulf. Bruce, the Resident, without authority from Bombay or anywhere else, went to Shiraz and signed an agreement in which, *inter alia*, he recognised the disputed Persian claims to the islands of Bahrain and Qishm.

Bruce has been described as 'the last of the old-style Company's Residents at Bushire' (2). His successors would be forbidden to indulge in private trade and would carry the new title of 'Resident in the Persian Gulf', the adjective 'Political' being added somewhat later. The Resident's duties would, in any case, become increasingly political in nature by virtue of the treaties and agreements negotiated with the Arab shaikhs in pursuit of the British Government's aim of stamping out piracy and the African slave trade, the main scourge of the Persian Gulf in the first half of the nineteenth century.

Bruce's successor, Lieutenant John Macleod of the Bombay Engineers, was informed by the Governor of Bombay that his principal task would be 'the permanent suppression of piracy and the conservation of the peace of the Gulf by the friendly interposition of our power and influence' (3). He was also expected to protect British and Indian trade and shipping with southern Persia, but was instructed not to concern himself with Persian politics. However, it was often impossible to avoid becoming involved in political affairs, given that Persia had her own interests in the Gulf, which sometimes clashed with those of the British. In such a situation the Resident was often at loggerheads with the Persian authorities as well as with the British envoy in Tehran. At one stage it was thought that differences might be avoided if the Resident became directly subordinate to the Minister in Tehran, but there was no possibility of the Government of India accepting this idea when, in 1836, they surrendered responsibility for the Tehran Mission to the Foreign Office. It was, however, then agreed that on Persian affairs the Resident would report direct to the Minister in Tehran, though he might continue dealing with the local authorities on piracy matters and cases affecting the lives and properties of British subjects in the southern province of Fars.*

Throughout the Qajar period the Resident remained virtually independent of the Foreign Office and Legation as far as Persian Gulf affairs were concerned. Even in the years 1839-42, when the British Minister withdrew from Persia because of the Herat dispute, the Resident remained *en poste* although, because of anti-British hostility and violence at Bushire, he transferred the Residency temporarily to Kharg Island, where he remained until 1842. Nor was the Residency closed in 1855 when Charles Murray broke off relations with the Persian Government.

This divided loyalty of the Resident did not make for easy relations with the Minister in Tehran. The young Lieutenant A. T. Wilson, on his first visit to Tehran in 1907, noted that the attitude of the British Minister and his Vice-Consul towards the Government of India and its officers in Persia was 'critical, almost hostile' (4). Generally speaking this was the Legation attitude towards the Residency and *vice versa* throughout the Qajar period. Perhaps it was unavoidable owing to their different responsibilities and the difficulties of communication—there was no telegraph until the 1860s, while the journey from Bushire to Tehran normally took between five and six weeks. Isolated from the Persian capital and thinking primarily of Britain's self-imposed role as guardian of tranquillity in the waters of the Persian Gulf, the Resident inevitably paid less attention to Persian interests and susceptibilities than either the Persians or the Legation would wish.

But for the pirates—mostly Qasimi Arabs centred round the little shaikhdom of Ras al-Khaimah—who preyed mercilessly on British and Indian shipping, and the inability of the Persian authorities, for lack of a navy, to suppress them, Britain would probably never have become deeply involved in the Persian Gulf. Punitive expeditions by the East India Company's Navy against the pirates in the years 1808-10 had only a momentary success; ten years later the Government of Bombay decided to take drastic measures in an effort to put an end to what had become a highly organised business. In 1819 a combined naval and military force under the command of Major-General Sir William Keir sailed for the Gulf from Bombay and, after some hard fighting and a six-day siege, captured Ras al-Khaimah which was then razed to the

---

* It was not until 1878, however, that the Persian authorities officially recognised the Resident's consular authority by granting him an *exaquatur* as 'Consul-General for Fars, and the coasts and islands of the Persian Gulf within the dominions of Persia'. In 1890 the provinces of Khuzistan and Luristan were added.

ground and the pirates' ships burnt or captured. The peace negotiations which followed resulted in January 1820 in a 'General Treaty of Peace with the Arab Tribes' signed by all the principal shaikhs of what was then known as the Pirate Coast. They undertook that there would be 'a cessation of plunder and piracy' and accepted that, in order to provide identification when challenged by ships of the Indian Navy, their vessels should fly a distinctive flag and carry a register and port clearance signed by the ruling shaikh. This treaty, and Britain's determination to ensure that its terms were honoured, was the first milestone in the establishment in the Persian Gulf of the *Pax Britannica* which was to endure until 1971 when the last of the British forces stationed in the Gulf by virtue of Britain's various treaties with the Arab shaikhs were withdrawn. The Treaty of 1820 transformed the role of the East India Company's Resident—from now on he was to carry the main responsibility for ensuring that this and subsequent treaties made with the Arab shaikhs were honoured. He was no longer a trader but an important political figure able, with the help of naval forces now permanently stationed in the Gulf, to assert the authority with which he was entrusted.

The pirates, though based on the Arabian shores of the Gulf, had close ties with the Persian shore where the Shaikh of Lingeh was also of the Qasimi tribe. They would often hide in the little inlets along the Persian coast. Ships of the Indian Navy during their 1809–10 anti-pirate operations attacked Lingeh and other Persian harbours, destroying any pirate shipping they found there. Although their authority in those parts was minimal, the Persian Government were sensitive to action of this sort, taken without their leave. When Keir's expedition was launched from Bombay they informed Willock, the Chargé d'Affaires in Tehran, that they were unwilling to countenance punitive action against pirates in Persian harbours. The Bombay Government had, however, already decided to ignore any Persian objections and had authorised Keir to enter Persian ports if necessary. In January 1820 the *Eden*, carrying twenty-six guns, sailed into two small Persian harbours and set fire to the pirate boats found there. The Persian Government protested strongly and asked for the recall of Bruce, the Resident at Bushire, whom they held responsible.

There was further trouble with the Persian authorities shortly afterwards when the Bombay Government decided 'whatsoever may be the sentiments of the Persian Government on the subject' (5) to transfer the considerable force, originally 1,200 strong, of British and Indian troops left behind by Keir at Ras al-Khaimah after his successful action there, to Qishm Island close to the Persian coast. By the time Willock

The English Amongst the Persians

had taken soundings in Tehran and learnt of the strong Persian objections the move to Qishm had been carried out. The Persians, though they had no navy of their own,* maintained that they had no need for any foreign help in suppressing piracy: they protested at the British action and called for the immediate evacuation of the island and, once again, demanded Bruce's removal. Both appeals were ignored. The base was, however, abandoned three years later, mainly because of the appalling climate and the havoc played by cholera and other diseases with the troops. When J. B. Fraser† visited the island in 1821, less than a year after the transfer from Ras al-Khaimah, he found that owing to illness barely 300 sepoys and a handful of British were fit for duty. He noted many deaths among the British and Indian garrison and queried the usefulness of 'retaining so unhealthy, so fatal a position' (6). However, though the cherished idea of a permanent anti-pirate base commanding the Straits of Hormuz was now abandoned, the British established in 1823 a naval supply depot at Basidu on the north-western tip of the island. They did so without seeking Persian permission and regarded the depot as sovereign British territory.

Basidu—or Bassadore as the British called it—remained the headquarters of the Persian Gulf Naval Squadron until 1879 after which it served for some time as a coaling station over which the Union Jack continued to fly. The Persian authorities had little choice than to acquiesce and to leave the policing of the Gulf waters in British hands.

The British themselves were often in two minds about the merits of Persian and Arab claims in the Persian Gulf over which, at different periods of history, the Persians had ruled supreme. Not surprisingly, the Persians sometimes questioned Britain's good faith in supporting Arab claims. The British argued that their occupation of Qishm Island in 1820 was by virtue of a written agreement with the Sultan of Muscat to whom, they said, the island belonged. Yet when Malcolm was in Tehran negotiating his 1801 Treaty he had recognised Persian sovereignty by seeking—albeit unsuccessfully—to persuade the Shah to cede or lease Qishm and Henjam Islands for use as British bases. Fath Ali Shah's unwillingness then, and later, to cede any island base to the British was due to his fear that this might lead to British control over his foreign policy and, as was happening in India at the time, to the gradual annexation of his own territory. The British therefore found it convenient to assert that both Qishm and the adjacent Henjam Island were the property of the Sultan of Muscat and were not, as the Persians claimed, dependencies of Bandar Abbas which the Sultan of Muscat

* Not until 1885, when they acquired two small ships from Germany.
† See p. 153.

had, since the end of the eighteenth century, leased from the Shah. Later, after fighting between Persian and Muscat forces in Bandar Abbas in 1854, the British supported the Sultan in trying to persuade the Persians to cede rather than lease Bandar Abbas to him. The Persians, weak though they were, were not prepared even under strong British pressure to surrender any of their territory: indeed, in return for renewing the lease of Bandar Abbas and its dependencies they secured the Sultan's recognition of their sovereignty over Qishm and Henjam.

The British, therefore, negotiated in 1868 with the Persian authorities and not with the Sultan of Muscat for a cable station on Henjam. For reasons of their own they closed the station in 1880 but twenty-four years later decided to re-open it. Despite the lapse of time British telegraph officials returned to the island without notifying the Persian authorities, re-occupied their old site, removed (according to the Persians) the Persian flag they found flying there and hoisted the Union Jack in its place. To assert their authority the Persian Government sent one of their customs officials to the island; the official in charge of the telegraph station was authorised from India to deny him water from the Telegraph Department's tanks. Grant Duff, the Chargé d'Affaires in Tehran, found it necessary to remind the Government of India that the island was Persian territory and that the Persian Government were fully entitled to place customs officials and coastguards on it. Some years later, in 1911, the Royal Navy quietly transferred their coaling station from Basidu to Henjam* and, again without Persian permission, established a naval canteen and recreation ground within the boundaries of the telegraph compound, taking it for granted that no customs duties would be payable on imported stores.

British officials in the Gulf were all too inclined to ignore Persian rights and susceptibilities. When, in 1879, the navy decided to give up using Basidu as a base the Government of India transferred the large sepoy guard there to Jask on the Makran coast, where the Indo-European Telegraph Department had a station. Barracks were built for the soldiers. Seven years passed before the Persian Government woke up to what had happened and demanded the withdrawal of the sepoys. The Indian authorities, aware of the weakness of their case, complied but some years later, in 1898, following the murder near Jask of a British telegraph official, parties of sepoys were landed at Jask and Chahbahar for the protection of the telegraph stations and their staffs. This time the Persian Government, conscious of their own inability to maintain

* Henjam remained the Navy's principal base in the Persian Gulf until 1935 when the British Government reluctantly surrendered their enclaves on both Qishm and Henjam.

law and order in these remote corners, acquiesced: barracks were built and the soldiers remained on Persian soil until the end of the Qajar period.

From the 1880s there was a running dispute between the British and Persians over the ownership of four little islands, Greater and Lesser Tunb, Sirri and Abu Musa, all of them situated in the Straits of Hormuz about mid-way between the Persian and Arab shores of the Gulf. So long as the Qasimi shaikhs acted as governors of Lingeh and paid taxes to the Persian Government there had been no dispute over these islands, which were generally regarded as belonging to Persia. But when, following inter-Qasimi quarrels and murders and the appointment of a Persian Governor of Lingeh, the Qasimi shaikhs crossed to the Arab shore the British supported their claim that these islands were part of their patrimony and that sovereignty over them now lay with the Qasimi shaikhs of Ras al-Khaimah and Sharjah; it was argued that the jurisdiction hitherto exercised over them by the Governor of Lingeh was not in his capacity as Governor but as a Qasimi shaikh. In Persian eyes the argument was spurious: as they saw it the islanders, even though they might all be Arabs, had recognised Persian sovereignty by paying taxes: what had been Persian one day could not suddenly become Arab. To make their point they occupied Sirri Island in 1887 where, although challenged by the British, they remained undisturbed. A War Office map, presented by the British Minister to the Shah in 1888, showed all the islands in Persian colours: the Persian case was further strengthened with the publication in 1892 of Curzon's two-volume *Persia and the Persian Question* in which the map, prepared by the Royal Geographical Society under Curzon's own supervision, also showed the islands as Persian territory. But an attempt in 1904 by the Persians to establish customs posts and hoist their flag on Tunb and Abu Musa was short-lived due to strong British pressure. They did not return to these islands until the withdrawal of British forces from the Gulf in 1971. In the years between these little islands were the cause of considerable friction between Britain and Persia.

The question of sovereignty over the island of Bahrain, situated close to the Arab shore, was a much longer-standing irritant in Anglo-Persian relations, dating from the early days of the nineteenth century when the British supported the claims of the al-Khalifah family. Here, too, in Persian eyes the British position was equivocal. In 1820, when seeking the Shah's agreement to the occupation of Qishm the British had held out the prospect of recognising Persian sovereignty over Bahrain as a *quid pro quo*. Two years later the Bushire Resident had formally recognised this sovereignty in a written agreement with the

Prince-Governor of Fars—it mattered little to the Persians that the Governor of Bombay had immediately repudiated the agreement and dismissed the Resident. Later, the Persians construed an ill-drafted letter from Clarendon to their Ambassador in London in 1869 as recognition of Persian sovereignty. Carelessness on the part of British Ministers and officials played into the hands of the Persians who lost no opportunity of asserting their sovereignty over Bahrain.

Although the British, no less than the French, had at various times cast covetous eyes on Kharg Island (spelt variously as Carrack, Kharruck, Kharak, Karaq) they never questioned Persian sovereignty over the island. Malcolm, who was said by Harford Jones to have a 'furious passion for the possession of an island in the Gulf' (7), tried unsuccessfully in 1801 to persuade Fath Ali Shah to cede the island to Britain; and in 1808-9, after the failure of his second mission to Persia, he was only prevented by Harford Jones' successful activities in Tehran from capturing the island with a large force standing by for the purpose in Bombay. Again in 1828, when back in Bombay as Governor, Malcolm reverted to the possibility of acquiring Kharg Island. He considered it would make a better British headquarters than Bushire since, as he presciently wrote to the Resident 'an insular position would free us of all that mingling in local disputes and policies which it is quite impossible for the representative to escape from as long as he is stationed at Abushire and which, besides other bad effects, has and will continue to embarrass our general interests in Persia'. Malcolm hoped, somewhat less presciently, that the British envoy in Tehran would be instructed 'to obtain the grant of this island. It neither has nor ever can have any value to Persia, and in our hands it must early become an emporium of trade' (8). Malcolm can hardly be blamed for not foreseeing the day when Kharg would become one of the world's great oil ports. Though British forces occupied the island in 1838 and again in 1856 they were withdrawn when their objective—Persian withdrawal from Herat—had been achieved: a proposal by the Indian Government in 1841 that the island be purchased was rejected by Palmerston who feared that it might lead to a Russian demand for territory on the Caspian coast.

By the 1840s, thanks to the combined efforts of the Resident in Bushire and the Persian Gulf Squadron's activities, piracy had been largely eliminated, leaving time for both to concentrate on suppressing the trade in African slaves imported into the Gulf mainly by Omani and Qasimi Arabs for sale on both shores. The British Government, which had set an example to the world in 1833 by abolishing slavery in the British Empire, now sought to end it elsewhere. Command of the seas was a powerful weapon in their hand and enabled Samuel Hennell, the most able and effective of all British Residents, to conclude anti-slave-trade agreements with the Sultan of Muscat and the Gulf shaikhs. Subsequently Sheil, the Minister in Tehran, was instructed to persuade the Shah to issue a *farman* prohibiting the trade at Persian ports and allowing British naval vessels to enforce the ban. The Shah at first resolutely refused to interfere with a long-established Persian institution, allegedly hallowed by Koranic precept, but two years later, in 1848, suddenly gave way and agreed to prohibit the importation of African slaves by sea; because of strong opposition from the religious classes he would not, however, impose a total ban, nor allow British naval ships to intercept Persian vessels. In 1851, again under strong British pressure, Nasir ed-Din Shah agreed to permit search of Persian merchant vessels on condition that a Persian official was aboard the British ship and that any vessels found carrying slaves were handed over to the Persian authorities while the British removed the slaves. A further Anglo-Persian Convention regarding slavery was signed in 1882 under which British search of Persian vessels without the presence of a Persian official was allowed; Persians taking their own slaves with them on the Mecca pilgrimage were to be provided with a special passport countersigned by the British Resident or a consul, while the Shah undertook to punish severely all Persian subjects engaged in the slave traffic.

Under the terms of the 1851 agreement British naval vessels could enter Persian ports and exact fines from those engaged in the slave trade. Until the beginning of World War I British consuls, particularly in south Persia, were kept busy issuing certificates of manumission to slaves who could prove they were entitled to their freedom: others, not so entitled, often sought asylum in the consulates and were a cause of embarrassment to the consul. Inevitably these British activities were unpopular, particularly with slave dealers and owners who resented foreign intervention in their affairs. For the British, however, there was eventually the satisfaction of knowing that, largely as a result of their efforts and perseverance, the Gulf slave trade, like piracy, was stamped out.

Gun-running, both to unruly Persian tribes and to Afghanistan for the tribes of the North-West Frontier of India had, by the 1880s, replaced slave trading as a lucrative Gulf occupation and caused the British and Persian authorities to co-operate in trying to stop an activity which threatened both their interests. At first the trade was carried on almost openly through Bushire where two firms, both enjoying British protection, imported arms from England, France and Belgium. Later, as British and Persian controls tightened, the business was largely conducted from Muscat, whence the arms were smuggled into little harbours along the Makran coast. Vice-Consulates were opened at Bandar Abbas in 1900 and Bam in 1906 in the hope of providing intelligence about the traffic but were no more effective than were regular anti-gun-running operations by forces from India in putting an end to a business which provided a source of arms in World War I for the Tangistani and other tribes of southern Persia.

The central figure in seeking to suppress gun-running, no less than piracy and slave-trading, was the Political Resident. At no time during the Qajar period was there any serious challenge to his authority in the Persian Gulf either from the Persians, on whose soil he resided, or the Arabs with whom he mostly dealt, or from jealous European powers, particularly Russia, France and Germany, who at times seemed poised to challenge the British position.* For Britain the Persian Gulf, like Herat and Afghanistan, had become part of the outer bastion protecting her precious Indian Empire. Lord Lansdowne spoke for the British Government when he warned the world in 1903 that 'we should regard the establishment of a naval base, or of a fortified port, in the Persian Gulf, by any other Power as a very grave menace to British interests, and we should certainly resist it with all the means at our disposal' (9).

British interests, in addition to trade and shipping, now included the operation and protection of the Indo-European telegraph lines and cables; the British-Indian post offices which provided the Gulf's only reliable postal service; a quarantine service; a lighting and buoying service for shipping; and, after 1908, the oil of the Anglo-Persian Oil Company. The day-to-day protection of these interests and of individuals from the Arab shaikhdoms, who were given the status of British Protected Persons, was the responsibility of the Political Resident. He needed to keep in close, if not always friendly, contact not only with the local Persian authorities but also with tribal chiefs up and down the Persian coast without whose goodwill telegraph wires were liable to be cut and travellers robbed.

By far the most important of these local chiefs was an Arab, Shaikh Khazal of Mohammerah, who enjoyed the allegiance of the predominantly Arab population of much of Khuzistan (then generally known as Arabistan) province. The Political Resident, Percy Cox, and the Anglo-Persian Oil Company negotiated with him rather than with the authorities in Tehran for the oil company's first pipe line and the land on which to build the refinery at Abadan. The deal completed, Cox steamed up to Mohammerah in his official launch, the *Lawrence*, to bestow on the Shaikh, with all the ceremony of a full-dress Indian

---

* The Russians opened a Consulate-General at Bushire in 1889 and the French a Vice-Consulate. The Germans followed in 1897.

The English Amongst the Persians

durbar, the insignia of a Knight Commander of the Most Eminent Order of the Indian Empire. There was no doubt about the beneficent effect on the Shaikh himself—over three years later Cox, in a report to Calcutta, rejoiced in the repeated signs of confidence and goodwill displayed by the Shaikh 'since his decoration with the K.C.I.E. in 1910' (10). The Persian Government were less impressed. They had long been distrustful of the Shaikh's close relations with the British, whose ships, as they steamed up the Shatt al-Arab past his palace, had for years fired a salute in memory of some helpful action by his father. Shaikh Khazal, who had no love for the Persian authorities, had deliberately neglected seeking the permission of the Shah, whose subject he was, before accepting his British decoration. Not surprisingly the Tehran press were critical of his behaviour while the Persian Government correctly suspected that, in addition to the K.C.I.E., he had reached some understanding with the British for the protection of his semi-independent position. When in December 1910, three months after the investiture, the Persian Minister for Foreign Affairs asked the British Minister in Tehran whether it was true that the Shaikh enjoyed the British Government's protection, he was told that the Shaikh was not a British Protected Person but that the British had special relations with him and in the event of any encroachment on his rights they would give him their support. The Persian Government were at the time far too weak to react strongly to this admission of British support for one of their more independent and powerful tribal chiefs. For their part the British had given their assurances reluctantly to an importunate Shaikh in the knowledge that without his goodwill Britain's political and commercial interests in southern Persia were at risk, since the authority of the Tehran Government in those parts was totally ineffective. In 1919, at the end of World War I, the British Government presented the Shaikh with a river steamer for his services during the war: they also gave him 3,000 rifles and ammunition to enable him to protect the installations of the Anglo-Persian Oil Company and cover the withdrawal of British forces from Khuzistan. But neither these nor the 1910 promise, albeit carefully qualified, of support 'in the event of any encroachment by the Persian Government on your jurisdiction and recognised rights, or on your property in Persia' were of any avail against the determined centralising policy of Reza Shah, in whose hands Shaikh Khazal died a virtual prisoner in 1936.

Despite his wide responsibilities the Resident had a small British staff of only three or four, including a doctor, all appointed from India: his 'native' staff was mostly Indian but included Persian and Arab *munshis* or translators. From the time when Bushire first became the

Uncrowned King of the Persian Gulf

East India Company's Gulf headquarters the Resident had been provided with a sepoy guard, later increased by the addition of *sowars* and Bombay Marines. They would parade at sunset, to the sound of drum and fife, to lower the large Union Jack fluttering over the Residency.

The life-style at the Residency in Bushire owed much to its close links with India—'everything is run on Indian lines' (11) was the first impression of an official of the Imperial Bank of Persia when he arrived in Bushire in 1913; an American visitor coming from Tehran at about the same time remarked that the Residency was 'filled with well-trained Indian servants, whose quiet ways and spotless white clothes seem miraculous after inefficient Persians in frock coats' (12). Even the Indian rupee circulated until 1922 as current coin in this and other Persian ports. The Residency was rebuilt in conventional Anglo-Indian style after the 1856–7 war, when the original building on the sea front was destroyed by British gunfire. At the same time a more splendid edifice, also in the spacious style of British India, was built at Sabzabad on higher ground about six miles from the town on land acquired by the Resident. Originally planned as a summer residence in the course of time this building became the Resident's permanent home and office: it was connected with the down-town offices first by telegraph and, in 1905, by telephone. Houses for other senior members of the Residency staff were also built at Sabzabad, which became a British enclave. Apart from the humidity and searing summer heat there was always a shortage of drinking water. Local supplies were brackish and often contaminated so that, until well into the twentieth century, drinking water was imported by ship in casks from Karachi. To escape the heat the Resident and families were in the habit of spending the summer in Shiraz where the Resident maintained a house for some years.

Lying off-shore, within sight of the town Residency which had its own jetty, would be one or more gunboats of the Persian Gulf Naval Squadron. These ships were ready to move off at a moment's notice in case of need. They were also used by the Resident—until he acquired his own 900-ton paddle-steamer, the *Lawrence*, in 1887—to take him on his annual spring tour of the Arab shaikhdoms. There he would be received with the pomp and ceremony due to the representative of the paramount power with whom the shaikhs now had treaties which guaranteed their independence against all and sundry. On the Persian side of the Gulf, too, the Resident was a figure who inspired considerable awe and carried more weight than local officials. A visitor in 1875 concluded that 'Bushire, though Persian, is under the entire control of the British Resident and the native Governor would not think of acting contrary to the wishes of the English sahib' (13). Curzon, who visited

The English Amongst the Persians

the Gulf for the first time in 1890, was immensely impressed with what he saw—'the Union Jack', he wrote, 'fluttering from the summit of the Residency flagstaff is no vain symbol of British ascendancy in Bushire ... the British Resident at Bushire is to this hour the umpire to whom all parties appeal, and who has by treaties been intrusted with the duty of preserving the peace of the waters ... Not a week passes but, by Persians and Arabs alike, disputes are referred to his arbitration; and he may with a greater truth than the phrase sometimes conveys, be entitled the Uncrowned King of the Persian Gulf' (14).

Unlike the British Minister in Tehran, who had to rely on his own powers of persuasion and the support of a distant government, the Political Resident had at his ready command an effective naval force which he could, and did, use to impose his will when necessary. For forty years the Indian Navy provided a Persian Gulf Squadron of seven ships, divided between Basra and Bushire with their base at Basidu, which kept constant vigil on the waters of the Gulf. Following the abolition in 1863 of the Indian Navy, mainly on grounds of expense, the Admiralty in London, prompted by fears that the Shah might create his own Gulf navy, allocated three gunboats of the Royal Navy for permanent service in the Gulf. Their commander was instructed that 'as difficulties are apt to rise suddenly, requiring prompt action for the maintenance of order in these waters, you are to consider yourself at the disposal of the British Resident for the support of British authority' (15). This force, like that of the Indian Navy earlier, gave the Resident a unique position as a powerful and virtually independent ruler. It was not a position which endeared him to the Persians. As the years went by they increasingly resented the presence on their soil* of a foreign representative who, by the nature of his responsibilities, acted —or so it seemed to them—with more solicitude for Arab than for Persian interests.

---

* The Residency was eventually, in 1946, transferred to Bahrain.

6

Consuls, Khans and Communities

NOWADAYS THERE IS only one British consul in all Persia. Based on Tehran his responsibilities cover the length and breadth of the land. Apart from the routine registry of births, marriages and deaths he is there, if need be, to help and protect all British subjects resident in Persia. He and his staff also spend much time dealing with the problems of tourists and other travellers, of which there are many, not least those caught drug-smuggling. The position was very different in Qajar times when, from having no consulates at all before 1841, the number had risen to twenty-three in 1921 despite the fact that the number of British residents was comparatively few, travellers rare birds of passage, and drug-smuggling unknown. It is true that in those days Britain extended her consular protection to embrace her Indian subjects and a variety of Protected Persons, but their numbers and distribution hardly justified the multitude of Consul-Generals, Consuls, Vice-Consuls and Consular Agents scattered all over Persia. Their story, told here, illustrates one side of the Great Game the British and Russians were then playing for influence in Persia, and also the different parts, varying greatly from post to post, played by the consuls of those days in contrast to the more circumscribed and humdrum role of their solitary modern successor.

Unlike the Levant Company in neighbouring Turkey, where consuls had been established under its aegis since the seventeenth century, the East India Company in the early days relied on the protection provided by its own factors and agents. Later, when Gore Ouseley went to Persia as Ambassador, he was instructed by the Foreign Office to draw up a list of towns where 'agents or consuls' might be established for the promotion of trade and the protection of British subjects. Nothing, in fact, came of the treaty of commerce which the British Government

The English Amongst the Persians

hoped he would negotiate for this purpose. The first foreigners to be given the right to appoint agents to reside in Persian cities for the assistance of their merchants were the Russians under the terms of the 1813 Treaty of Gulestan. Later, in 1828, the Treaty of Turkmanchai permitted them to appoint 'consuls or commercial agents wherever the good of commerce may require'.

Commercial and political rivalry with the Russians provided much of the impetus behind British pressure on the Persians for equal treaty rights in respect of consuls. The British first opened a consulate at the Turkish Black Sea port of Trebizond in 1830* with a view to developing trade with northern Persia, but found themselves at a disadvantage so long as they had no consulate in Tabriz, then the main commercial city in Persia. An English traveller, writing in 1832 after a visit to Persia, called on the British Government to pay more attention to British interests there and to 'the great advantages that might accrue from the appointment of a consul in Tabriz, both with a view to the protection of trade and to its encouragement' (1). The following year Campbell, the British envoy, was instructed by the Foreign Office to negotiate a commercial treaty with the Persian Government. This he proceeded to do and in February 1835 presented a draft to the Shah who seemed happy with it until he came to the passage dealing with the appointment of consuls: he then paused and commented 'this is not good and the right Russia has acquired of placing consuls is most injurious to Persia' (2). The Shah thereupon rejected the proposed treaty. A few days later one of his ministers explained that this was due to the Shah's fears that the establishment of British, alongside Russian, consuls on Persian soil would result in the country 'being entirely partitioned' by the two Powers (3). The steady annexation of Caucasian and Indian territory then going on provided a warning which Fath Ali Shah and his successor took to heart, and accounted for their stubborn resistance to British demands for a commercial treaty with consular rights.

However, the British Government were determined to get on equal terms with the Russians and instructed Henry Ellis to pursue, if opportunity arose during his special mission to Persia in 1835, the commercial treaty which Campbell had failed to secure. Ellis was, however, no more successful than Campbell whose successor, McNeill, was equally disappointed when in 1838 the Shah brusquely withdrew his approval of a treaty which would have permitted the appointment of a consul to Tabriz. Only after diplomatic relations had been broken, Kharg Island occupied, and Persian troops forced to abandon their siege of Herat was McNeill able to return to the charge: in 1841 he negotiated

* See pp. 95-6.

a commercial treaty which allowed British commercial agents or consuls to reside at Tabriz and Tehran in return for similar Persian appointments in London and Bombay. In addition, the anomalous position of the Resident in Bushire was regularised, it being stipulated in the treaty that he might continue to reside there.

The British, however, with only two consuls, still remained at a disadvantage compared with the Russians, who had the right to appoint consuls where they pleased. It was not until the Persians suffered another defeat at British hands in the 1856-7 war that they conceded, under the terms of the Treaty of Paris, 'most favoured nation treatment' in respect of the whole hierarchy 'General-Consuls, Consuls, Vice-Consuls and Consular Agents'.* Thereafter the British and Russians were on equal terms.

Both before and after this the British—and the Russians—made frequent use, in lieu of consuls, of locally recruited agents to protect their interests and report on local events. The system originated with the agents employed by the East India Company at their trading posts in southern Persia. Malcolm's and Harford Jones' missions resulted in the Company's man in Shiraz, Ja'far Ali Khan, becoming a figure of considerable importance as intermediary and negotiator on their behalf with the Prince-Governor of Fars. Jones was delighted with his performance and improved his status by issuing him a 'patent constituting him the Agent for the British affairs at the Court of Shiraz' (4). As British interest in the country increased the system was extended so that, in the course of time, these Native Agents (also known as Mission News Writers) were to be found in all the more important Persian towns.

The Persian authorities tacitly accepted the existence of these men and their right to act on behalf of the British and Indian Governments, though there was no official recognition of their status. When trouble blew up over the appointment of a Native Agent in Shiraz in 1855† the Persian Prime Minister sent a stiff note to the British Minister pointing out that he had no treaty right to appoint an Agent there. Murray replied that 'although by Treaty Bushire, Tabreez, and Tehran are the only places in Persia where British Consular Agents can reside, the British Mission has for many years entertained Agents in Shiraz, Ispahan and other cities of Persia, to assist British subjects in their affairs, and to transmit to the Mission intelligence of passing events' (5). The system, which was of convenience to both countries, was allowed to continue.

* For the sake of simplicity they are usually all referred to as Consuls in the following pages.
† See p. 23.

The English Amongst the Persians

Native Agents were selected by the Tehran Legation or the Resident in Bushire from well-known local figures, preferably with a British connection; often they were not of Persian descent. In Shiraz the Agency remained for several generations in the hands of the high-born and affluent Nawab family who were Shi'i Moslems of Indian origin; in Isfahan members of a well-to-do Christian Armenian family, the Aganoors, acted as Native Agents, son succeeding father*; in Mashad the British Agent, or *vakil ul-dowleh* as the Persians called these men, was *Mirza* Abbas Khan, a Government of India pensioner whose family had served the British well at Kandahar during the Afghan War; at Lingeh on the Persian Gulf he was a prosperous Arab merchant. The first Native Agent to be appointed to Kermanshah was an Arab, Hajji Khalil, who, it was said, had come to Persia from Baghdad as a muleteer with Rawlinson. According to legend he had saved Rawlinson's life when he fell from scaffolding when copying the rock inscriptions at Bisitun. The muleteer settled down at Kermanshah, prospered greatly and was in due course succeeded as British Agent by both his son and grandson. An English traveller who passed through Kermanshah in 1890 noted that both father and son were the only men in Kermanshah 'not afraid to show their wealth, and for the simple reason that it cannot be touched, because they are British subjects. . . . British protection has been in fact the making of these men' (6).

Native Agents were recognised by the Persian authorities as being under British protection. The status and privileges thus acquired and the decorations sometimes bestowed on them by a grateful British or Indian Government helped them greatly in their own private affairs: most of them grew rich in consequence. By the nature of things they were usually regarded with jealousy and dislike, mingled with awe, by the Persians among whom they lived. Nor did the locally resident British always take kindly to them. Dr C. J. Wills, who spent a number of years in Persia with the Indo-European Telegraph Department, complained that 'at Kermanshah, Hamadan, Ispahan, Shiraz, Yazd and Kerman, all great commercial centres, we have only native agents: these men exercise no influence, and are held in contempt by natives and Europeans alike, as powerless' (7). In their stead he wanted full-time British-born consuls. A few years later, in 1886, a member of the Legation staff, after a tour of the country, reported on 'the utter inefficiency of our native Agents' (8), while Durand, when Minister in Tehran, considered that these same Agents 'often do more harm than

* Stephen P. Aganoor, educated in Bombay, was British Agent for nearly forty years; the son who succeeded him trained as a doctor in Edinburgh and had a busy medical practice in Isfahan.

Gateway to the British Legation, Tehran, *circa* 1890.

The British Minister's Residence, Tehran.

The British Minister's summer Residence, Gulhek.
By courtesy of Stephen Whitwell.

The great *bast* in the grounds of the British Legation, Tehran, 15 July–5 August 1906.

The battle of Khoshab, 5 February 1857.

British bombardment of Mohammerah, March 1857.
From G. H. Hunt's *Outram and Havelock's Persian Campaign*.

THE ANGLO-PERSIAN WAR OF 1856–7.

THE BRITISH CONSULATE-GENERAL, MASHAD, *circa* 1895.

(Top) Entrance gateway. (Centre) The Consul-General's house. (Bottom) The Charitable Dispensary with men and women awaiting treatment. From C. E. Yate's *Khurasan and Sistan*.

good' (9) and called for the opening of more consulates as a means of countering Russian influence and enhancing British prestige. His recommendations, put forward in 1899, were supported by the Government of India and were largely responsible for the proliferation of consulates which followed.

The first consulates had been opened at Tabriz and Tehran in 1841. In those days, when there was no regular Consular Service, the usual practice was to appoint a consul from among the resident British community, if there was one, and to allow him to combine his consular duties, which were not normally likely to be very heavy, with his own business activities. Later, with the creation of a Consular Service, these trading consuls were, as a general rule, replaced by career men drawn from that Service and also, in the case of Persia, from the Indian Political Service.

Edward Bonham, who was officially recognised by the Persians as Consul at Tabriz in 1841, had been trading there for the past nine years. The Foreign Office, in their hurry to open a consulate, had anticipated Persian permission by nominating him to the post in 1837 at an annual salary of £500 and £100 for expenses with instructions to afford 'efficient Consular Protection to His Majesty's subjects trading with Persia'(10). He was at the same time authorised to engage in mercantile pursuits of his own and to move into what had previously been the British Minister's Tabriz residence—a large, rambling building of seventeen rooms and innumerable passages built round three courtyards with an attractive garden laid out in the front courtyard.

Keith Abbott, appointed Consul at Tehran at the same time, had a Turkish background and was associated in business with James Brant, a Smyrna merchant who had opened the Consulate at Trebizond in 1830. Abbott had previously worked for Brant at Trebizond, Erzerum and Tabriz. From Tehran he made periodic visits to the Caspian province of Gilan in order to report on and encourage the cultivation of silk which was exported to England. He also made long exploratory trips to Khiva in Transcaspia and to central and south-eastern Persia, collecting information about places almost unknown to Europeans.

When Bonham, after the death of his young wife in 1844 from typhus, decided to return to Europe, a Mr Richard White Stevens was appointed to Tabriz in his place. He, like Abbott, had previously been associated with Brant in Turkey. He went to Tabriz as Consul in 1847 accompanied by a younger brother, George, as his business partner. Meanwhile another Stevens brother, Francis, had taken Brant's place in Trebizond after Brant had moved to Erzerum, an important trading

The English Amongst the Persians

centre on the road to Tabriz. All three Stevens brothers* were associated with Brant in developing trade with Persia.

Richard Stevens was not, however, a success at Tabriz. Though both he and his brother, George, were said to be 'clever, shrewd fellows' (11), the fact that he had never been to England and was regarded as a Levantine told against him as far as the Foreign Office and the Legation were concerned, as did his reputation for being on too friendly terms with the Russians. Sheil thought him unreliable, 'credulous and easily misled in what relates to self love' (12). He upset the Persian authorities to such an extent that the Shah himself referred in one of his rescripts to 'Mr Stevens whose proceedings and mischief-making while living in Tabriz, would fill ten books' (13). Because of these short-comings the Legation arranged, in 1854, for him to exchange places with Abbott, Tabriz being in those days far more important as a consular post than Tehran, both commercially and as a vantage point from which to report on the Russians. Abbott was well thought of by the Legation though the Foreign Office were inclined to regard him as 'an out-and-out Persian' (14). Abbott remained at Tabriz fourteen years before being transferred as Consul to Odessa.

It was not until after the signature of the Treaty of Paris in 1857 that the British were permitted to open a third consulate, this time at Rasht, the capital of the Caspian province of Gilan. Rasht was chosen partly because of the important silk trade of which it was the centre and partly as an observation post from which to watch Russian activities in Transcaspia. Here, in the heart of the Caspian rainbelt, the sloping roofs and white-washed, thatched cottages set amongst luxuriant vegetation, were in striking contrast to the flat-roofed adobe dwellings of the plateau south of the Elburz mountains. The first consul, Captain Charles Mackenzie, fresh from the Crimean War, got into financial trouble and stayed only four years, a very short time in those days. His successor was William George Abbott, a cousin of Keith Abbott and, like him, previously resident in Turkey, where he had also worked for Brant. He first went to Persia in 1863 at the suggestion of his cousin to take charge of the consulate at Tabriz while the latter went on leave: later he spent some months on 'special service' at Astarabad (now Gorgan) with the Persian army then campaigning against the Turkoman tribes. In 1865 he was appointed Consul at Rasht: he remained there

---

* Members of the Stevens family continued, even after the Qajar period, to play a role in Anglo-Persian trade. According to family tradition the three brothers mentioned above were the sons of a Reading man who went as a Prize Officer during the Napoleonic Wars to Malta, where he married and settled. Francis Stevens went to Trebizond in 1837 and was Consul there 1841-67. See p. 100.

Consuls, Khans and Communities

ten years before promotion to Consul-General at Tabriz where he stayed another fifteen years before Drummond Wolff, his chief in Tehran who considered him 'utterly incompetent' (15), had him exiled to Rio de Janeiro. Abbott was followed at Rasht by H. A. Churchill who, before making a name for himself in the defence of Kars during the Crimean War, had served two years as attaché and translator at the Tehran Legation.* Later, three of his sons were to be employed in the Tehran Legation which for many years was never without a Churchill. One son, Harry, followed in his father's footsteps by serving as Consul at Rasht from 1891 to 1899. Another, Sidney, who joined the Legation after some years with the Indo-European Telegraph Company, greatly impressed young Miss Gertrude Bell on her first visit to the east in 1892. In a letter home she described him in glowing terms as speaking 'Persian like a Persian, having lived in every part of this country, disguised and undisguised: knows the people and their habits and prejudices as no European does: rides anything and anywhere and is one of the most capable people withal that I have ever come across' (16). He provided the British Museum with a rich collection of Persian manuscripts and drawings. A third son, George, was Oriental Secretary at the Legation during the 1907 constitutional crisis when a servant brought news that the Shah had arrested the Prime Minister† and was about to have him killed. Churchill‡ rushed to the Palace and by his personal intervention saved the Prime Minister's life.

After Rasht the British, alarmed by Russian expansion eastwards, wished to open a consulate at Astarabad as an observation post. Astarabad was at the eastern end of the Caspian on the fringe of the steppes inhabited by the Yamut and Tekke Turkomans whose independence was now being threatened. The Persians were reluctant to meet the British request for fear of provoking the Russians, even though the Turkomans were nominally the Shah's subjects. However, in 1879, they gave way and three British officers from India served as consuls at Astarabad in quick succession.§ Following the Russian defeat of the Tekke Turkomans at Goek Tepe in 1881 and annexation of Transcaspia the post lost its *raison d'être* and was closed in 1883.

* Previously attached, as surveyor and interpreter, to the British Commission for the delimitation of the Turco-Persian frontier. See p. 141.

† Abol Ghassem Khan, Nasir ul-Mulk, head of the influential Qaragozlu family and the first Persian to enter Oxford University. He was at Balliol under Dr Jowett from 1879 to 1882. Among his contemporaries there were G. N. Curzon, Edward Grey and Cecil Spring-Rice who described him as one of Jowett's 'oriental pets, a good historian, immensely hard working, and an eloquent opponent of Curzon's in our debating society . . . we used to call him Kasim Khan, or Curs'im for short' (17).

‡ George Churchill later became a Persian specialist in the Foreign Office, 1919–24.

§ Major O. B. St. John, Captain C. B. Lovett and Colonel C. E. Stewart.

The English Amongst the Persians

The Russians, in their drive eastwards, now pressed the Persians for permission to open a consulate at Mashad, the holiest city in Persia and the capital of the strategically important province of Khorasan bordering Transcaspia and Afghanistan. At first the Shah resisted the Russian demand but, as part of his difficult balancing act between the two Powers, he felt constrained to give way after succumbing to British pressure for the opening of the Karun river. Then, to redress the balance once more, he invited the British to open a consulate at Mashad as he had no wish to see the Russian flag fly there alone. This the British were quick to do and scored a minor scoop by getting their man, Colonel Charles MacLean, into Mashad in 1889 a few weeks ahead of the Russian consul. MacLean, an Indian Army officer, was conveniently on the spot, serving with the Persian-Afghan Frontier Commission which had provided him with useful cover when establishing an espionage network, based on Herat, against the Russians. He was now to do the same thing in Mashad and was the first of a long line of officers of the Indian Political Service to serve in a city which, because of its location, became the most politically important of all British consulates in Persia.

When Curzon passed through Mashad in the autumn of 1889 he was unimpressed by what he saw of the British presence there: in a despatch to *The Times* he called on the Government to provide for the maintenance of the Consul-General 'in a style and in quarters better fitted to represent to the native mind the prestige of a great and wealthy power' (18). This letter had its effect and MacLean's successor, Ney Elias, was authorised to build offices, staff quarters and stabling on an eight-acre site which were to make Mashad by far the most impressive of the consulates. The Consul-General carried the additional title of 'Agent for the Government of India in Khorasan' and, like the Political Resident in Bushire, looked on the Governor-General in India rather than the Minister in Tehran as his real chief. He, like other 'Indian Politicals' appointed to some of the consulates opened later,* was better paid and able to live on a far grander scale than his Foreign Office counterparts elsewhere in Persia. His domestic and office retinues were on the lavish scale of Anglo-India. Also, in addition to the usual ragged guard provided by the Persian Government, he could boast a small sepoy guard, decked in the colourful uniforms of the Queen's Own Corps of Guides, and twenty-two Turkoman *sowars* who provided a courier service between Mashad and Herat. Some idea of the difference

* Officers of the Indian Political Service normally filled the following consular posts: Ahwaz, Bushire, Bandar Abbas, Kerman, Mashad and Sistan (Zabol and Birjand). They also were appointed to the short-lived posts at Astarabad and Bam.

Consuls, Khans and Communities

in the scale of Mashad's style and that of the Consul-General in Tabriz can be gained from the fact that the cost of running the two posts in 1899 was officially estimated at £8,600 and £920 respectively! Another unsatisfactory element in this diarchal system was that the 'Indian Politicals' usually went direct to their posts from India without visiting Tehran or meeting the Minister there. More often than not they were ignorant of the niceties of Anglo-Persian diplomacy as seen by the Foreign Office and the Legation. The actions of these consuls, in obedience to instructions from India, could be a serious embarrassment to the Legation. Such was the case in 1905 when the Consul-General in Mashad, without the prior knowledge of the Legation, was involved in recruiting local tribesmen for service in British-Indian regiments. So too when, following disturbances in Sistan, the Government of India sent mule-loads of rifles and ammunition to be used for the defence of the Mashad and Sistan Consulates if needed: when the Persian Government got wind of this they could hardly be blamed for officially objecting to the 'smuggling' of arms by British officials across their eastern frontier.

The Consul-General's duties in Mashad varied from dealing with the problems of the thousands of Shi'i pilgrims from India who flocked annually to the shrine of Imam Reza, to producing an annual trade report and acting as intermediary between the Governors of Mashad and Herat. His main task, however, was the collection of intelligence about Russian military activities across the border, for which purpose he was liberally supplied with secret funds from India. Mashad, a large city swarming with pilgrims from all the countries bordering India, was considered an ideal centre 'for obtaining Secret Agents without attracting any special attention. . . . The Persians, for all their faults, make on the whole better Secret Service Agents than the Afghans or the natives of India' (19).* When, by 1905, intelligence work became too much for the consul alone, a full-time Military Attaché from the Indian Army was appointed to his staff for the purpose. The Military Attaché had his agents on both sides of the frontier and reported weekly to the Intelligence Branch in India on military and other activities in Bokhara, Samarkand, Tashkent and elsewhere in Central Asia.

Commercial no less than political rivalry with the Russians prompted the opening of other consulates. As early as 1875 Messrs Gray, Dawes and Company, of Austin Friars, London, had petitioned the British Government to secure the opening of the Karun river for British ship-

* On the other hand Curzon, who was at this time Viceroy in India, had doubts about the value of 'procuring unreliable and almost worthless information through native and ill-informed agents' (20).

ping and to appoint a consul at Isfahan. They considered both steps necessary if British trade with southern Persia was to compete successfully with Russian trade there. When, fourteen years later, the Shah eventually gave way to British pressure and agreed to open the Karun the British were quick to establish consulates at Mohammerah (1890), the port where the waters of the Karun and Shatt al-Arab meet, and at Isfahan (1891) which, it was expected, would become the main inland centre for the Karun river trade. In 1904, again with this trade in mind, a consulate was opened at Ahwaz on the Karun, seventy-five miles upstream from Mohammerah, where the overland route to Isfahan began. When, four years later, oil was discovered at Maidan-e-Naftun both Ahwaz and Mohammerah acquired a new importance.

The first Vice-Consul at Mohammerah was William McDouall, who had originally gone as a young telegraph clerk to Persia from a Suffolk vicarage. After nearly twenty years at Mohammerah he had more or less 'gone native' and after the discovery of oil was not considered up to the new demands of the post. He was therefore transferred to Kermanshah, on the trade route from Baghdad to Tehran, where a consulate had been opened in 1903. His place at Mohammerah was taken by Lieutenant A. T. Wilson, then attached to the Ahwaz Consulate.* Wilson, a young man of boundless energy and keen intelligence, had already made a name for himself in Ahwaz by the assiduity with which he travelled, surveyed and amassed information. At Mohammerah he became actively involved in negotiations with the Shaikh over the oil company's pipe line and refinery site.

Wilson's chief at Ahwaz had been a fellow member of the Indian Political Service, Captain David L. R. Lorimer, a scholarly figure much interested in languages, books, maps and people. When Lorimer first went to Ahwaz he was instructed to devote himself 'chiefly to travel; to the cultivation of intimate relations with the Bakhtiaris and other Lur tribes; and to the promotion of British enterprise in Arabistan, of which the main artery is the Karun River and its present radiating base, Ahwaz' (21). The importance of friendly relations with the tribes then lay in the fact that, in the absence of a strong central government, they controlled the trade routes leading inland; in particular the Ahwaz–Isfahan route, on which the British set much store, ran through Bakhtiari territory.

The Consuls at Ahwaz and Isfahan, on the south-western and north-eastern extremities of Bakhtiari country, soon became deeply involved in tribal affairs—not because of any desire of the British or Indian Governments to undermine the authority of Tehran, but because the

* See p. 41.

Consuls, Khans and Communities

absence of any such authority made it essential, if British interests were to be promoted and protected in south-western Persia, to come to terms with those elements there who could help maintain law and order. Similarly the Consul at Mohammerah sought to secure the goodwill of the Shaikh of Mohammerah, while all three consuls devoted much time to promoting peace and harmony between the Shaikh and his powerful but quarrelsome Bakhtiari neighbours.

Previously there had only been spasmodic and infrequent contact between the British and the migratory Bakhtiari and Lur tribes of south-western Persia. Captain Isaac Hart had helped raise and train 3,000 of them in the early days of the British Military Mission. In 1831 Stocqueler, a journalist and writer travelling from India, had traversed Bakhtiari country from west to east; in 1835 Henry Rawlinson had marched from Kermanshah to suppress a tribal rising among the Bakhtiari; in 1840-1 a young Englishman, Henry Layard, spent an adventurous ten months living among them and getting to know them as no other Englishman had done*; and in the spring of 1875 an enterprising young Scot, George Mackenzie,† then working in the Isfahan office of Gray, Paul and Company, had reconnoitred a possible road from Isfahan through the heart of Bakhtiari country to Shustar on the Karun. The first official British contact with the Bakhtiaris took place only at the very end of the nineteenth century when the British Consul in Isfahan‡ helped a British firm, Lynch Bros, reach agreement with the Bakhtiari khans for the construction of a road linking Ahwaz with Isfahan. Resultant disputes over costs, repairs and other such problems were usually laid at the feet of the Consuls in Isfahan and Ahwaz, who thus became increasingly enmeshed in Bakhtiari affairs.

It was, however, the discovery of oil, deep in the winter grazing grounds of the Bakhtiari, that led to that close association with the British which was the cause of so much suspicion in Tehran.

Before the British oil prospectors§ could begin drilling permission had to be obtained from the Bakhtiari khans in whose territory the oil lands lay. Unlike the road, for which the khans had first obtained—with British assistance—a sixty-year concession from the Shah, the khans held no such royal concession for oil. Nevertheless, they negotiated direct with the British with whom, thanks largely to the support of Consul Preece, an agreement was signed in 1905. The Persian Government, however, refused to recognise it. Thus, from the beginning, the

---

* See pp. 159-61.

† Sir George Mackenzie, K.C.M.G. (1844-1910). Successful merchant: partner in Gray, Dawes & Co. of London.

‡ John Preece, previously employed by the Indo-European Telegraph Department.

§ See pp. 108-9.

85

The English Amongst the Persians

authorities in Tehran looked with suspicion on the activities of the oil company in Khuzistan. They were also inclined to blame the British for their own difficulties with the unruly khans. Money from the Lynch road tolls and oil company subsidies, coupled with expectations of official British support, encouraged the khans in their traditional defiance of the central government.

In their quest for stability in south-western Persia the British not infrequently felt obliged to take steps which, in Persian eyes, could only appear as unwarranted interference in their country's internal affairs. Because the Bakhtiari khans at first dismally failed to provide the security for which they were paid an annual subsidy of £2,000 by the oil company, the British sent Wilson and his Bengal Lancers to the oilfields where robbery and disorder were such that oil drilling was in jeopardy. In 1912, in an effort to secure some continuity and responsibility in the tribal leadership, the British Legation played an active role in securing an agreement between the senior khans whereby the *Ilkhan*, or paramount chief, would be appointed for a five-year period. Sardar-e-Jang, the first *Ilkhan* so appointed, was strongly and openly backed by the British. A measure of the authority the British then wielded in Bakhtiari affairs is apparent from a despatch of the British Minister informing the Foreign Office that he had sent a message through the Consul in Isfahan to the younger Bakhtiari khans 'ordering them to behave themselves . . . this I have done at the request of the khans here who say that they will pay attention to the orders of the British Minister although they would snap their fingers at the commands of the Persian Government' (22). Likewise, it was with the British authorities in Bushire and Mohammerah and not with the Persian Government in Tehran that the Shaikh of Mohammerah and Sardar-e-Jang insisted later in the year on registering an agreement in settlement of one of their frequent disputes. The British had brought the two parties together. During the Great War, in order to safeguard vital oil supplies at a time when the Tehran Government's neutrality was in doubt, a secret agreement was signed in February 1916 by the British Minister with the Bakhtiari khans. In return for down payments of £5,000 each to the two main branches of the tribe and the promise of another £10,000 each at the end of the War, they undertook to protect the Anglo-Persian Oil Company's interests, to maintain friendly relations with the Shaikh of Mohammerah and not to take up arms against Britain or her allies. For their part the British undertook to maintain their 'traditional relations of friendship with the khans' and to sponsor Bakhtiari candidates 'for Governorships in provinces where British interests are paramount' (23). In the spring of 1918 the British

Consuls, Khans and Communities

Government sent a quantity of rifles and ammunition and two mountain guns to enable certain friendly khans to re-establish their authority and quell disorder.

It was not surprising if the Persian authorities regarded these Bakhtiari khans as British protégés and an obstacle to the unification of Persia—a situation which Reza Khan quickly sought to rectify when he came to power. The British, for all their friendship with the Bakhtiaris, never found them easy to deal with—'fickle and money-loving' was how the British Minister described them in 1914 (24).

A consulate had been opened at Shiraz, the capital of the southern province of Fars, in 1903. However, though there were powerful tribes in the province there was not the same imperative as in Khuzistan to enlist their support until German intrigues among them in the early years of the Great War caused much trouble for the British. In the years immediately before the war the Consul in Shiraz had become the virtual paymaster of the provincial government in Fars; from 1911 onwards the provincial government was largely dependent on an annual subsidy from the British Government to keep going. British assistance even extended to supporting, to the tune of £100,000 in 1913 alone, a Swedish-officered gendarmerie. The Consul who controlled the purse strings was thus in a unique position of power.

Consulates were also opened in central and eastern Persia. In 1893 the Manager of the Imperial Bank's newly-opened branch in Yazd was appointed honorary Vice-Consul there. The following year Lieutenant Percy Sykes of the 2nd Dragoon Guards,* who had already done some discreet travelling in Persia on behalf of the War Office, was sent from London to open a consulate at Kerman, the remote desert town on the caravan route from Bandar Abbas to Mashad. He and his sister Ella were the only Europeans there. The object was to strengthen the British position in Persian Baluchistan and to encourage Anglo-Indian trade, there being about forty Hindu traders resident in the town. Four years later, when it was learnt that the Russians were establishing a consulate in Sistan on the southern borders of Afghanistan, Sykes was hurried there from Kerman to open a consulate at Nusratabad. A consulate was next opened in 1903 at Torbat-e-Haidari, some eighty miles south of Mashad, by way of riposte to Russian activities there. In 1909 another was opened at Birjand, lying athwart the road from Sistan to Mashad, the seat of the powerful Alam family who dominated this corner of

---

* Brigadier Sir Percy Sykes, K.C.I.E. etc. (1867–1945). Early service in India. In 1892 travelled in disguise with a fellow officer to Samarkand. Consul-General, Mashad, 1905–13. Raised and commanded the South Persia Rifles 1916–20. Author of *A History of Persia* etc.

The English Amongst the Persians

Persia where the British and Russians were now face to face. The British were lucky to enjoy the friendship of Amir Muhammad Ibrahim Khan Alam, Shaukat ul-Mulk, the head of the family and father of a future Prime Minister.

Although many of the British consuls made close friends of those Persians with whom they had contact and were often respected locally, consuls *qua* consuls were not liked, particularly those from India. Their powers and privileges were a constant reminder to a sensitive and proud people of their own inferior position. The Persians hated the consuls' *sowar* escorts and resented the fact that under the capitulatory regime not only were disputes between British subjects and Protected Persons settled in consular courts totally removed from Persian control, but disputes between Persians and British were referred to special tribunals presided over by officials known as the *karguzars*, appointed by the Ministry of Foreign Affairs. The consul or his representative had the right to appear at these tribunals; he could also settle disputes direct with the *karguzar*. The Persians soon discovered that, though the original 1841 agreement on consuls had provided for reciprocity, in practice Persian consuls, whether in London or Bombay, were not permitted by the law of the land to interfere in judicial matters to the extent permitted to British consuls in Persia.

By to-day's standards the consuls were not overworked. Their duties, varied though they were, rarely demanded much of their time for long and except for the trading consuls, who had their own businesses to foster, they were often idle by force of circumstances. They had plenty of leisure for travel and sport, chiefly shooting game. But it was a lonely life for them and their wives, even in Tabriz and Tehran* where there were always a few Europeans. Elsewhere there was often none at all, except perhaps the Russian Consul and his wife, with whom it was not always politic to be too close. The 'Indian Politicals' in their remote east Persian posts, amid the barren hills and sandy wastes of Khorasan and Sistan, must have been hard put to fill their time or find sufficient material for their weekly reports or 'diaries'. The arrival of some unexpected European traveller, the movements of the Russian Consul, crop prospects, the depredations of a swarm of locusts—all such tit-bits served to fill their pages.†

---

* The total number of Europeans in Tehran during the 1860s and 1870s was, according to travellers' accounts, between fifty and sixty; mostly British, Russian and French. By 1909 their numbers had grown to about 200. Curzon's estimate of 500 in 1889 seems too high.

† 'Indian Politicals' who subsequently wrote reminiscences of consular life in Persia include R. L. Kennion, Frederick O'Connor, Clarmont Skrine, P. M. Sykes, Arnold Wilson and C. E. Yate. See Bibliography.

Consuls, Khans and Communities

After the withdrawal of the Military Mission in 1839 the British-born community in Persia dwindled to about twenty souls and remained at that figure for the next quarter of a century. Except for the odd trader or gentleman of fortune in the Shah's service* they were all connected either with the Legation and Consulates or the Residency at Bushire. Most were unmarried or grass widowers, though a few had wives with them.† The British community increased considerably in the 1860s with the arrival of staff to erect and maintain the telegraph line from London to India, but even as late as 1886 there were only about seventy British in all Persia, fifty of them Telegraph employees. In due time missionaries, managers and clerks of the Imperial Bank, and oil men swelled the ranks of the British who must have accounted for a large proportion of the 1,200 Europeans estimated to be living in Persia on the eve of World War I.

Already in 1889 the British Government considered there were sufficient British and British Protected Persons residing in Persia to warrant the promulgation of two Orders in Council establishing consular control over them. Consuls were given power to convene their own courts for this purpose.

In Qajar times Persia was too remote and 'uncivilised' to be a favourite posting either with diplomats or others. According to Curzon young attachés from the Foreign Office were apt to regard Tehran as a penal settlement. The few Europeans there kept very much to themselves and were regarded with suspicion and hostility by most Persians, who had little or no contact with them. The situation was even more difficult in the smaller towns where religious fanaticism tended to be more extreme. In Isfahan, for instance, the British and other Europeans were obliged at first to reside in the Armenian suburb of Julfa which Isabella Bishop, an intrepid and hardened traveller, described as 'a haven from the howling bigots of Isfahan' (25). The Manager of the Imperial Bank was the first European to set up house in Isfahan proper when the Bank opened a branch there in 1890; he was soon followed by the Consul and, in 1904, by the missionaries.

Left to their own devices the British took the lead among the Europeans in Tehran in organising recreation and amusement in what

* In the 1848-9 the Shah employed a British gardener, Burton, who also helped Lady Sheil with the Legation garden. In the early 1860s a Col. J. de G. Dolmage, ex-British army doctor and vet who had served in the Crimean War, was superintendent of the royal gunpowder factory in Mashad.

† Lady Ouseley was the first Englishwoman to accompany her husband to Persia during the Qajar period. Other early envoys—Willock, McDonald, Campbell, McNeill and Sheil—also had wives with them during some of their time in Persia.

The English Amongst the Persians

was essentially a male society. There were few European women in Tehran and no possibility of meeting Persian women, who lived in total seclusion from the opposite sex. On the other hand horses were cheap and almost all could afford to ride, so that hunting for fox and hare as well as hawking and shooting were popular sports. Alison, the eccentric British Minister of the 1860s, had his own hawks and a small pack of greyhounds; he would provide a hunt breakfast for the dozen or so Europeans who met at the British Mission before setting out for the chase, each accompanied by a couple of mounted servants. Later, when Durand arrived from India, he introduced weekly paper-chases, gymkhanas and tent-pegging: and Percy Sykes, coming to Tehran from Kerman in 1897, brought polo sticks and balls to revive a game which had its home in Persia but had not been played there since the Afghan invasions of the eighteenth century. Although it would be some years before the Persians themselves took up polo again they enjoyed watching the British, with teams representing the Legation, the Imperial Bank, and the Indo-European Telegraph Department playing against each other on the big army parade ground, the Maidan-e-Mashq. Thanks to the enthusiasm of Horace Rumbold and a fellow secretary in the Legation a race track was built in 1896 at Gulhek where the Legation organised a two-day race meeting each September. Tennis, on mud courts, became the rage in the 1870s and was played almost daily by the British who also introduced cricket, football and hockey to Persia.

But the evenings were long and tedious. Dining out, before the advent of carriages and cars, was a tiresome and hazardous business since it meant walking or riding, often long distances, through filthy, unlit streets, muddy in winter, dusty in summer and full of potholes. Those who did venture out were preceded by servants, each carrying a lantern which varied in size according to the rank of the person before whom it was borne. At the Legation the unmarried secretaries were expected to dine each night with the Minister and his wife. Afterwards there were billiards and cards but, as the young Rumbold recorded, 'after a time the inevitable happened—we exhausted all topics of conversation' (26). Other members of the British community were inclined, not for the first or last time, to regard the diplomats as stand-offish and self-important. It was the lively and more numerous Telegraph set who, despite the shortage of women, organised amateur theatricals and weekly dances to which they invited other members of the European community. Tehran had its social sets, centring round the Telegraph, the Imperial Bank, and the Legations. A visitor at the turn of the century noted there was 'an uncommon deal of social etiquette, and people are most particular regarding calls, dress, and the number of cards left at each door. It looks somewhat incongruous to see men in their black frock-coats and silk tall hats, prowling about the streets, with mud up to their knees if wet, or blinded with dust if dry, among strings of camels, mules, or donkeys. But that is the fashion, and people have to abide by it' (27).

In winter skating was a popular pastime, on one occasion the Shah himself coming to see how the Europeans amused themselves. In summer, to escape the enervating heat of Tehran, the British Minister with his diplomatic secretaries used to camp high up in the Lar valley, usually a two-day ride into the Elburz mountains to the north. There the river Lar abounded with trout and the surrounding hills with ibex, mouflon and partridge. The clear mountain air was fresh with the scent of wild mint and thyme, while the cold, star-lit nights possessed a rare invigorating quality. The Legation would pitch their spacious Indian tents on greensward close to the river near a great cliff of rock from which a spring of ice-cold water gushed. A few miles away the majestic form of Demavend, its dome usually capped in cloud, dominated the beautiful, treeless valley through which the river meandered before curving round the great mountain to cut its way through a series of narrow gorges to the Caspian. When Charles Murray camped there in 1858 he, like many others before and since, enthused over 'the fine stream which flows in front of our tents and which abounds so much in trout that I frequently kill fifty in an hour with a fly' (28). Although other members of the European community also discovered the delights of the Lar valley it was mainly the British* who, year after year, spent much of each July and August there, keeping in touch with Tehran through a daily messenger service.

Despite their healthy outdoor life the British, like everyone else, suffered greatly from the unhygienic conditions of the time and the very limited medical facilities then available. Home leave was a rare luxury since it entailed long and expensive travel for which the individual himself had to pay. When Justin Sheil applied for leave in 1846 he had been seven and a half years away from home: a Legation clerk, who later died in Tehran, was seventeen years without home leave: the head of the Indo-European Telegraph Department went home only twice in the course of twenty-two years. Such was the rule, not the exception. Cholera, typhus, dysentery and malaria took toll of young and old, often striking them down even before they reached their destination. Charles Scott, the second son of Sir Walter Scott the writer, died of dysentery within days of reaching Tehran to join the

* By 1837, if not before, the British Legation had a summer camp in the Lar valley. Nasir ed-Din Shah used also to camp there each summer.

The English Amongst the Persians

Legation staff in 1841. Twenty years earlier, Claudius Rich,* on his way to Bombay from Baghdad, died suddenly of cholera in Shiraz. His diary entry, shortly before the epidemic reached Shiraz, conveys something of its horror: 'News from Bushire. The cholera is raging there and carries off thirty persons a day. It is all over the Ghermaseer: Mr Sturmey, on his way down, saw the road from Burauzgoon to Bushire strewed with dead bodies. The Liverpool frigate, which arrived at Bushire, lost three lieutenants in fifteen hours. The surgeon and a great part of the crew we hear are also dead' (29).

Seventy years later fear of cholera still haunted Europeans and Persians alike. Gertrude Bell,† who had been staying with her aunt and uncle, Sir Frank and Lady Lascelles, at the British Legation wrote home in September 1892 about the epidemic which had raged all that summer in Tehran:

> The long lines of new mounds in the graveyard gave one a sudden shiver of realising what it had been . . . at the back of one's mind I think there must have always been a feeling that everyone was carrying his life in his hand. It was so hideously sudden sometimes: in the evenings you were well and merry, and the next morning, dead . . . None of our immediate acquaintances had it, but many Europeans died, people whom we knew slightly. Telegraph clerks who had been playing cricket the day before . . . The panic of some of the servants has been rather curious. It takes the form of religious scruples, they think there will be divine vengeance upon them because they serve Europeans (30).

Memorials and gravestones in the Armenian churchyards and cemeteries where, until the 1880s, the British were buried‡—at Bushire, Shiraz, Isfahan, Tehran and Tabriz—have each a story to tell. Sufficient here to record perhaps the saddest story of all, that of the Murdoch Smith family.

---

* Resident of the East India Company in Baghdad 1808–21. Brilliant linguist, orientalist and archaeologist.

† Gertrude Bell (1868–1926). Traveller, writer and administrator. This was her first visit to the Middle East where she was to make her name. During her six months in Tehran she learnt Persian and translated Hafez's poems. She also became engaged to one of the Legation secretaries, Henry Cadogan, who died suddenly the following year.

‡ In 1884 the British joined with other Protestant communities in acquiring ground for a Protestant cemetery at Akbarabad, then a village on the western outskirts of Tehran. The cemetery was managed by an international committee presided over by the British envoy. In 1970 a new cemetery, south of Tehran, was consecrated to replace the Akbarabad site which was then deep within the city limits and no longer suitable for burials. The British Ambassador still presides over the Cemetery Committee.

Consuls, Khans and Communities

Major Robert Murdoch Smith* of the Royal Engineers had gone to Persia in 1863 at the age of twenty-eight to help establish and run the new telegraph line. Six years later he married in Tehran Eleanor Baker, the sister of one of his colleagues. They had nine children, all but one born in Persia where four of them died in infancy. Then in November 1883 Murdoch-Smith's wife died, as also did her mother, who was living with them, three months later. Murdoch Smith was now alone in Tehran with five young children on his hands, the oldest a boy of seven years and the youngest a girl of four months. He decided that he must send them home to be cared for by one of his family and in March 1884 set off with the five children and the Telegraph Department's doctor on the long journey to Bushire where they were to take a boat for Bombay and home. But at Kashan, only seven stages out of Tehran, tragedy struck and three of the children died on successive days of diphtheria. Poor Murdoch Smith went on to Bushire with his two remaining children, both girls, to put them on their ship. He then returned to the empty house in Tehran. The following year, perhaps because he could stand the solitude no longer, he left for his native Scotland.

Such were the hazards and sorrows of life in Persia in those days.

---

* Major-General Sir Robert Murdoch Smith, K.C.M.G. (1835-1900). See Chapter 9.

7

The World of Business

AT THE BEGINNING of the nineteenth century there was little trade between Britain and Persia. This was mainly due to the geographical isolation of the country, the chaos that followed the collapse of the Safavid dynasty in the early eighteenth century, and the lack of any compensating Persian exports. Unlike neighbouring Turkey, where prosperous British mercantile communities were well established in Smyrna and Constantinople, the sole British trader in Persia was the East India Company's Resident at Bushire. Even after the abolition in 1811 of the Company's monopoly of trade in the Persian Gulf, some years elapsed before any British firms were tempted to establish themselves at Bushire or elsewhere.

The East India Company's Persian trade was more directed towards India than England. Persian horses and donkeys, raw wool, silk and cotton, grains, skins and hides were shipped to India in return for sugar and spices, dyes and oils. Some English woollens and cotton fabrics, the staple British export in those days, reached Persia from Bombay where they were trans-shipped after the long voyage round the Cape into sailing vessels serving the Persian Gulf. An even smaller volume of English goods found their way into northern Persia through British and Greek merchants in Constantinople who onward shipped them to Poti on the Black Sea whence they travelled overland through Tiflis to Tabriz, or else across the Caspian to Enzeli (now Bandar Pahlavi).

The awakening of political interest in Persia in the early days of the Qajar period revived British commercial interest in the country. Malcolm had been instructed before leaving India on his first mission to the Qajar court to secure a commercial as well as a political treaty. Though he succeeded, the treaty was never ratified and was cancelled by the Shah in 1807 when he did his deal with the French. Thereafter,

The World of Business

despite several attempts, in response to appeals from British merchants, to secure a commercial treaty that would encourage and protect British trade, this was not achieved until 1841 when the British Government made the resumption of diplomatic relations conditional on the signature of such a treaty.

Without a treaty* the British were at a disadvantage compared with the Russians who, under the terms of the Treaty of Turkmanchai, had secured important commercial privileges including an undertaking that customs duties on all their exports would not exceed 5% *ad valorem*. Both countries saw in Persia a profitable market for the cheap products of their factories whose processes had been revolutionised by the inventions of the previous century. In southern Persia the British, because of their position in India and their control of the Gulf, could remain fairly confident of holding their own. But the situation was very different in the north, which was on the Russian doorstep. To have any chance of competing there British merchants would need to use a quicker and cheaper route than that provided by the Persian Gulf. This meant seeking to reach Persia by way of the Mediterranean and Black Seas and then overland through Georgia or Turkey. In 1809 Harford Jones drew the attention of the Foreign Office to the advantages of using the ancient caravan route which led from Trebizond over the thickly forested Pontic Alps and the bleak, treeless plateau to Erzerum and Tabriz. This route, which was 200 miles shorter than the Russian-controlled Georgian route, passed entirely through friendly Turkish territory. By using it Harford Jones believed that Britain could capture much of the north Persian market from Russia, particularly as the Crown Prince, Abbas *Mirza*, had promised to send Tabriz merchants to Trebizond to buy any cargoes landed there. This same route could also be used to export silk and other Persian products at an economic cost. But though Jones' successors also championed the use of Trebizond and the opening of consulates there and at Erzerum as a means of developing trade with northern Persia their recommendations were not implemented until 1830. This was due less to official inertia than to reluctance to act until Turkey could be persuaded, or compelled, to open her Black Sea ports to foreign shipping—a step only achieved in 1829 with the signing of the Treaty of Adrianople at the conclusion of the Turco-Russian War. In the next year James Brant, an enterprising Smyrna merchant, was appointed by the British Government as the first British consul in

---

* A first step had been taken in 1836 when the Shah issued a *farman* placing British merchants on the same footing as Russian merchants in respect of customs duties. However it was not until the signature of the 1841 Anglo-Persian Commercial Treaty that Britain acquired full 'most favoured nation' treatment.

The English Amongst the Persians

Trebizond. Brant quickly began exerting himself to develop Trebizond as a base for the transit trade with northern Persia. He and his partners chartered ships to bring British and other merchandise from Constantinople, then the main distribution centre in the Near East for European goods. Their efforts were further helped in 1836 with the introduction of fortnightly steamship sailings between the two ports. British merchandise, mainly 'Manchester goods', soon found its way in increasing volume to the bazaars of Tabriz.

One solitary English trader had already established himself in Tabriz, at the other end of the caravan route, before Brant went to Trebizond. This was Charles Burgess, the son of a London banker. Burgess' interest in Persia had been aroused by a plausible Armenian* whom he had met in London and who had persuaded him to accompany a valuable consignment of British merchandise, which the Armenian was shipping to Tabriz by the Black Sea–Georgian route. It was one of the first such shipments direct from London. Charles Burgess, then only nineteen years old, successfully accomplished what was undoubtedly a difficult task for so young a man with no previous experience of oriental ways. He reached Tabriz with his precious goods in July 1828 and for the next eight years was to busy himself, albeit unsuccessfully, in seeking his fortune by trading with England.

The curious and sad story of Charles Burgess and his young brother Edward, whom Charles persuaded two years later to join him in Tabriz, is recorded in a series of letters they wrote to their family in England. Whether Charles first went to Tabriz with the intention of embarking on a commercial career is uncertain. More probably he was attracted by his Armenian friend's promise of a commission in the Crown Prince's army once he reached Tabriz—a promise that was fulfilled. Charles was then attached to the British Military Mission in Tabriz and quickly entered into a business partnership with his commanding officer, Major Isaac Hart, there being no problems in those days about officers dabbling in business. The partnership was short-lived and unsuccessful as Hart died in 1830 leaving Charles Burgess in his debt to the tune of £1,600. By this time Charles, after spending part of the previous year helping to train the armed followers of a Kurdish chieftain, had decided to concentrate with his young brother on trading. To this end he visited Trebizond and England despite the difficulties of the journey. He also travelled in Persia looking for goods to sell in England—apart from silk, on which he counted most, he contemplated exporting wool, opium,

* Known as Sadık Bey in Turkey and Sayyed Khan in Persia. He had connections in Constantinople and London with the firm of Hamson Bros., and in Tabriz with the Crown Prince whose agent he claimed to be when in London.

The World of Business

'yellow berries', gums and even caviar. But he was not a good businessman and was soon in trouble. By 1833 his brother Edward was writing home that 'Charles appears to have taken any goods he could lay his hands on without any regard as to whether these were suited to the Persian taste or not' (1). The brothers also had bad luck when, in an effort to protect local merchants and manufacturers, the Shah at one moment forbade his subjects to buy any of the Burgess imports. But, as Edward pointed out, his brother was wrong to embark on speculative silk deals before paying off his English creditors. Charles might, however, have made good in 1836 when the Crown Prince entrusted him with the task of buying some £30,000 worth of muskets and other military equipment in London. Instead he absconded with the money advanced to him for this purpose and never returned to Persia, leaving behind not only debts but two illegitimate children by an Armenian mistress and, most tragic of all, his brother Edward, whom the Persians held hostage on Charles' account for the rest of his life.

Edward Burgess shines through his letters home as a devoted son and saintly character, rarely complaining about his fate and insisting that 'I cannot leave Persia without coming to some arrangement with my creditors, that is without running away, which you know I would never do' (2). For years he helped provide for the children and mistress his brother had abandoned. He bore no ill-will towards the Persians who refused to let him leave the country until his brother returned, preferring them to the Greek merchants of Tabriz* who, he said, 'have the insolence to call the Persians barbarians' (3). To make a living he worked for a time with Edward Bonham, then the only other British merchant in Tabriz. Later he became translator for one of the royal princes and also helped to tutor the prince's children and manage his stables. This in turn led to translation work for the Crown Prince, Nasir ed-Din *Mirza*, whom, on succeeding to the throne in 1848, Edward accompanied to Tehran as chief interpreter. In Tehran Edward Burgess was to secure for himself a permanent niche in Persian history when he was appointed editor of the first newspaper† to be published in Persia. Edward had the delicate task of selecting and translating extracts from the European and Turkish press for publication in the paper, sometimes getting into trouble for his selections. Lady Sheil, the observant wife of the British Minister, noted the uncritical nature of the paper whose

---

* By the 1840s the European community in Tabriz consisted almost entirely of Greeks, ten to fifteen in number, who had moved there from Constantinople about 1837.

† *Ruznameh Vaqayi-e-Ittifaqiyyeh*, founded by the Prime Minister *Mirza* Taqi Khan, Amir Kabir Nizam, and published weekly in Tehran between 1850 and 1860.

The English Amongst the Persians

leading articles were 'often the composition of the Prime Minister himself, and were chiefly in praise of the Shah's Government' (4). She thought it would be at least another five hundred years before the Persians enjoyed a free press. Another of Edward Burgess' jobs was to translate for the Shah's and his Prime Minister's own benefit press articles not considered suitable for the public.

Despite the royal favour he now enjoyed and the efforts of Sheil to secure permission for him to visit England this was not granted until 1855. At long last, with arrears of pay made good, he was able to set off with his Armenian wife and young daughter on the longed-for journey home. He yearned to see his old father who had done his best through the Foreign Office to secure his release. It was not to be. Already in poor health before leaving Tehran, Edward got no further than Tabriz where he died and was buried in the Armenian cemetery. His wayward brother Charles, who had been living for some years at Aix-la-Chapelle, passed away at about the same time, suffering dreadfully from the advanced stages of syphilis.

At the time of Edward Burgess' death there were no British merchants left in Persia: the consuls, first Stevens and then Abbott, had withdrawn from commercial activity. Stevens' young brother George had gone to Trebizond, leaving behind a number of debts which were to embarrass Consul Stevens, though not to the same extent that Charles Burgess' debts had embarrassed his brother. Imports from Britain by the Trebizond route were now largely in the hands of five Greek firms, enjoying either Russian or Turkish protection, in Tabriz. A London firm, Mills and Co., which in 1848 had secured a large Persian Government order for 100,000 muskets, considered opening branches in Shiraz and Isfahan 'for the purpose', as they explained to the Foreign Office, 'of introducing English manufacturers to compete with the Russians who monopolise the whole import trade through the north' (5) but they were deterred by the absence of any form of consular protection in either town. Periodic visits were paid to Tehran by a Mr Alexander Hector, an English trader established in Baghdad.* He also managed to sell a quantity of muskets—of inferior quality according to Sheil—but he was a tiresome visitor, complaining that the Legation had deprived him of further arms sales and would not allow him to use their courier service. He, like Mills and Co., employed Armenian agents, it being unusual in those days for European merchants to employ Persians.

The leading Greek firm in Tabriz at this time was Ralli and Angelasto, linked abroad with other Ralli firms founded by five enterprising

---

* Alexander Hector first set himself up as a merchant in Baghdad in 1832. He acted as storekeeper and purser of Chesney's Euphrates Expedition in 1835.

The World of Business

brothers, two of whom had settled in Britain in 1818 and become naturalised British subjects. A Swiss firm, Ziegler and Co., had also started business in Tabriz. Having no diplomatic or consular representative of their own to turn to in case of need both firms sought, and were duly granted, British protection. Later a Dutch firm, Hotz and Son, based on Bushire, also secured British protection.* Though it was rare for any of these three firms to employ British staff in Persia they were regarded as British and undoubtedly profited from the security and advantages that this position gave them. In a country which possessed no commercial code redress for debts and other losses, such as highway robbery of caravans, could normally only be obtained by direct appeal to the Persian authorities or by the seizure of some of the debtor's property. The knowledge that the British Minister or consul stood behind the claimant was an invaluable help in settling disputes which sometimes dragged on for years.

Ralli and Angelasto did a brisk business importing piece goods from Manchester and exporting silk from the Caspian region, where they had a large and comfortable establishment at Rasht. However, successive failures of the silk crop together with the frustrations of dealing with unhelpful officials caused them to close down in 1871. Zieglers also concentrated at first on exporting Gilan silk and importing cotton goods from Manchester (where they had their head office) but difficulties in remitting the proceeds of their sales led them to start buying carpets for export. This proved so successful that by the 1880s Zieglers, in addition to their general business as import-export merchants, were playing a major role in reviving the centuries-old, but moribund, Persian carpet industry. They established themselves at Sultanabad (now Arak) in the heart of an important carpet weaving area and placed orders for carpets and rugs with cottage weavers in the town and surrounding villages. They supplied the weavers with wool yarn already dyed and persuaded them to modify traditional designs and sizes to meet European tastes. By 1900 Zieglers controlled some 2,500 looms in the Sultanabad area where their own large compound, complete with staff houses, dyeing works and warehouses, was said to be 'on a European scale of style and comfort only surpassed in all Persia by the British Legation in Tehran' (6).

The Persian Carpet Manufacturing Co., a subsidiary of Hotz and Son, soon followed Zieglers into the carpet business at Sultanabad and

* Ralli and Angelasto, previously under Russian protection, were granted British protection in 1860 on the grounds that the two senior partners were then British subjects. Zieglers and Hotz secured British protection after registering their head offices in England.

were joined by others including The Oriental Carpet Manufacturers Ltd, (O.C.M.).* Zieglers† and O.C.M. became the leaders in the carpet trade and opened branches in all the main weaving centres. Some deplored their commercialisation and attempted standardisation of the weaving industry feeling, like Curzon, that it was 'at the expense alike of originality and excellence' (7). But without some form of standardisation Persian rugs and carpets would never have captured the European and American markets to the extent they did. Well before the end of the Qajar period carpets had become one of Persia's principal exports. Zieglers deserve much credit for having pioneered this business which, long before oil, became an important factor in balancing Persian trade with Europe.

One of the few Englishmen to be employed by Zieglers in Persia was Hildebrand Stevens, son of Francis Stevens mentioned in the previous chapter. Hildebrand, who came to Persia from Turkey about 1875, soon left Zieglers and established himself on his own in Tabriz. After a few years he was running a thriving import-export business, Hild. F. Stevens and Son, with branches throughout the country in competition with his former employers. Hildebrand Stevens and his son Charles‡ were held in high esteem in Tabriz by British and Persians alike: both became honorary Vice-Consuls and would take charge of British interests in the absence of the Consul-General. At one time the firm had a concession for running ferry boats on Lake Urumiyah but nothing came of the project.

There were two other British firms, Gray, Paul and Co. and Lynch Bros, trading principally in south and south-western Persia, who played an important role in developing Persia's foreign trade at this time.§ The former had been established at Bushire since 1866 and were associated with Gray, Dawes and Co., merchants and ships' agents of London. At Bushire and other Gulf ports they acted as agents for the ships of the British India Steam Navigation Co. which plied between

* O.C.M., the largest of the carpet firms, was formed in London in 1906 by a merger of six companies mainly engaged in the Turkish carpet trade. Their first representative in Persia, A. C. Edwards, established his headquarters in Hamadan. He was the author of *The Persian Carpet* and *A Persian Caravan*, the latter a delightful account of some of his experiences.

† Zieglers sold the famous Ardebil carpet to a London dealer who, in turn, sold it in 1893 to the Victoria and Albert Museum for £2,500.

‡ Charles Stevens died in 1934, leaving no heir to carry on the family business, which was wound up. Zieglers withdrew from Persia about the same time.

§ Other British firms operating in south Persia in the late nineteenth century were The Persian Gulf Trading Co. (formerly Muir, Tweedy and Co.), David Sassoon and Co., and Strick and Co. (engaged mainly in shipping red oxide from the islands of Hormuz and Abu Musa).

The World of Business

Bombay and the Persian Gulf. They also shipped carpets, dates, wool, grain, opium and other Persian products, and imported 'colonial' goods such as tea and sugar, as well as dye stuffs and manufactures from India and Europe. In 1871 Gray, Paul made the first practical proposals for regular steam navigation on the Karun river.*

However it was a rival firm, Lynch Bros, established in Baghdad since 1841, which first managed to sail a paddle-steamer up the Karun when it was opened to foreign shipping in 1888. Assisted by annual subsidies from both the British and Indian Governments Lynch, who were already running a steamer service on the Euphrates and Tigris, now inaugurated a regular fortnightly service between Mohammerah, Ahwaz and Shustar. Ten years later, in a further effort to develop trade with the interior by this route, they built the 270-mile-long 'Lynch' road between Ahwaz and Isfahan. Both the Legation in Tehran and the Consul in Isfahan had strongly supported them in their negotiations with the Bakhtiari khans for this project. Though the road they built was little more than a mule track, the engineering and transport problems to be overcome were considerable. Men and mules alone could be used to transport heavy steel girders to bridge two gorges high up in the mountains. Lynch opened offices at Dizful as well as Ahwaz and Shustar where local produce, such as sesame seed and wool, was bought for export and caravans assembled for the two-week journey to Isfahan. Their representatives in these towns, without other European company, led solitary lives and suffered much from the religious fanaticism of those amongst whom they lived and the hostility of local shaikhs and merchants, who resented foreign intrusion on their preserves.

Both Gray, Paul and Lynch† played a pioneer role in the early economic development of a remote and almost totally neglected corner of Persia. More might have been achieved if ambitious British plans for irrigation and railway construction had matured.

It looked for a time as if the Karun route would fulfil the high hopes of influential figures in Britain who for years had lobbied hard in its favour. They saw the opening of the Batum–Baku railway as destroying the competitiveness of the Trebizond route and giving the Russians a big advantage over other users of the Black Sea route into Persia; they

---

* As far back as 1831 Francis Chesney had explored the Karun from Mohammerah to Ahwaz. In 1835 Lt. Alexander Burnes of the Indian Army drew attention to the possibilities of sending goods into the heart of Persia via the Karun. The first detailed survey of the river was made in 1841-2 by Lt. W. B. Selby of the Indian Navy, assisted by Henry Layard.

† Gray, Paul and Co. still flourish in Persia under the name of Gray Mackenzie and Co., a member of the Inchcape Group: Lynch Bros. were wound up about 1960.

The English Amongst the Persians

feared that unless some better alternative to 'the terrible road from Bushire' (8) into the interior was found the Russians would soon capture the southern as well as the northern Persian market. The Karun-Isfahan route seemed to provide just that alternative, being only about half as long as the road from Bushire to Isfahan, the principal commercial centre south of Tehran and the northern limit of British commercial predominance. But though there was some increase in trade, particularly in exports from Persia, expectations were never fulfilled—apart from obstruction by Persian officials and local merchants, the port facilities at Mohammerah were bad, communications between Ahwaz and the interior even worse, and navigation on the river often impeded by obstacles such as sand banks and shallow waters: in addition snow blocked the passes on the Lynch road for five months each year, and the cost of fodder for mules was higher than expected.

The Shah had only reluctantly, under prolonged and persistent British pressure, agreed in 1888 to allow foreign shipping to use the Karun river. Nine years earlier he had turned down a British request for exclusive rights on the river and curtly reminded the British Minister that 'Persia was not a dependent but an independent Power' (9). Behind the Shah's refusal and resentment of outside pressure lay fear of Russian reaction should he favour the British in this way. He was still smarting from the effects of his enforced cancellation in 1873 of a concession he had all-too-willingly granted to Baron Julius de Reuter—a concession which Curzon described as 'the most complete and extraordinary surrender of the entire industrial resources of a kingdom into foreign hands that has probably ever been dreamed of, much less accomplished, in history' (10).

Reuter was a German Jew who had become a naturalised British subject in 1857 and subsequently made a fortune with his news agency business. He obtained his Persian concession almost by chance and without any encouragement or support from the British Government. The commercially-minded, rather sharp Persian Minister in London, General Hajü Mohsen Khan, had for some time been unsuccessfully hawking a concession round the City; he eventually turned to Reuter, an outsider in the City's eyes, and interested him in a seventy-year railway concession from the Caspian to the Persian Gulf. Reuter, who knew nothing about Persia, sent a representative to Tehran to negotiate details and ended up in July 1872 with a concession which, in addition to the railway, gave him exclusive rights for seventy years throughout Persia for tramways, mining, irrigation, water works and exploitation of the state forests. He was also given a twenty-year monopoly over the Persian Customs and the first option on any further concessions for public utilities, roads, postal services, manufacturing plants and banks. In return, 20% of the railway's profits and 15% of the profits of other activities undertaken by Reuter were to go to the Shah. Reuter, as evidence of his good faith, agreed to put down £40,000, to be forfeited if he had not begun work on the railway within fifteen months.

The Shah's interest in the concession was by no means only pecuniary. He and his Prime Minister were worried by the Russian threat to Persian independence. They believed—or hoped—that by giving the British a large economic stake in the country they would become committed to defending that independence.

Announcement of the concession's terms startled Europe. Thiers, the French statesman, commented that they left nothing of Persia to the Shah except the atmosphere. Both the British and Indian Governments, whom Reuter had kept in the dark until the last moment, were much alarmed, fearing in particular Russian reaction. The Russians were predictably opposed to what amounted to their exclusion from any part in Persia's economic development. They made their views known to the Shah when he visited Moscow the following year. In Persia popular feeling against the surrender of the nation's birthright to foreigners was stirred up both by the *mullahs* and the Russians. The Shah bowed to the mounting opposition and in November 1873 cancelled the concession on the grounds that Reuter had failed to start work on the railway within the stipulated fifteen months' period. Reuter, who had in fact hurriedly embarked on this work a few weeks earlier, refused to accept the Shah's cancellation. By threatening to sell part of his concession to the Russians he virtually blackmailed a reluctant and suspicious Foreign Office into taking up the cudgels on his behalf. When the Shah subsequently sought to grant concessions to other business adventurers—Russian, French, German or American—who flocked to Tehran at this time in pursuit of profitable outlets for surplus capital the British Minister would protest and insist that any new concessions were invalid so long as Reuter's remained in force.

Reuter was certainly entitled to expect some compensation for the treatment he had received. However, it was not until 1889 that he was eventually offered a new concession, giving him exclusive banking and mining rights for sixty years. Although not to be compared in sweep with his first concession it was, nonetheless, a very valuable one. He had been greatly helped in reaching this satisfactory settlement of his claims by the energetic support of the British Minister, Drummond Wolff, who was an old friend.

Reuter's mining rights were taken up by The Persian Bank Mining

The English Amongst the Persians

Rights Corporation Ltd, a company which was floated on his behalf by Messrs J. Henry Schroder and Co. and David Sassoon and Co: then, as now, well-known City names. Curzon became a director. The company's prospectus referred to the 'exclusive and definitive privilege of working throughout the Persian Empire the iron, copper, lead, mercury, coal, petroleum, manganese, borax and asbestos mines belonging to the State, and which had not been previously ceded to others'. Gold, silver and precious stones were excluded from what otherwise was a virtual monopoly of Persia's mineral wealth. British geologists and engineers as well as Cornish miners arrived to prospect for coal, oil, mercury and manganese but they had little success. Furthermore, they were discouraged by local hostility and by the enormous problems, physical as well as financial, created by the almost total lack of communications and consequent inaccessibility of the mining areas. After three years of effort the company decided to cut its losses and went into voluntary liquidation.*

The story of Reuter's sixty-year banking concession is a much happier one. The Bank was established under the chairmanship in London of Mr William Keswick of the well-known Far Eastern firm of Jardine, Matheson and Co. and was given the exclusive right to issue bank notes which would be legal tender throughout the country. The Imperial Bank of Persia, as it was to be called, became in effect the State bank and controlled the country's note circulation. In addition it was permitted to carry on normal banking business. It was exempted from all taxes and import dues in Persia. Not surprisingly the Bank's initial capital of £1 million was heavily over-subscribed within a few hours of the lists being open to the public—an augury of the success which, after a shaky start, attended the Bank's operations in Persia for over sixty years.

The Imperial Bank opened its doors in Tehran in September 1889 and in the following year, by taking over the New Oriental Banking Corporation Ltd of London and India,† acquired a network of branches in all the main Persian towns. Later other branches were opened according to need. In one case, however, pressure from the Government of India and the attraction of an annual subsidy of £1,500 rather than commercial judgement caused the bank to open a branch. This was in

---

* Two earlier British mining ventures proved equally unsuccessful. In 1810, with the backing of the Crown Prince, a Mr Williamson had tried to mine copper south of Tabriz. In 1836 Lindesay-Bethune with the help of a two-year loan from the British Government started an iron mine and foundry in the Karadagh district of Azarbaijan: he brought machinery and 8 or 9 miners from Scotland for the purpose.

† The New Oriental Banking Corporation opened up in Tehran in 1888, the first European bank to do so.

The World of Business

1903 at Nusratabad in Sistan following rumours that the Russians were opening a bank there. Apart from forestalling the Russians, the Government of India was anxious to promote trade with Sistan, where a number of Indian merchants had been encouraged to establish themselves.

The Imperial Bank's first Chief Manager in Tehran was Mr Joseph Rabino di Borgomale,* born in London of an Italian father and English mother who had previously worked with Crédit Lyonnais in Cairo and become a naturalised British subject. He proved an admirable choice and during his eighteen years in Persia did much to build up the Bank's reputation. He instructed all his managers that the first essential of success was to establish 'a good circulation of notes particularly of the smaller denominations . . . We have to inspire confidence in the public, and to this end must impress upon them at all times that our notes are cash' (11). Rabino's second essential was the accumulation of fixed deposits, without which the bank could not expand its commercial banking activities. He had a higher opinion of the Persians than most Europeans and wisely urged his managers to learn Persian. It was no mean achievement that Rabino and his British staff should have succeeded relatively quickly in introducing European banking ideas into a country where they were previously unknown. Bank notes came to be accepted instead of coin. To achieve this the bank's branches, many of them several days' or weeks' journey from Tehran, were kept supplied with silver coins ready to be paid out should there be a run on the bank. Such runs did occur, sometimes inspired by the Russians, whose own bank had the advantage of official backing from the Russian Government† and was a deadly rival, both commercial and political, of the Imperial Bank. As a precaution against these runs the Bank's notes were clearly marked with the name of the sole branch where any one note was encashable. By a combination of good management and luck not one of the great caravans of mules or camels, escorted by Persian soldiers, which carried the coin across the mountains and deserts of Persia to district branches was ever plundered. Nor, for lack of coin, was any branch ever forced to close its doors—one advantage of there being only one small silver coin in circulation (the *kran*, worth about fourpence in those days) was the physical impossibility of customers carrying away large quantities at a time.

* His son, Hyacinth L. Rabino, after a spell with the Bank at Kermanshah, joined the Consular Service and was Vice-Consul at Rasht, 1906–12; he published a number of interesting papers on the Caspian provinces, Persian press and coinage.

† *The Banque des Prêts*, later named *Banque d'Escompte de Perse*. The Russians obtained their banking concession in 1890.

The English Amongst the Persians

The astute Reuter took on as the Bank's high-level contact man in Tehran General Albert Houtum Schindler, like himself a naturalised British subject of German origin. Schindler had lived in Persia for many years. After first being employed by the Indo-European Telegraph Company he joined the Persian Telegraph service. He was also said to have served in the Persian army and to be an admiral in the Shah's miniature navy. In the course of his duties he had travelled all over Persia and written a number of learned papers and articles for the *Encyclopaedia Britannica* about the country's geography and resources. Curzon, who drew heavily on Schindler for the detailed information which so greatly impresses readers of *Persia and the Persian Question*, described him in that book as 'a sort of *deus ex machina* required to assist in the solution of most Persian problems' (12). Drummond Wolff thought so highly of him that he tried hard, but unsuccessfully, to persuade the Foreign Office to engage him as a member of the Legation staff. Reuter employed him instead. Schindler and Rabino were popular figures in Tehran and were regarded by travellers who met them as the two best informed members of the European community. The fact that they were both employed by the Imperial Bank contributed much to the Bank's high standing. So, too, did its ornate head office, once a private residence, with a façade of gay Persian tiles and arcaded balcony which dominated the eastern end of Maidan-e-Topkhaneh, Tehran's principal thoroughfare.

The Bank, despite its foreign ownership, became a respected national institution with an enviable reputation throughout the country for commercial integrity. There were, however, those who noticed that no Persians occupied positions of authority either in the Bank's head office or in any of its numerous branches. It was the instrument through which three British loans were provided for the Shah between 1892 and 1911. These loans, raised against the security of the Caspian fisheries and the Customs dues of the Persian Gulf ports, attracted—as did Russian loans—the odium of Persian nationalists, who saw them as strangling Persia. Yet the Imperial Bank,* though involved, managed to keep its reputation unimpaired.

Drummond Wolff was soon assisting another old City friend to land an important concession, this time with disastrous consequences. The new concessionaire was Major Gerald Talbot, who, after an audience with the Shah and two heavy down payments,† was granted a concession

---

* The Bank lost its note issuing right in 1931. On the expiration of its original charter in 1949 it was renamed The British Bank of Iran and the Middle East. It withdrew from Persia in 1952 but returned in 1958.

† The Shah was paid £25,000 and his Prime Minister £15,000.

The World of Business

in 1890 for a fifty-year monopoly of the production, sale and export of Persia's entire tobacco crop. In return the Persian treasury was to receive an annual rent of £15,000 and a quarter of the net annual profits. Talbot, after forming the Imperial Tobacco Corporation of Persia in London, returned to Tehran early in 1891 with staff to organise what was known as the Tobacco Regie. Details of the concession soon leaked out and quickly provoked a popular outcry when the extent of foreign control over the country's tobacco became known. Once again the *mullahs*, with the Russians active in the background, stirred up feelings against the British. There were disturbances as far afield as Mashad and Shiraz, Isfahan and Yazd. The Consul in Tabriz feared a massacre of the Christians. He also reported that 'this Tobacco Concession has done much to raise a hostile feeling against the British who till recently were undoubtedly looked upon by very many here as friends of Persia . . . now every vile epithet is used towards them' (13). There was a remarkable response when a leading religious divine called on all Persians to abstain from tobacco until the concession should be repealed. 'Suddenly', a French observer recorded at the time, 'with perfect accord all the tobacco merchants have closed their shops, all the *qalyans* have been put aside and no one smokes any longer' (14). In December 1891 the Shah gave way to public opinion and cancelled the concession, causing a great loss of face to the British and a corresponding rise in Russian prestige. Even then there was rioting and shooting in Tehran. For the Persians it was, in a sense, the beginning of a national awakening and demonstrated, as Professor E. G. Browne wrote later, 'that there was a limit to what they would endure, that they were not the spiritless creatures which they had been supposed to be, and that henceforth they would have to be reckoned with' (15). For Major Talbot and his Imperial Tobacco Corporation there was to be half a million pounds of compensation for their loss, paid from a loan negotiated by the Persians with the Imperial Bank. It was the first of several humiliating foreign loans the Persians were to raise in the coming years to get themselves out of financial troubles largely of their own making.

The City of London's fingers had been burnt by the cancellation of the Tobacco Concession and the failure of the Persian Bank Mining Rights Corporation. They had also been badly caught in 1889 in a swindle involving Malkom Khan, the Persian envoy to London, who had pocketed large sums subscribed for what proved to be a non-existent National Lottery Concession. It was hardly surprising therefore if the City was chary of investing in further Persian adventures. Thus it was William D'Arcy, who had gone to Australia as a young man and made a fortune there in gold-mining, rather than the top-hatted gentlemen of Lombard Street, who acquired what became Britain's most valuable concession in Persia.

Once again Drummond Wolff, now recovered from the mental breakdown which had ended his Tehran career in 1890, was involved. So, too, were two Frenchmen*—one of them an archaeologist who had noticed many oil seepages during his wanderings in Persia: the other a former agent for Reuter in Persia. The latter and a retired Persian Armenian Customs official,† who held a temporary post as the Persian Commissioner-General at the 1900 Paris Exposition, approached Drummond Wolff in Paris with a highly speculative oil concession. They asked him, in return for a suitable commission, to find them a rich buyer. Wolff thought of D'Arcy, now settled in England with money to burn, and persuaded him to take up the concession. D'Arcy, who never set foot in Persia himself, sent a representative to Tehran early in 1901 to negotiate on his behalf. By May, despite active Russian opposition, he had acquired a sixty-year concession, covering all but the five northern provinces of Persia, to search for, develop, and sell all natural gas, petroleum, asphalt, and ozokerite: also to construct pipe lines from anywhere in Persia to the south coast. He paid £20,000 in cash for his exclusive rights; in addition the Persian Government were promised 20,000 £1 shares in the company D'Arcy was to form to exploit the concession and 16% of the net profits.

Hardinge, the Minister in Tehran, strongly supported D'Arcy and in a despatch to the Foreign Office guardedly prophesied that 'if the hopes of the concessionaires are realised, and petroleum is discovered . . . in sufficient quantities to compete with Baku, the concession may be fraught with important economic and indeed political results' (16). Curzon, the acknowledged expert on Persia and then Viceroy of India, took a different view. He poured cold water on Hardinge's hopes: he thought D'Arcy was no more likely to be successful than the Mining Rights Corporation with which he, Curzon, had been associated. 'I advise you, therefore', he wrote magisterially to the Secretary of State for India, 'not to think that the industrial regeneration of Persia is going to make a new start in Mr D'Arcy's hands' (17).

It looked for a time as if Curzon's prediction would prove right. Drilling, which had begun near Qasr-e-Shirin in western Persia at the end of 1902, proved unsuccessful after an encouraging start. The next effort on another site further south ended in failure in 1907. After five years D'Arcy had nothing to show for the quarter of a million pounds spent in his search for oil. He had, in the meantime, come to an arrangement with the Burmah Oil Company and formed The Conces-

* Jacques de Morgan and Edouard Cotte.　　† General Antone Ketabchi Khan.

The World of Business

sions Syndicate Ltd. which relieved him of some of his financial worries and ensured further exploration of southern Persia. An access road was built to enable equipment to be transported for one final effort, at Maidan-e-Naftun near an ancient ruin known as Masjid-e-Suleiman set in a treeless, lunar landscape, over eighty miles north-east of Ahwaz. Drilling began there in January 1908 and was crowned with success when a gusher was struck in May of the same year, just when the directors of the Concessions Syndicate at home were considering abandoning the quest for oil altogether.

This discovery marked a turning point in Persian history as well as the beginning of the Persian, and indeed the Middle Eastern, oil industry. The credit belongs largely to two Englishmen—William D'Arcy, who risked all but persevered, and G. B. Reynolds, who had been selected by D'Arcy to take charge of the operations in Persia. Reynolds was an engineer who had prospected for oil in Sumatra and been employed by the Indian Public Works Department. Though he was past fifty when he went to Persia his energy and single-minded determination to find oil enabled him to endure heat, rough living conditions and formidable logistic problems which would have daunted many a younger man. Arnold Wilson, who saw much of him during these early days, regarded him as 'a great man, who inspires real respect in Englishmen and Canadians and real affection in Persians and Arabs, he also has remarkable gifts of organisation and management' (18). Reynolds' determination and drive overcame the enormous difficulties of moving heavy equipment, such as boilers and steel pipes, across trackless mountains and bridgeless rivers. To get equipment to M.I.S. (as all oilmen came to call the site of the first well) it was first landed at Mohammerah, then shipped up the Karun to Ahwaz for carriage by a specially built tramway to a point above the rapids where it was put aboard a small stern-wheeler boat belonging to Lynch Bros which took it to Shustar, where it was landed once more and then transported by mule and cart to M.I.S.

The certainty that oil had been found in commercial quantities at M.I.S. led to some quick and impressive developments. A route for a pipe line to carry the crude oil to the coast was surveyed and the site chosen for a terminal and refinery on Abadan Island, close to Mohammerah. Agreement was reached with the Shaikh of Mohammerah and the Bakhtiari khans on the use of the land. In London the Anglo-Persian Oil Company Ltd. (A.P.O.C.) was formed* to take over the Concessions

---

* The Anglo-Persian Oil Company Ltd. in turn registered two subsidiary companies, The First Exploitation Co. Ltd., and the Bakhtiari Oil Co. Ltd., from both of which the Bakhtiari khans were to receive 3% of the profits.

The English Amongst the Persians

Syndicate's interests and provide the large sums now required to produce and market the oil. Houses, schools and a hospital—far better than existed elsewhere in Persia—were built for the staff. By 1911 the 130-mile-long pipe line was completed and two years later the refinery was in operation. The output of oil was increased from 43,000 tons in 1912 to 272,000 tons in 1914: by 1920 it was 1,385,000 tons and over 20,000 Persians and 500 British were employed by the A.P.O.C. This was no small achievement after starting from scratch without any of the facilities such as roads, railways, port facilities and electricity that exist to-day. Nor had the Persian authorities been at all helpful. They had refused to recognise the company's original agreement with the Bakhtiari khans and disputed the Shaikh of Mohammerah's right to lease or sell land at Abadan: they questioned the company's right to lay telephone lines to connect M.I.S. with the refinery or use their own barges on the Upper Karun; they accused the company of secretly importing arms and building a fort at Abadan. Despite official obstruction and enormous physical difficulties A.P.O.C. pushed ahead. By 1914, on the eve of the Great War, it was clear that Lord Fisher's decision to convert the Royal Navy's ships from coal to oil-burning was the right one and that Persian oil would be a major factor in their supply. It was because of this that Winston Churchill, then First Lord of the Admiralty, persuaded the British Government to invest £2 million in A.P.O.C. and thus acquire a 51% share in what was to become Britain's largest overseas asset.

Through nationalist Persian eyes, as the years went by and the company prospered, the picture looked rather different. For them the A.P.O.C. was a remote and privileged foreign body. They saw it by-passing the Tehran Government and making its own arrangements with local khans and shaikhs. They noticed that the British held all but the unskilled jobs and lived apart from the company's Persian employees. They disputed, sometimes with good reason, the company's interpretation of the customs exemptions granted under the concession. They noted the importation of large numbers of Indian labour though, under the terms of the concession, only Persians were to be employed for non-technical work. They questioned the basis on which the company calculated its net profits, of which 16% were payable to the Persian Government and of which a much larger share went to the British Treasury and shareholders. They resented the occupation of the oil fields and refinery by British and Indian troops during the Great War and the company's refusal, while hostilities lasted, to pay for the Royal Navy's large oil liftings. Those few Persians who then took any interest in these matters regarded, in the words of one of them, the eventual settlement

On parade at Nusratabad, Sistan.

THE CONSUL'S *sowar* ESCORT.

Paying a visit to the Governor-General, Isfahan.
From A. H. Savage-Landor's *Across Coveted Lands* and V. Chirol's *The Middle Eastern Question*.

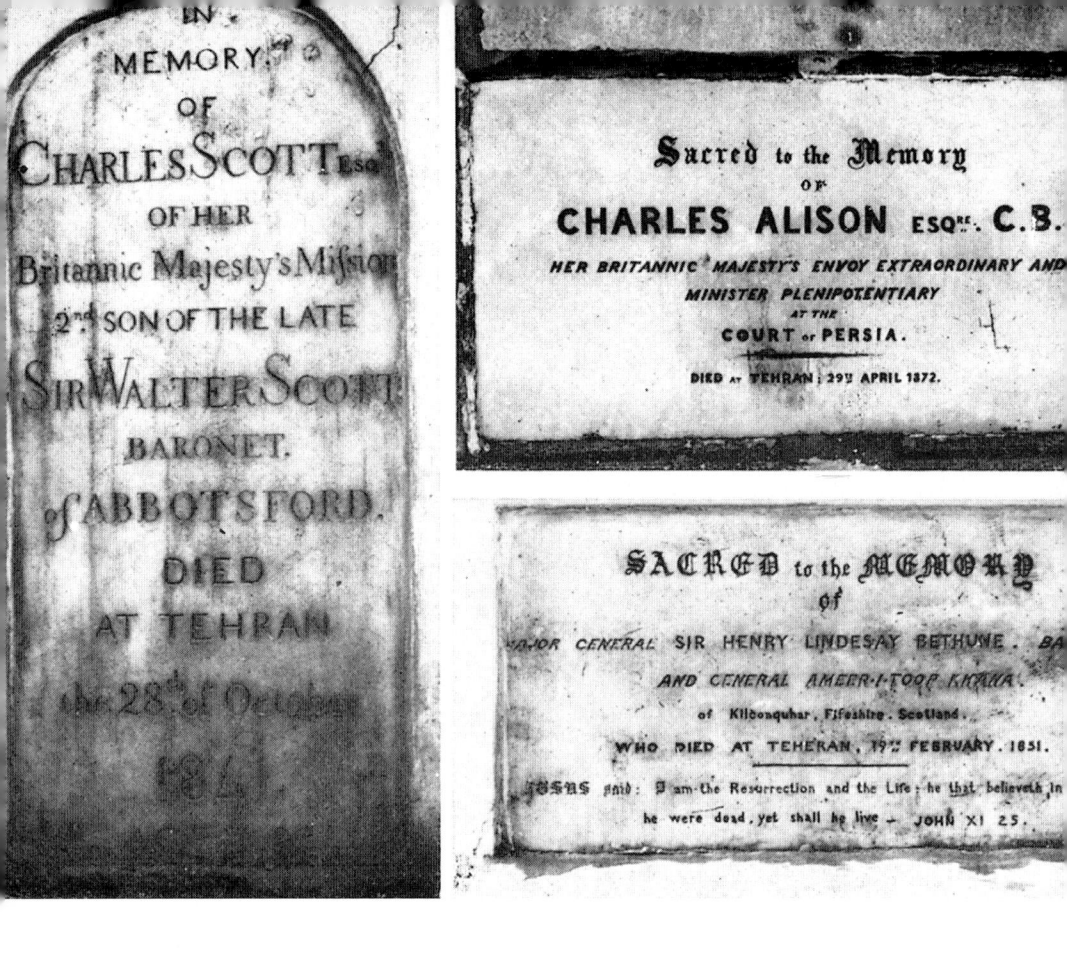

Memorials and grave stones in the old Armenian Church, Tehran.
By courtesy of Desmond Harney and Roger Wood.

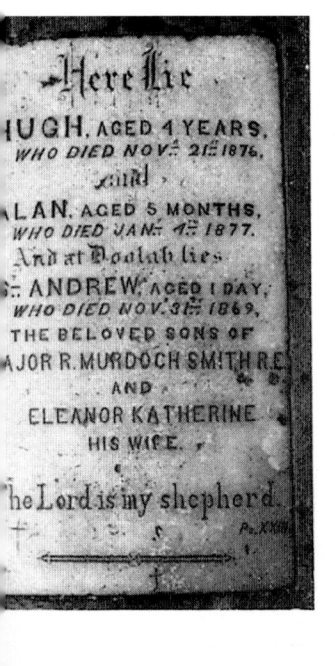

The head office of the Imperial Bank of Persia, *circa* 1890.

One of the banknotes issued by the Imperial Bank.
By courtesy of the British Bank of the Middle East.

The Indo-European Telegraph Department's station at Jask.
From E. A. Floyer's *Unexplored Baluchistan*.

Stamps of the British-Indian post offices in Persia.
By courtesy of E. Fraser-Smith.

The World of Business

in 1920 of claims and counter-claims as 'entirely inadequate' (19).

There were, however, few signs in those early days of the troubles that lay ahead for the oil company. Because of the specialist nature of their business and their physical isolation from the rest of the country the British oilmen had little cause to bother with what went on elsewhere. The Persians themselves cared little about Khuzistan, still very much the fief of Shaikh Khazal and the Bakhtiari khans. Almost unconsciously the A.P.O.C. developed into a semi-autonomous body, a virtual law unto itself, and became an easy target in due time for the politicians and nationalists in Tehran.

The impact of British and other European businessmen on Persia during the Qajar period was not altogether a happy one. Sheil noted in 1853 that 'English merchants in Persia have not been conspicuous for scrupulous straight-forwardness in their dealings, or for moderation in their gains' (20). Ten years earlier Consuls Abbott and Bonham were reporting from Tehran and Tabriz that Persians there were protesting about the damage to their livelihoods caused by imports of cheap, machine-made European goods. The Persians also complained that foreign merchants only had to pay a 5% *ad valorem* duty on their imports whereas they themselves had to pay a *rahdari* or road toll on imported goods at every town through which they passed, thus making it easy for the foreign merchant to undercut his Persian competitor. Sheil considered this so unjust that he took the unusual step of writing to the Persian Prime Minister and urging him to end a practice whereby 'the Persian merchant suffers intolerably and is deprived of all powers of competition with foreigners' (21).

Many of the European concession hunters who descended, like vultures, on Tehran towards the end of the nineteenth century were unscrupulous adventurers keen to make easy money. Their wheeling and dealing together with the memory of the cancelled Reuter and Tobacco Concessions sank deep into the Persian mind and accounted for what Harding, the British Minister, described in 1904 as 'an attitude of distrust and hostility to all foreign enterprise' (22). The activities of these hard-headed businessmen and adventurers, by no means only British, were often frowned on by the British Government, whose Persian policy was inspired more by political than commercial considerations. Lord Salisbury had defined that policy, in a letter written to Lascelles on the latter's appointment to Tehran in 1891, as being 'to make Persia as strong as we can by internal development' so that she might be able to resist possible Russian aggression. At the same time the sensible Salisbury warned that 'we have to guard against the suspicion that we are not labouring for the development but only for the exploitation of Persia. It is a suspicion which the Persians obviously entertain . . . Nothing must be pushed merely because it will favour a British speculation, unless you are certain that it will do good, or at least no harm to Persia itself' (23).

Looking back, the British record was not a bad one. Traders such as Burgess, Brant, Lynch and Stevens did much to develop Persia's foreign trade, often in the face of formidable difficulties and at great financial risk. The opening of the Karun river to shipping, the introduction of modern banking, the revival of a moribund carpet industry and the building of a great new oil industry were notable achievements at a time of chronic instability.

8

Missionaries and Doctors

SHORTLY AFTER ARRIVING in Shiraz on his way to Tehran in 1811 Sir Gore Ouseley was called upon by a young Church of England clergyman, the Rev. Henry Martyn, then aged thirty, who had been a Senior Wrangler at Cambridge and gone to Calcutta as chaplain to the East India Company in 1805. While there he had helped translate the New Testament into Persian and Arabic and was now sent to Persia so that he might revise these translations. He came armed with an introduction to Ouseley from no less a person than John Malcolm, who commended him as an excellent oriental scholar who had, Malcolm wrote, 'assured me, and begged I would mention it to you, that he had no thought of preaching to the Persians, or to entering into theological controversies: but means to confine himself to two objects—a research after old Gospels, and the endeavour to qualify himself for giving a correct version of the Scriptures into Arabic and Persian, on the plan proposed by the Bible Society. I have not hesitated to tell him that I thought you would require that he should act with great caution, and not allow his zeal to run away with him' (1).

His zeal did, however, run away with him and he was soon engaged in fierce theological argument with the *ulema* or religious leaders of Shiraz. During his year there he wrote and distributed tracts in explanation and defence of Christianity, to which the *ulema* replied with tracts of their own. Yet despite these disputations Martyn, unlike some of the missionaries who were to follow later, seems by his humility and patience to have won the affection of those with whom he argued. They recognised his obvious sincerity and called him 'a Man of God'. Sometimes they came to visit him in such numbers that he had to decline to see them so that he could continue his translation work. However, when he went to Tehran early in 1812 in the hope of presenting a copy

The English Amongst the Persians

of his translation of the New Testament to the Shah he ran foul of the *mullahs* around the Court and had to leave without making the presentation. Shortly afterwards he died at Tokat in Turkey on his way to England.

Martyn left his mark in Persia. John McNeill, who was not a man to give praise lightly, wrote from Tabriz in 1825 that 'Henry Martyn produced in Persia a greater impression than any other man could now hope to do, for he was not only admirably calculated for the undertaking, but he was perhaps the first Christian divine who showed himself superior to the Persians in all the learning on which they most valued themselves. I doubt whether Martyn made any converts, but he elicited a spirit of enquiry and discussion which had not existed before his time, and he taught the Persians to respect a religion that instilled in its votaries the lofty principles of virtue and benevolence which they admired in him' (2).

Martyn was the first of many Protestant clergymen fired with missionary fervour to visit Persia in the nineteenth century. However, many years passed before any British missionary society established itself in the country: French Catholics and American Presbyterians were first in the field by a long way. British missionary effort during much of the century was undertaken by individuals on relatively short visits, either freelancing on their own, or as representatives of the London Society for Promoting Christianity among the Jews. These latter were usually converted German Jews who had settled in England.

The first of the freelancers, a curious character named Captain Peter Gordon, was a sea captain who, having failed with a trading venture which had taken him from Calcutta to Russia, decided to wander through Persia evangelising as he went. Before leaving Russia in 1820 he established contact with the Edinburgh Missionary Society, which then had a station at Astrakhan at the mouth of the Volga, and provided him with tracts and Bibles for distribution in Persia. At Qum, Persia's second holy city, he was disappointed to find that no one would accept his tracts and that he was not even allowed to touch a Koran. He had better luck at Kashan: at Isfahan he was convinced that the distribution of religious literature was the best way to introduce the Gospel into Persia. He was also much impressed by the reputation left behind by 'the amiable Mullah Martyn' and thought that 'some living teachers would be invaluable whatever their qualifications; some to confound the wise, but others to instruct the simple' (3). He recognised, however, after an argument with a *mullah* that the story of Christ's miraculous birth was likely to prove a stumbling block.

By the time he reached Shiraz in July 1820 Gordon apparently

Missionaries and Doctors

believed that between 15,000 and 16,000 Persians there were 'inclined to Christianity, the New Testament being publicly read by the Mullahs, and well understood; a teacher and a deliverer are alone wanted for the public profession of Christianity' (4). He did not stay long enough to discover how wrong he was. However a number of his ideas were adopted by later missionaries and were summed up in a short 'Memorandum concerning the propagation of Christianity in Persia', in which he wrote that 'Shirauz ought to be reoccupied by a quiet meek minister. Persian and Arabic would be the languages of most use to him. Hebrew would be extremely desirable on account of the Jews in and about the town. . . . To attend to the poor degraded Jews would be a great means of introducing Christianity amongst their Moslem oppressors, by shewing its chief excellency—that to the poor the Gospel is preached'. Isfahan differed from Shiraz and needed 'a preacher, who might in time sit with his testaments, and eventually with his tracts, in some part of the bazaar, and thus be at hand to let strangers know the new doctrine. Persian alone would be necessary: next to it a knowledge of Armenian, might render him useful to that wandering body of Christians, whose chief seat is in the Julfa suburb'. Gordon considered Shiraz the most suitable base for missionary activity, being relatively accessible to India and remote from the authorities in Tehran 'as it might be improper for them to countenance a Missionary'. He anticipated that missionary success in either Isfahan or Shiraz 'would cause disquietude, but after the seed sown began to bring forth fruit, would be too late for rooting it out; it would become a tree, and its branches would cover the earth' (5).

In 1829 two British missionaries, Anthony Groves and a young Scot named Bothie, passed through Tabriz on their way to Baghdad, which they considered would be a good centre for the evangelisation of Persia. Groves, an Exeter dentist who sold up and financed the expedition from a £10,000 legacy, was accompanied by his wife, sister and two young children: also a Miss Taylor and a young deaf-mute, John Kitto, whose job was to look after the children. They* must have provided an unusual sight for the Persians, who in those days rarely saw European women or children. Groves planned to visit Shiraz and Isfahan in the missionary cause, but nothing seems to have come of this and, after nearly three years in Baghdad, where his wife died of cholera, he moved on to India: Kitto returned to England, passing through Tehran and Tabriz in 1833 on his way home.

* Groves was a co-founder of the Plymouth Brethren: Miss Taylor got no further than Tabriz where she married Nisbet, the store-keeper of the British Military Mission. Kitto eventually became a Doctor of Divinity and prolific religious writer. He also wrote *The Court of Persia viewed in connexion with scriptural usages* and *The People of Persia*.

The English Amongst the Persians

In the meantime the London Society for Promoting Christianity among the Jews had set their sights on the Middle East including Persia where several thousand Jews were living in squalid conditions in many of the bigger towns. The first missionary from London to visit them was Joseph Wolff.

Wolff was one of the most remarkable missionaries of all time. Born in 1796, the son of a Bavarian rabbi, his inquisitive mind and early interest in theology led him to enter the Roman Catholic Church at the age of seventeen. He went to Rome to study theology but his natural contentiousness did not endear him to the Vatican, which decided that he was unsuitable for the priesthood and bundled him out of the Holy City. He next went to England where Henry Drummond, an influential banker and Member of Parliament whom he had met in Rome, befriended him. He now joined the Anglican Church and at the same time applied to the London Society for Promoting Christianity among the Jews to be taken on as a missionary. After a spell at Cambridge studying oriental languages he set out in 1821 for the Middle East as a lay preacher on behalf of the London Society. He was absent from England five years on this first mission, travelling through Persia from Bushire to Tabriz in 1824–5. A British officer who met him by chance in Baghdad was fascinated by Wolff's account of the perils he had encountered on his hazardous journey across the desert. Wolff, who quickly made friends wherever he went, impressed this young officer with his 'inexhaustible fund of anecdote, and showed such enthusiasm in the laborious and perilous office in which he was employed, that, though we might not agree with him in the efficacy of his mission, we could not help admiring his unaffected piety, and the sincerity of his religious zeal' (6).

Back in England in 1826 Wolff married Lady Georgina Walpole, the sister of the Earl of Orford. In 1827 he was off again, accompanied as far as Alexandria by Lady Georgina. There she gave birth to a son, destined in time to become a Member of Parliament and the Queen of England's envoy in Tehran: he was christened Henry Drummond after his father's kind friend. Joseph Wolff, restless as ever, left his wife and child in Egypt and, styling himself the 'Apostle of our Lord Jesus Christ for Palestine, Persia, Bukhara and Balkh' spent the next four years searching for the lost tribes of Israel and trying, with small success, to convert Jews and others to Christianity. In his quest Wolff had more than his fair share of adventure and hardship, being shipwrecked, robbed, bastinadoed and nearly sold into slavery when seized and robbed by a gang of slave dealers in Khorasan. But nothing daunted this extraordinary man who was able, through his gift of tongues and love

Missionaries and Doctors

of argument, to reach Bokhara safely before turning south into Afghanistan and India.

Eventually, in 1838, Wolff was ordained priest and given a quiet Yorkshire living but six years later he was back in Persia, once again on his way to Bokhara. He had volunteered to help discover the fate of two British officers* taken prisoner by the Emir of Bokhara. All he asked was that his expenses should be paid. Wolff reached Tabriz in January 1844, travelling from Trebizond in terrible winter weather which took toll of the lives of a number of other travellers. He then went to Tehran where, wearing the canonical dress in which he travelled throughout his journey, he was granted an audience by the Shah. He stayed with Sheil in the Legation, where he held a service for members of the British and Russian communities. By the time he reached Bokhara both Englishmen were dead, murdered by the Emir's command. Wolff himself was imprisoned and all but lost his life before being released and allowed to return through Persia to England, where he ended his days quietly as a country parson in Somerset.

For all his pertinacity and enthusiasm Wolff made few, if any, converts in Persia. However, on his first journey he did manage to establish schools for Armenian children in Bushire and Shiraz. He was also an early advocate of the medical missionary and recommended the sending of 'some Christian-minded physicians into Khorasan' (7) which he regarded as a good field for missionary work. Above all, though, he saw the Jews of Persia as ripe for conversion and wanted a mission sent to them as soon as possible. This happened in 1844, when the London Society for the Promotion of Christianity among the Jews sent a three-man 'Mission to the Jews in Chaldea and Persia'. Their headquarters were in Baghdad. Only one of the three, Murray Vicars, was born an Englishman, the other two—Aaron Stern and Sternschuss—being converted German Jews. Stern in particular suffered much harassment and hardship during the course of three long journeys in Persia when he travelled all over the country trying—with occasional success—to make converts. At one point he recommended setting up a central mission in Isfahan but the idea was dropped when it was realised that there was no consul there to provide protection in a town noted for its bigotry.†
The mission in Baghdad was closed in 1865 but work among the Persian

---

* Col. Charles Stoddart and Capt. Arthur Conolly. Both had Persian connections. Stoddart had come to Persia with the 1833 Military Mission and been sent to intercede with the Shah outside Herat in 1838: Conolly had tried to reach Khiva from Persia in disguise in 1830.

† Stern subsequently went to work among the Falashas or 'Black Jews' of Ethiopia. He was among the prisoners held by King Theodore at Magdala to secure whose release Britain went to war with Ethiopia in 1867.

The English Amongst the Persians

Jews was continued by a handful of converts, one of whom went to England in 1888 to train as a missionary: some years later the London Society established a permanent mission in Isfahan.

The Church Missionary Society of London (C.M.S.), which was to become the main instrument of British missionary effort in Persia, took a first hesitant step in 1869 when it authorised one of its missionaries, the Rev. Robert Bruce, to spend two years in Isfahan learning Persian and revising Martyn's New Testament translations. Bruce, a tall, spare, scholarly Irishman, who had served with the C.M.S. in India for a number of years, was in Isfahan at the time of the terrible famine and cholera epidemic in 1870–1. He and his wife took the lead in organising relief work, more especially among the Armenians. They had at their disposal funds collected in London by the Mansion House Persian Relief Fund, to which the British public had subscribed generously. As part of this work Bruce started a small orphanage and trade school for Armenians and Moslems alike and soon felt the call to remain permanently in Persia. In London the C.M.S. agreed that he might do so provided he continued his work on the New Testament and also translated the rest of the Bible into Persian. This Bruce undertook to do, maintaining himself largely from his own private means until 1875 when the C.M.S. decided to provide support for a permanent mission in Isfahan.

In 1880 Bruce received his first assistant from London, an Edinburgh-trained doctor, E. F. Hoernle. Before this he and his wife carried on alone, working mainly among the Armenians of Julfa* where they lived. With the help of Armenian teachers Mr and Mrs Bruce founded a boys' and a girls' school in Julfa. In 1876, despite local opposition, Bruce bought a large plot of land where for the next thirty years the Mission had its headquarters before moving across the river into Isfahan proper.

A steady flow of missionaries, male and female, including doctors and nurses, began to arrive. By 1896 there were seventeen of them in Julfa, where they lived a cloistered life of their own in the spacious C.M.S. compound which contained church, dispensary, hospital and library as well as the boys' and girls' schools. Between 1897 and 1900 some of these men and women moved to Kerman, Yazd and Shiraz where they also established dispensaries, hospitals and schools as a basis for their missionary work. These towns, together with Isfahan, were the centres from which the British missionaries operated in Persia. They made no

---

* Following successful campaigns in Armenia and Georgia in the early seventeenth century Shah Abbas I forcibly transferred thousands of Armenians from Julfa on the Araxes to this New Julfa on the south bank of the Zaindeh river opposite Isfahan, of which it was a suburb. By 1880 their numbers had dwindled to about 2,000.

Missionaries and Doctors

attempt to establish themselves in Tehran or any of the towns of northern Persia which, under the terms of an agreement reached with the American Presbyterian Mission in 1895, were recognised as an American preserve. In return the Americans undertook not to poach on C.M.S. ground in the south.

The missionaries were a motley group*—some educated, others hardly at all: some broad-minded and tolerant, others as bigoted and narrow-minded as the most fanatic Moslem. Life was far from easy for them, especially the unmarried ladies† with no experience of life in a Moslem country. Socially they tended to keep much to themselves and to regard Persians and Armenians more as children to be pitied and helped than as equals. They were, perhaps, doing no more than reflect the spirit of an age which believed in the white man's burden and superiority, but it was an attitude which had no appeal to the Persians, who were inclined to regard the missionaries either with intense hostility as interfering infidels or else with tolerance as harmless, well-meaning curiosities from another continent.

In the early days of the C.M.S. no Christian dared live in Isfahan proper because of the hostility of the Moslem population. The missionaries had no choice but to join the small European community already living in Julfa among the Armenians. Thus, though the Moslems were their real target, they found themselves concentrating most of their attention on the Armenians, some of whom—for one reason or another—were happy to place themselves under the wing of the British missionaries. By 1883 about two hundred Armenians had joined the Anglican Church. Bruce, who disclaimed trying to convert them, nevertheless hoped, in his own words, to create 'a living spiritual Church in the centre of Persia, in place of the dead, corrupt Armenian Church' (8). This would, he believed, in due season bear fruit among the Moslems.

The successful activities of the C.M.S. among the Armenians brought down on its head the wrath of the Armenian clergy of Julfa who combined with a Roman Catholic priest and the *mullahs* to make life as difficult as possible for the missionaries. In 1876 the boys' school was closed by order of the Prince-Governor of Isfahan after the *mullahs* had denounced it as a British engine for the destruction of Islam. It was only reopened after the intervention of the British Minister in Tehran and on condition that no Moslem child was to be admitted and

---

* By 1919 they numbered forty including wives: nine were doctors and seventeen unmarried women, mostly nurses and teachers.

† One of their number, Dr Elizabeth Ross, found the narrowness of life in Julfa so unbearable that she went to work as a doctor with the womenfolk of the leading Bakhtiari khans among whom she lived between 1909 and 1914.

no religious instruction given to Armenian children under the age of twenty-one.* Eventually, in 1921, the C.M.S. made its peace with the Armenian Bishop of Julfa by assuring him that they would accept no further Armenians into the Anglican Church.

As far back as 1835 the British Minister had warned the first American missionaries to come to Persia of 'the indispensable necessity of avoiding interference with the religious belief of the Muhammedan population' (9). Yet that was what, by the very nature of their calling, missionaries most wanted to do. Most of them, like Henry Martyn in 1811, found it difficult to resist the temptation. Because of this the C.M.S. missionaries often proved an unsettling element among the conservative Moslem populations where they worked. The dispensaries they opened were regarded with distrust by the Persian authorities, who frequently insisted on their closure. The opening of a bookshop and the use of Armenian colporteurs to distribute religious literature printed on the C.M.S.'s own small press at Isfahan inevitably aroused suspicion. The missionaries sometimes seemed—for the best of motives —to invite trouble as, for instance, when they gave asylum to persecuted Bahais whose lives were in danger. The British Legation found their activities an embarrassment—'The Church Missionary Society here', wrote one of the diplomats in 1897, 'are a dreadful thorn in our side and are always giving rise to rows owing to their tactlessness and desire to proselytise amongst Moslems' (10). Yet one cannot but admire the obstinate courage and single-minded determination of women like Mary Bird who, shortly after joining the Mission in 1891, opened a dispensary for Moslem women deep in the Isfahan bazaar where Christians rarely penetrated. She had no medical training yet, once the ice was broken, women flocked to her for treatment. The *mullahs* preached against her in the mosques and encouraged their followers to insult her as she rode unveiled through the bazaar's crowded alleyways: they tried to shut and bolt her doors: with the help of her patients she reopened them. Despite all opposition Maryan Khanum, as she was known, persisted in her good works and won the devotion of her many patients. She died in Kerman in 1914.

Medical missionary work was, in the words of one of their number 'the golden key that opens the door of the heart of the most fanatical Moslem' (11). And indeed Persians of all classes crowded the C.M.S. hospitals and dispensaries, knowing that there was nowhere else where

* This ban was relaxed later. By the early 1920s the C.M.S.'s Stuart Memorial College for Boys and Stileman Memorial School for Girls were, with the American Presbyterian Mission's Alborz College in Tehran, the three outstanding schools in the country.

Missionaries and Doctors

they could get such excellent medical care. For over thirty years Doctors George Dodson in Kerman and Donald Carr in Isfahan did memorable work for the sick. The Persians were grateful to the missionaries for this but gratitude rarely led to a change of religion. The number of genuine converts to Christianity which resulted from so much effort and prayer was infinitesimal. Nonetheless, more as an act of faith in the future than in response to any need, the Anglican authorities in England decided in 1913 to constitute Persia a full diocese of the Church of England. The Rev. C. H. Stileman, Secretary to the C.M.S. in London, was consecrated the first Bishop in Isfahan.

The only other British missionary activity in Persia during the Qajar period was that of The Archbishop of Canterbury's Assyrian Mission. Its purpose and methods were very different from those of the C.M.S.

The Anglican Church had first made contact with the Christian Assyrians of eastern Turkey and north-western Persia in 1843 when the Rev. G. P. Badger was sent on an exploratory journey among them by the Society for the Promotion of Christian Knowledge. Following this the Assyrian Patriarch, known as Mar Shimun, and some of his bishops made periodic appeals for British support, addressing themselves sometimes to the Archbishop of Canterbury, sometimes to the consul in Tabriz. They sought British assistance partly in order to help resist the proselytising activities of American Presbyterians and French Catholic missionaries: partly in order to secure British political protection against the Turks, Persians and Kurds amongst whom they lived and suffered. The Archbishop of Canterbury eventually agreed to establish at Urumiyah a small educational mission designed to revitalise a fossilised church by educating the young and training men for the priesthood.

The first two Anglican priests reached Urumiyah in 1885: by 1890 there were four of them under Canon A. J. Maclean, all celibates and graduates of Oxford or Cambridge, prepared to live simply and frugally as the Assyrians lived. They quickly established four schools for boys, mostly boarders, two in Urumiyah itself and two outside on the plain. One of the schools, to which the others were in a way subsidiary, was exclusively for ordinands for the priesthood through whom the missionaries hoped to breathe new life into the Church. Any imitation of western ways and manners was forbidden, as was proselytising in the Anglican cause either among the Assyrians or Moslems. A hand-printing press enabled the mission to supply pupils with text books, portions of the scriptures, a catechism and, most important of all in many ways, a uniform church service book compiled by Maclean from the diverse manuscript service books then in use. The missionaries also produced a Persian-Assyrian grammar for the use of those who knew no Persian.

The English Amongst the Persians

They were joined in 1890 by four Anglican nuns from England who started a boarding school for Assyrian girls.

The Great War put an end to the Archbishop's Mission to the Assyrians. The missionaries working in Turkey* withdrew to join their colleagues in Urumiyah when Turkey entered the war. In October 1914 about 350 Assyrians took refuge in the Urumiyya Mission house when Kurds and Turks attacked and pillaged the town until stopped by the arrival of Russian troops. Chaos and massacre however soon followed when these Russian forces retreated in January 1915. The British missionaries left at the same time and never returned.

The C.M.S. missionaries in southern Persia provided medical services —qualified doctors, nurses, dispensaries and hospitals—where none had previously existed. Their hospitals, for men and women, were the first by many years to be opened in Isfahan, Kerman, Yazd and Shiraz. They were not, however, the first to introduce western medicine to Persia. Long before the arrival of the C.M.S. British doctors in the service of the East India Company had been active in Persia.

Doctors had been attached to the East India Company's factories since the early seventeenth century and when the Residency was established at Bushire late in the following century it had its own surgeon and hospital. Doctors appointed from the East India Company's Bombay establishment accompanied all three of Malcolm's missions to Persia, as well as that of Harford Jones. Two of them, James Campbell and John Cormick, remained in Tehran and Tabriz, attached to the British missions there while a third, Andrew Jukes, was appointed 'Surgeon, Acting Assistant and Translator' to the Bushire Residency where he combined medical with political work. Thereafter, throughout the Qajar period, the Legation in Tehran and the Residency in Bushire always had a doctor on their staff. From the 1860s the Indo-European Telegraph Department also had one or more English doctors resident in Persia for the care of its employees. Later still the A.P.O.C. had its own doctor and hospital in Abadan.

The early British doctors, who treated Persian as well as British patients, gradually broke down deep-rooted prejudices against western medicine. An idea of the difficulties they had to overcome can be obtained from Morier's account of Jukes' attempt to treat a Persian member of Harford Jones' staff in 1810:

> Our head Persian writer was long laid up with a fever, which brought him to the point of death. He was bled copiously six times

---

* The Mission's headquarters had been transferred to Turkey, where most of the Assyrians lived, in 1903. For lack of funds the four nuns had been withdrawn by 1890.

in six days. These people put no faith in our medicines, and therefore he would not allow the Physician of the Mission to visit him. At length however he was persuaded by a *'fall'* which he took in Hafiz, and which pointed out, that he should 'trust in the stranger'. The superstitious faith with which Persians observe these *falls* is inconceivable: the oracle consists in taking the book of Hafiz, wherever it may chance to open, and reading the passage on which the eye may first happen to alight. That, by which the attention is thus attracted, is the prediction. Before they open the book, they make certain invocations to God. Dr Jukes accordingly prescribed; but his patient I believe disregarded his advice; and we were despairing about him, when we were told that the King's physician had been with him, and had given him a water-melon to eat, and that the sick man was now recovering. The theory of Persian medicine is somewhat that of Galen: they attribute all sickness to one of two causes, heat or cold. If the patient is supposed to suffer from too much heat, they bleed him beyond measure; if from cold, they give him cathartics in the same proportion (12).

However Jukes did manage to get permission to vaccinate a number of children against smallpox—all of them Armenians since the Persians were not prepared to risk their own children, vaccination then being unknown to them. Two years later the doctors attached to Ouseley's mission met opposition from Persian doctors when they proposed more vaccinations: they were however able to treat about 300 children, though whether they included Persians as well as Armenians is not known. That same year James Campbell won the gratitude of the Crown Prince, whom 'he entirely cured of a venereal complaint and vaccinated the whole of His Highness' family' (13). This was an important success which opened the royal door to a succession of the Company's doctors—John Cormick, John McNeill and James Riach.*

Cormick was particularly close to the Crown Prince and accompanied him everywhere. McNeill became the most influential of all British doctors in Persia. A brilliant all-rounder, he had first come to Tehran as assistant surgeon to the Legation in 1821. He showed his metal that same year when, on hearing that Jukes was dangerously ill at Isfahan, he rode there, over 250 miles away, on the same horse in less than four days only to find Jukes dead. Soon McNeill was occupied mainly on

---

* Gordon, the lone missionary, recorded in his 1820 journal that 'the benevolent offices of the medical gentlemen, who are or have been in the country, have tended as much as aught else to give the people a more favourable opinion of Europeans than their prophet would be pleased with'.

The English Amongst the Persians

political work, for which he showed a remarkable aptitude, but he did not neglect medicine. He operated on the Crown Prince for cirrhosis of the liver more than once and, by successfully treating the Shah's favourite wife in 1826, seems finally to have overcome Fath Ali Shah's suspicions of western medical practice. Thereafter McNeill, by regularly attending the Shah's large harem and other members of his family, acquired exceptional influence at the Court. Even after his appointment as Minister in Tehran he would, in the absence of Riach, the Legation doctor, treat the Shah and his family. Riach, who had served as surgeon at Bushire for a number of years, marched to Mashad in 1836 with Muhammad Shah as his personal doctor, but, along with a number of British officers, was summarily dismissed by the pro-Russian monarch and returned to Tehran.

None knew better than McNeill the political usefulness of a doctor who could, to use his own words, act 'as a medium of a confidential intercourse between the Mission and the Shah' (14). Unfortunately, after the rupture in diplomatic relations between Britain and Persia in 1838 British doctors lost, for a number of years, the position they had previously enjoyed as the royal family's closest medical advisers. A succession of French doctors filled this role, though the British were not entirely left out of the picture. From time to time the doctors attached to the Legation and the Indo-European Telegraph Department were consulted. Also Cormick's son William, who had trained as a doctor in England and subsequently practised in London and Paris, was summoned back to Persia by the Shah in 1844. He settled down in Tabriz, the home-town of his Armenian mother and wife* where, in addition to attending the family of the late Abbas *Mirza*, he ran a profitable apothecary's business. Joseph Dickson, who succeeded two Bell brothers from Edinburgh as Legation doctor in 1848, held the appointment for almost forty years and, with his brother William, became a well-known figure in Tehran.† He was called in at times to treat Nasir ed-Din Shah and, at the Shah's request, accompanied him on his first European tour in 1873. In England both Dickson and the Shah's personal physician, a Frenchman, were awarded knighthoods by the Queen—an honour which must have delighted Dickson whom some of the British were apt to despise as a Levantine. Dickson's successors at

* His mother had been married to John Cormick by the Rev. Henry Martyn in 1812. William, who married the sister of Edward Burgess' wife, died in 1875 at Tabriz.

† Joseph Dickson was Legation doctor from 1848–87: his brother William was appointed translator and interpreter at the Legation in 1852 and remained there over thirty years. Both brothers were born in Tripoli, Libya, and previously served under Brant in Erzerum. William was the father of Major-General W. E. R. Dickson who headed the British Military Mission to Persia in 1920.

Missionaries and Doctors

the Legation, Thomas Odling and A. R. Neligan,* also spent long years in Persia during which they built up big reputations and became closely associated with many leading Tehran families who trusted their medical skills.

In the 1890s another British doctor, Hugh Adcock, was appointed personal physician in Tabriz to the Crown Prince. When Muzaffar ed-Din *Mirza* became Shah in 1896 Adcock went with him to Tehran and for the next ten years held the important post of Consulting Physician-in-Chief to the monarch. Like Dickson and the other doctors he proved a useful confidential channel for communication between the British Legation and the Shah. Adcock† accompanied the Shah on his visit to England in 1902 when Edward VII greatly offended the Persian king by declining to give him the Order of the Garter which Hardinge, the Minister in Tehran, had unwisely promised him. Edward VII maintained that the Order was reserved for Christian monarchs though, as the Shah well knew, both the Turkish Sultan and Nasir ed-Din Shah had received it from the hands of Queen Victoria. The Shah refused to be fobbed off with the Order of the Bath or with a miniature of the King set in a gold frame studded with diamonds: he also made all his suite reject the decorations offered to them and returned to Tehran boiling with indignation. However, this was not the end of the story. Fears that the incident might permanently alienate the Shah in favour of Russia caused the British Prime Minister to threaten resignation unless the King climbed down. Edward VII gave way with the greatest reluctance and early in 1903 Lord Downe was sent on a Special Mission to Tehran solely in order to invest the Shah with the Garter.

The last British doctor to be associated directly with the Qajar Court was the Hon. Lennox Lindley‡ who had first been appointed as assistant Court physician in 1900 and later took over from Adcock. He was physician at the Court of three successive Shahs including Ahmad Shah, the last of the Qajars.

Apart from the physicians close to the Shah there was one other British doctor who played an important political role in Persia. This was Dr M. Y. Young, a diminutive figure popularly known as the 'Little Doctor' who went to Persia for the Anglo-Persian Oil Company in 1907 and remained there throughout the Great War. He quickly learnt excellent Persian and by his medical skills and personality won the confidence of the Bakhtiari khans and their womenfolk to such an

* Odling came to Persia in 1872 as doctor to the Indo-European Telegraph Department: he became Legation doctor in 1891 and died in Tehran in 1906: his successor, Neligan, held the post from 1906–26.
† He was knighted in 1901.
‡ A younger son of Lord Lindley, sometime Master of the Rolls.

extent that the A.P.O.C. used him both as Political and Medical Officer. He became a key figure in the company's various negotiations with the Shaikh of Mohammerah and the Bakhtiaris: during the War the British Government preferred to use him rather than the consul in Isfahan to conduct secret negotiations with the khans. So great was Young's influence among the Bakhtiaris that Arnold Wilson, who was in a position to know, claimed that 'to him more than any other single man the Company and the British and Persian Governments owed the complete absence of trouble in the oil fields in the autumn of 1914 when communication with the coast was cut off by bands of insurgent Arabs under Turkish leadership' (15).

Let it not be thought however that the British doctors were only concerned with the high and the mighty. As early as 1837 a visitor to Tabriz remarked that 'from morning to night the steps of the British Palace were thronged with sick, who sought relief from the European skill. Both here and in Tehran the good which is done by the medical gentlemen belonging to the Embassy is incalculable' (16). The medical treatment offered by the British to the poor in Tabriz, Tehran and Bushire was later extended to other parts of the country when consulates were opened. Most of these consulates maintained 'Charitable Dispensaries' to which Persians flocked from far and wide for free treatment at the hands of trained Indian medical orderlies. At Mashad, where there was a British doctor on the consulate staff, some 6,000 patients were treated at the dispensary in one year alone; at Bushire, where the Residency hospital was also open to Persians, over 13,000 out-patients were treated in 1907: at Ahwaz the daily average was little short of one hundred. The Indo-European Telegraph Department doctors ran similar dispensaries for the poor, including one in the Isfahan bazaar. Consuls going on tour would frequently be accompanied by a medical orderly to provide medicines and treatment in remote corners of Persia. The goodwill created by this medical activity greatly impressed a trade mission to central and southern Persia sponsored by the Government of India in 1904; they subsequently recommended the opening of dispensaries and the appointment of medical officers to all the additional consular posts they wanted established in the interests of trade promotion.

Despite the activities of the British and the few other foreign doctors in Tehran the Persian Government did not begin to concern itself with public health until 1868. In that year a Sanitary Council was established in Tehran on which doctors from the British, French and Russian Legations served. The following year the Persian Government opened, with German help, its first hospital in Tehran. The Germans managed the hospital until the Great War, at the end of which the British

Government undertook to run it under a Persian director and to subsidise the purchase of its medical supplies. The Legation and the Indo-European Telegraph Department's doctors, Neligan and Scott, were placed in charge and an English matron and nurse brought out from England to help with what was intended to become an eighty-bed hospital. 'The English Hospital', as it was soon known, suffered terribly from neglect: food for patients often ran short: staff, unpaid for months on end, blamed the British for their plight: the two British doctors had no real authority and their position was undermined by intrigue. In despair the British Government decided in 1923 to withdraw from what was proving an expensive and embarrassing commitment. The British were more successful with a hospital they established at Bushire in 1916 with the help of voluntary contributions from local merchants: it was efficiently run for many years under the supervision of the Residency doctor and was highly regarded by the Persians who, at that time, had no other hospital in that region.

British doctors also became responsible for the administration of international quarantine regulations in the ports along the coast. In an attempt to curb the spread of plague and cholera, often carried by passengers arriving at these ports from Bombay and Karachi, agreement was reached between the Persian and British Governments in 1896 whereby the latter were placed in sole control of quarantine in the Persian ports. Doctors and assistants from the Indian Medical Service were posted to the main ports—Jask, Bandar Abbas, Lingeh, Bushire and Mohammerah—to work under the direction of the Residency doctor in Bushire: the Persian Government paid their salaries. It was, for the Persians, a one-sided arrangement which they never liked. Strict enforcement by the British of international regulations, which required ten days' quarantine for passengers and ships, was little understood and provoked intense hostility among local merchants and others whose livelihoods were often affected. In addition, pious Moslem families wishing, as many did, to ship the bodies of their dear ones to Basra for burial in the sacred precincts of Kerbela had first to obtain a sanitary certificate from the British authorities. Anti-British disturbances occurred in 1899 at Bushire, possibly encouraged by the Russian and other European consuls there who shared Persian resentment of British control over all shipping entering Persian ports and the opportunity it allegedly provided of favouring British traders.

By 1921 nationalist feeling had been thoroughly aroused against arrangements which were regarded as infringing Persia's sovereignty. It was only a matter of time before Reza Shah decided, in 1928, to remove all responsibility for port quarantine from British hands.

9

The Electric Telegraph and other Innovations

THE ANGLO-PERSIAN WAR of 1856–7, followed by the Indian Mutiny, served to bring home, as nothing else had done, the lamentable slowness of London's communications with an area that was at the geographical centre of the Empire and close to Russia, the bogy of the day. To remedy the situation the authorities in London and India created a telegraphic system in which Persia became a vital link. From the mid-1860s until the end of the Qajar period the Indo-European telegraph was Britain's most precious interest in Persia, outranking in importance both the Imperial Bank and the Anglo-Persian Oil Company.

The use of the electric telegraph was still in its infancy at the time of the Mutiny but enough progress had been made to demonstrate the feasibility of establishing a link between London and India. Already in 1851 a cable under the Channel had successfully connected London with Paris. By 1856 about 4,500 miles of telegraph wire linked the principal cities of India with each other. However, an attempt to connect London with India by submarine cable through the Mediterranean and Red Seas had been a dismal failure and strengthened the hands of those who advocated going overland as much as possible. Telegraphic connections across Europe already existed between London and Constantinople before the Turkish Government, with the help of British engineers, extended their own system to Baghdad between 1857–61 and thus opened up possibilities of reaching India via the Persian Gulf. However, because of the lawlessness of the Arab tribes and the pestilential climate of Lower Mesopotamia it was considered unsafe to rely exclusively on a route running from Baghdad through what was then known as Turkish Arabia. A second line, from Baghdad through Persia

The Electric Telegraph and other Innovations

to the Gulf, was considered essential in the interests of security. Separate negotiations therefore took place in the early 1860s with the Turkish and Persian Governments as a result of which the British managed to obtain alternative routes to the Gulf from Baghdad—from the Turks a line from Baghdad to Fao at the head of the Persian Gulf and from the Persians one from Khaniqin* on the Turkish frontier to Tehran and then on to Bushire. From Fao and Bushire the British proposed laying submarine cables down the Gulf to Gwadur on the undefined Makran border between India and Persia whence the line would run overland to Karachi, the terminal station in India.

The negotiations with the Persian Government had not been at all easy. Some Persians considered the existing telegraphic connection between Tehran and Tabriz more than enough and felt that there were better uses for public money. Conservative elements round the Court were strongly opposed to any extension of the new-fangled foreign invention to other parts of the country. Provincial officials feared that it would place a curb on their independence. Yet others suspected British motives in wanting to run a line through Persia and saw no reason to oblige a foreign country with whom they had so recently been at war.

When Alison, the Minister in Tehran, opened negotiations in 1861 the Shah made it clear that he saw little advantage for Persia in the proposed line even though the British were willing to bear half the cost. His lack of enthusiasm meant that negotiations dragged on until the end of 1862 when an agreement, in the form of an 'Engagement entered into by the Persian Minister for Foreign Affairs' was reached. This 'Engagement', remarkable more for its omissions than for its six short articles, was essentially a face-saving document designed to overcome the doubts and hesitations of Persian Ministers and to hide the real extent of British involvement. It enabled the British to get a foot in a door which they soon pushed wide open. Both sides must have known all too well that there was no possibility of observing the stipulation that the Persians themselves would build and run the cross-country telegraph line under the superintendence of a single English Engineer officer. And indeed within a matter of months the British had not only appointed Major J. E. Champain,† then serving with the Bengal Engineers, to take charge of the work as Director in Tehran of

---

* The Turks undertook to link Khaniqin with Baghdad.
† Col. Sir John Bateman-Champain, K.C.M.G. (1835–87). Saw service at Delhi and Lucknow during the Indian Mutiny. Deputy-Director in London of Indo-European Telegraph Department 1865–70 and Director-General 1870–87. Assumed additional name of Bateman, 1870.

the Indo-European Telegraph Department* but had recruited three fellow Royal Engineer officers† as well as eighteen NCOs and civilians to assist with the task. By early 1865 their number had swollen to about forty. No one was in any doubt that it was the British and not the Persians who were building the line, albeit with locally recruited labour and at Persian expense. The Persians were not pleased. Murdoch Smith, who was in charge of one of the five stretches into which the line was divided, later summed up the British position in forthright terms:

> The situation was altogether false and unsatisfactory. A line of 1,250 miles, through an extremely difficult and troublesome country, had, by hook or by crook, to be made with Persian materials, at Persian expense, by a handful of foreigners whom every man in the Kingdom, from the Shah downwards, then regarded as pestilent interlopers. Looking back with the knowledge of subsequent experience, the writer is astounded at the cool impudence of the whole undertaking. The marvel is that our throats were not promptly cut by patriotic brigands (1).

Nevertheless, despite official hostility and the almost total lack of help from the provincial authorities the British set about their task with great determination. By August 1863 large quantities of stores and equipment had been shipped from England to Bushire and Baghdad, where it was loaded on to hundreds of mules and carried great distances to points along the route, each section of which was under British supervision. Trees to serve as telegraph poles were bought and shaped, small telegraph stations with accommodation for staff were built every sixty miles or so, equipment installed, and poles erected to which a single wire was attached. While this work was progressing the British were also busy laying cables down the Gulf from Fao and Bushire to Gwadur. By October 1864, after little more than a year's work, the job was completed but, because of rows and misunderstandings with the Persian authorities, the telegraph did not become operational until the following spring.

There was trouble with the Governor of Kermanshah who maintained that Persian claims to a tract of frontier at Khaniqin had been prejudiced by the erection across it of iron telegraph poles, as used in Turkey,

* Though a department of the Government of India its headquarters were in London. Not to be confused with the Indo-European Telegraph *Company*, a commercial firm established in London in 1867 by Siemens and Co. of London and Siemens and Halske of Berlin.

† Majors R. Murdoch Smith and O. B. St. John; Capt. W. H. Pierson. Smith replaced Champain as Director in Tehran in 1865. Cheltenham College chapel contains, side by side on its walls, tablets to the memory of Champain and Pierson.

The Electric Telegraph and other Innovations

instead of wooden Persian poles. To make his point the Governor had the telegraph wires cut and was only pacified when alternate wooden and iron poles were erected across the disputed territory. At Shiraz Persian pride was hurt when the British maintained that the transmitting equipment was too complicated for a Persian signaller to operate. The Persians cut the line and removed the equipment. At Isfahan there was similar trouble. The British retaliated by disconnecting equipment both there and in Tehran. Local officials, opposed to the introduction of rapid communication with the capital, encouraged tribesmen and villagers to remove poles and cut wires—the Qashqai destroyed some twenty miles of line south of Shiraz, broke hundreds of insulators and cut the wires. Eventually another face-saving *modus vivendi* was devised whereby the British were permitted to manage the line for five months on the understanding that they would then hand it over to the Persians and withdraw all their personnel except three who might remain in an advisory capacity for another ten months. In return the British recognised the Persian Minister of Public Works as the head of all telegraphs in Persia on the understanding that he was not to issue any orders affecting the Khaniqin–Bushire line without British consent. The formula satisfied Persian pride while giving the British the control they wanted.

By the time the five months grace was up relations with the Persian authorities had greatly improved. The need for British help in running and maintaining a line which provided much needed revenue was recognised. It was thus possible towards the end of 1865 to negotiate a new agreement, or Convention as it was called, which, despite some window dressing to satisfy Persian sensitivity, gave the British most of what they wanted. They were permitted to instal a second wire, to be used exclusively for international messages in European languages, and were given control of this line for five years. To run it they were allowed to employ up to fifty expatriates. In filling vacancies among their own signallers they undertook to give preference to 'natives of Persia'. This they did, though the natives they employed were mostly Christian Armenians rather than Moslems, not so much by choice as because at that time Moslems showed little inclination to work with Europeans.

Colonel Frederic Goldsmid,* Director-General in London of the Indo-European Telegraph Department, had spent three months in

---

* Major-General Sir Frederic Goldsmid, K.C.S.I. etc. (1818–1908). Originally commissioned in the E.I.C.'s army but after service in China transferred to the civilian establishment. Served many years in Sind: from 1861–70 almost continuously employed on Indo-European Telegraph work. Makran and Sistan Boundary Commissioner 1871–2. A brilliant linguist.

Tehran negotiating the new Convention which, the Legation informed the Foreign Office, was only obtained 'with a great deal of trouble. All the Governors and petty Officials were rather averse to it, and it required a great deal of bullying to get them to help our officers' (2). The Persians, while agreeing privately with this or that proposal were, according to Goldsmid, 'loth to commit to paper, and especially in the form of a Treaty or Convention, to be read and commented on by other Powers, anything which might be construed into admission of need, whether of material, men or money, or whether of moral supervision and administrative control' (3). In short the Persians were a proud people unwilling to admit publicly that they needed outside help. The Turks worked their own telegraph, why not they?

The Legation in Tehran, greatly relieved when the Convention was signed, urged the Foreign Office to provide 'a few thousand pounds' for presents to the Shah and those Ministers and officials who had helped bring the negotiations to a successful conclusion 'in acknowledgment of a great service which Persia has rendered to the British Nation and to the Indian Government in particular' (4).

Once the British were in control and were seen to be running the line efficiently their presence came to be accepted. Instead of having to withdraw at the end of five years a series of further Conventions provided for successive extensions of their period of control as well as for a new international line to run from Tehran across central Persia, through Yazd and Kerman to the Baluchistan–India border. The Persians also allowed the British to build a landline from Jask to Gwadur—to protect which *danegeld*, in the shape of regular subsidies, was hopefully paid through the Consul in Bandar Abbas to local shaikhs and tribal chiefs along this wild and lawless stretch of coast. The problem of maintaining the lines in working order was not however confined to any one area. Throughout the country wooden telegraph poles and wires were at risk from the weather and from the other uses, such as house rafters and firewood, to which they could be put: white porcelain insulators were an irresistible target for trigger-happy tribesmen. To discourage theft and wanton damage iron poles and iron-clad insulators were introduced but in the last resort it was the Telegraph Department's Persian 'linesmen' or mounted guards, posted at each telegraph station, who kept the line working. As soon as a break was noticed these men, no matter what the weather, would gallop out from the stations at both ends of the broken stretch to find the fault and repair it.

However, owing to the number of European frontiers to be crossed before reaching Baghdad neither of the telegraphic routes to India, via Fao and Bushire, proved very satisfactory: long delays and mutilations

The Electric Telegraph and other Innovations

in the messages sent were frequent. To overcome this problem Messrs. Siemens, an Anglo-German firm, were encouraged by the British Government to erect an international line across Germany, southern Russia and Persia to join the Indo-European Telegraph Department's Indian line at Tehran. Siemens founded the Indo-European Telegraph Company in London in 1867 for this purpose: by 1870 the new line was in working order. It had the great advantage of only crossing two countries before reaching Persia and quickly became the chosen route for Indian telegraphic traffic from London.

The telegraph not only provided valuable revenue for the Persian treasury but also greatly strengthened the hand of the Shah in dealing with his far-flung provinces. Additionally it brought Persia into contact with the outside world as never before and was probably more responsible than any other single factor in stimulating those reformist and nationalist movements which began to stir in the last quarter of the nineteenth century. Tehran's first daily newspaper, which appeared in 1898, relied for its foreign news on the Reuter summaries transmitted daily from London for publication in India. On the other hand the popular belief that the telegraph wires all ended at the foot of the throne in Tehran encouraged resort to the telegraph stations by *bastis* in search of asylum or as a form of protest, often to the embarrassment of British and Persian officialdom. One such occasion occurred in 1893 at Shiraz when, following bread riots, a mob of 2,000 marched on the telegraph station and insisted that a message be sent to the Shah demanding the dismissal of the Mayor of Shiraz and a cut in the price of bread. The crowd swelled to about 10,000 and held the telegraph staff prisoner until an answer was received from Tehran.

In a country where hotels were non-existent and caravansarais were notoriously dirty European travellers were glad to accept the hospitality offered them by the British and Armenians who manned the lonely telegraph stations spread across the country. Curzon, after his travels in Persia in 1889, spoke for many other travellers when he wrote that 'it is among the most agreeable incidents of Persian travel to come, at intervals of 60 or more miles along the principal routes, upon a telegraph station occupied by an English official, who dispenses a generous hospitality, and as a rule is excellently informed about the country in which he has lived and worked so long. I entertain the most friendly recollections of evenings, lightened by the intercourse and rendered comfortable by the attentions of these gentlemen, upon whose amiability travellers, it is to be feared, have sometimes been disposed to presume' (5).

Curzon, who was much impressed by the calibre of the telegraph personnel he met, believed that 'the English telegraph officers in Persia

The English Amongst the Persians

may be considered mainly responsible for the high estimate in which English character and honour are held in that country' (6). Members of the Indo-European Telegraph Department themselves believed that, thanks to the telegraph, the British were much more popular in central and southern Persia than the Russians. Yet it would be wrong to assume from this that the Persians really welcomed the British or their control of the telegraph lines which crossed their countryside. An American, by no means ill-disposed towards the British, who travelled through Persia in 1875, was nearer the truth* in writing that 'to most Persians, the telegraph-wire put through their country by England, without regard to their wishes, thus binding their land by a cord of iron, was plainly an ill omen, an unmistakable harbinger of evil, and could mean nothing else than, sooner or later, a complete subjection of entire Persia to the British rule. Hence their determination to break, if possible, the spell, by their repeated attempts to destroy the telegraph line, and hence their antipathy to the "feringhis", or foreigners' (7). The Persians were too polite to say such things to the British.

For many years the telegraph families were the backbone of small British communities scattered about Persia. At Isfahan they lived in the Armenian suburb of Julfa: in Shiraz they were housed in Anglo-Indian-style bungalows behind high compound walls some way out of the town, while their offices were in the beautiful Audience Chamber of what had once been a royal palace. At Jask and Reshahr, close to Bushire, on the torrid coast where the landlines and submarine cables joined they formed little outposts of Empire complete with club, tennis court and croquet lawn. In Tehran, where there was a good deal of friction and jealousy between the Legation and the Telegraph Department, Murdoch Smith was the dominant figure for twenty years. He had taken over from Champain as Director of the Telegraph in 1865 and lived in some style in newly built houses in Tehran and, during the summer, at Gulhek, driving around in a four-in-hand phaeton brought from London. He liked the Persians, who returned the compliment. He was a good Persian scholar and soon became deeply interested in their art and antiquities—an interest probably stimulated by two archaeological expeditions† in which he had taken part before coming to Persia. When home on leave in 1873, after discovering how very little Persian material was possessed by the South Kensington Museum, he offered to collect

---

* Borne out by Reza Shah taking over all landlines from the British in 1931 despite a 1913 agreement extending British control until 1945.
† To Turkey and Cyrenica. In Turkey at Halicarnassus (now Bodrum) he was largely instrumental in discovering the site of Mausolus' tomb, one of the Seven Wonders of the Ancient World.

The Electric Telegraph and other Innovations

for the Museum; his offer was accepted and he was authorised to make a start with £100. In the course of the next few years he bought and shipped home, with the approval of the Persian authorities, a large variety of Persian antiquities ranging from ceramics and metalwork to textiles and lacquer work; also a number of Qajar paintings, bought for a few shillings each, discarded by Nasir ed-Din Shah on his return from Europe in favour of European pictures and bric-à-brac. A caravan of thirty-two mules was required in 1875 to carry important collections, bought from two Frenchmen, to Bushire for shipment home. The following year the South Kensington Museum put its now excellent Persian collection on display, the first exhibition of Persian art to be staged in London. Murdoch Smith wrote a descriptive handbook for the occasion. Shortly after leaving Tehran in 1885 he became Director of what is now the Royal Scottish Museum and was mainly responsible for establishing that Museum's Persian collection.

Apart from the telegraph other forms of communication within Persia were still, by the 1860s, mediaeval. There were no carriage roads, no railways and no post offices. Things were not much better by 1921.

In order to keep in regular touch with London and India the British Legation employed a body of mounted messengers, or *gholams*, who carried mail once a month both to Constantinople and Shiraz whence fresh couriers bore it to London and Bushire: from Bushire the mail went to Bombay by boat. The *gholams* were a very tough lot. They had to cover great distances in every sort of weather: rivers had to be forded and precipitous mountain tracks surmounted: sometimes they were caught in blizzards: and more than one *gholam* froze to death or died from exhaustion as he battled with the elements. They usually covered about a hundred miles a day, riding a relay of horses stabled along the route at the *chaparkhanehs* or post houses maintained by the Persian Government.

In the absence of any sort of postal service the British allowed their *gholams* to carry mail for approved Persian and European friends on their route. When, in 1862, regular steamship sailings between Bombay and the Persian Gulf were begun the Government of India decided to establish their own post offices in the Gulf ports. Under pressure from the British the Persians had little choice but to accept an arrangement for which they had little use themselves at the time. The first British – Indian post office was opened at Bushire, within the precincts of the Residency, in 1864 and was soon followed by others at the Persian ports* served by ships of the British India Steam Navigation Company.

* Bandar Abbas and Lingeh in 1867: Mohammerah 1892: Chahbahar and Henjam Island 1913.

The English Amongst the Persians

Until the Persian Government inaugurated its own postal service in 1876 the British provided what amounted to a semi-public postal service between Bushire and the interior of the country. Legation and Telegraph Department messengers would deliver letters for posting at Bushire where mail would be collected for delivery along the messengers' route back to Tehran. These British – Indian post offices were under the control of the Postmaster-General in Bombay and were run without reference to the Persian authorities: letters were franked with Indian stamps bearing the crowned head of Queen Victoria and her two successors: Indian inland postal rates were charged: and the stamps were cancelled with an English post-mark. It was inevitable that once the Persians had established their own post offices and joined the International Postal Union they would come into conflict with the British. They objected to the use of the Indian stamp and to the acceptance by these British post offices of mail for delivery within Persia: also to the delivery of parcels direct from ships without passing through Persian Customs. On their side the British post offices refused to accept or forward mail bearing Persian stamps. In the course of the Great War when British forces were stationed in Khuzistan, the British opened a post office in the oil fields for the use of the military and the oil company. The existence of this chain of foreign-run post offices was, for the Persians, a painful infringement of national sovereignty. As soon as the war was over the British came under strong pressure to close them and by the end of 1922 they had reluctantly agreed to do so.

If, by the end of the Qajar era, there were still no long-distance railways in Persia it was no fault of the British. Julius de Reuter's main interest in the sweeping concession he had obtained from the Shah in 1872 had been the railway he hoped to build from the Caspian to the Persian Gulf. The British Government, increasingly worried by the Russian threat to Persia, firmly believed that without a railway from the Persian Gulf into the interior it would be impossible for them to render effective military assistance to Persia in the event of Russian aggression from the north. City of London financiers no less than War Office strategists wanted railways to be built: both were happy that the British Minister in Tehran, Drummond Wolff, was willing to exert his considerable energies in the successful pursuit of a railway concession. Thus it was that after the Shah had felt obliged to balance the favour he had shown to the British, in opening the Karun river to foreign shipping, by granting the Russians a railway concession in the north, Drummond Wolff was able to insist that the British be given a railway concession in the south. The Shah was too weak to resist but, having given way to Drummond Wolff, again came under intense pressure from

The Electric Telegraph and other Innovations

the Russians who, for strategic and commercial reasons, were determined to prevent the British building any railway from the Persian Gulf. Once more the unhappy Shah gave way and in late 1890 a Russo-Persian Agreement was signed under which all railway construction in Persia for the next ten years was prohibited. The Agreement was renewed for another ten years in 1900, thus putting an end to any hope of railway construction for many years. When this second Agreement expired London's interest in railway construction in Persia quickly revived. A Persian Railway Syndicate was formed by a powerful group of City financiers and a concession obtained from the Shah to survey and construct railways from the Persian Gulf to the interior. The British Government put their weight behind the Syndicate, not only for military reasons but also because they believed that without railways and roads Persia's shaky economic position would go from bad to worse.

A measure of the British and Indian Governments' interest in railway construction was that they deputed one of their ablest officials, Arnold Wilson, to spend most of 1911–13 in surveying possible railway routes from the Persian Gulf to the interior.* However, the war and the events that followed put an end to any hope of the British playing a part in Persian railway development.†

Roads capable of taking wheeled traffic were few and far between in Qajar Persia—by the 1880s only two such roads existed and they were short and very rough, linking Tehran only with Qazvin and Qum. Such developments as took place later were the result of concessions granted to the British and Russians or action taken by the two countries' military engineers during the Great War. Road concessions reflected Anglo-Russian rivalry—those obtained by the Imperial Bank in 1890 to build a carriage road from Tehran to Ahwaz through Qum and Sultanabad were countered two years later by the grant to the Russians of a road concession from Enzeli to Qazvin. Further concessions granted to the Russians in north Persia were balanced by one to the Imperial Bank in 1898 for a road from Qum to Isfahan. Both were to be reimbursed by the levying of tolls on the stretches of road they built—an imposition which Persian travellers, unaware of the financial modalities, resented as yet another sign of British and Russian domination of their country.

The Imperial Bank spent so much money on survey work and repairs

---

* The British were interested in four possible railway lines: Bandar Abbas–Kerman: Mohammerah–Khorramabad: Bushire–Shiraz: Bandar Abbas–Shiraz–Ahwaz.

† It was not until 1927 that Reza Shah, with his customary drive, got work started on Persia's first major railway, the Trans-Iranian line that ran from the Gulf to the Caspian.

The English Amongst the Persians

to the existing Tehran–Qum stretch of road* that it decided, in the absence of any financial support from the British Government, to get rid of the concession. Fear that the Russians might acquire it prompted the British Government to persuade Lynch Bros to step in by founding the Persian Road and Transport Company in 1902. With the help of an annual subsidy from the British and Indian Governments Lynch proceeded to construct the first carriage road from Tehran to Isfahan and Sultanabad. The Great War put an end to their efforts to extend the road to Ahwaz and, when it was over, disputes with the Persian authorities led to the cancellation of the concession.

During and immediately after the war the British Army built a number of roads to suit their own military requirements and thus provided southern and eastern Persia with a nucleus of rough but motorable roads. The newly-appointed British Consul to Shiraz had, as early as 1914, been able to motor in a Ford car from Tehran to his post: by 1919 British military vehicles had travelled from Bushire to Shiraz and across central Persia from Khaniqin to Qazvin and Tehran: they also plied between Isfahan, Yazd and Kerman and up Persia's eastern border from Zahedan to Mashad.

The British can, therefore, claim the doubtful distinction of having introduced the internal combustion engine to the remoter corners of Persia.

---

* The Bank for a time ran a carriage service between Tehran and Qum.

10

Frontier Makers

No RECORD OF the British in Persia during the Qajar period would be complete without a short account of the role they played in drawing the frontiers within which, with few changes, Persia thrives to-day. A measure of the British interest in Persia is the fact that they had a hand in settling all her frontiers with the single exception of the northern boundary with Russia lying to the east of the Caspian Sea. Even here the British tried hard to take part but the Russians would not agree.

Britain herself had no territorial ambitions to satisfy. Her involvement in Persian frontier-making was due to an over-riding concern for the defence of India and fear of Russian expansion in that direction. Unsettled Persian frontiers, whether on the west or east, were a temptation to trouble-makers and a threat to peace and stability. Although the Persians were far from happy with some of the frontiers drawn at British insistence, they were, in the first half of the nineteenth century at any rate, glad of British participation if for no other reason than as a counter-weight to Russian ambitions and intrigues. It had been at Persian insistence that a stipulation had been included in the Anglo-Persian Treaty of 1814 to the effect that 'The limits of the territories of the two States of Russia and Persia shall be determined according to the admission of Great Britain, Persia and Russia'.

Persia's loss of her Caucasian provinces following her two wars with Russia meant drawing a new frontier in that region. The British had played an important part behind the scenes in securing peace for Persia on both occasions, though only at the price of the humiliating Treaties of Gulestan and Turkmanchai. Colonel William Monteith of the Madras Engineers, who had spent much of his time with Persian forces on the Caucasian front since 1810, assisted in delimiting the new

The English Amongst the Persians

frontier after the signature of both treaties. He only left the country in late 1829 when the boundary, which has remained unchanged to this day, had been finally determined.

Settlement of Persia's long western frontier with the Ottoman Empire, over which the Persians and Turks had been at each other's throats for years, was to be a much more protracted affair. It suited neither the Russians with their newly acquired Caucasian interests, nor the British, with their interests in the Persian Gulf and India, that the Persians and Turks should be at loggerheads. The two great Powers, rivals though they were, therefore offered to mediate. The offer was accepted and a Mixed Boundary Commission, on which all four Powers were represented, met in Erzerum early in 1843. There, despite the bitter cold winters and the scorching summer heat, they remained for the next four years, engaged in the tedious business of examining documents and hearing witnesses in an effort to reach agreement on a frontier running from the Persian Gulf to Mount Ararat, a distance of over 700 miles as the crow flies.

There were three British Commissioners, the senior being Lieutenant Colonel Fenwick Williams of the Royal Artillery, assisted by Major Francis Farrant of the Tehran Legation and the Hon. Robert Curzon* of the Constantinople Embassy. They and the Russian Commissioners had to put up with every sort of difficulty, particularly from the Turks, but at length in June 1847 agreement on the broad lines of the frontier was reached and embodied in the Treaty of Erzerum. Thanks largely to the efforts of the British Commissioners the Turks recognised Persian sovereignty over Mohammerah and the small off-shore island of Khizr (now Abadan).

But this was not the end of the matter. It was one thing to agree on the broad lines of the frontier, and quite another on the details. Nearly seventy years passed before this happened. The trouble was that much of the frontier was unknown, wild, tribal country where the writ of neither Government ran. No surveys had ever been made and the old maps and place names on which the Commissioners had based their findings were unreliable and misleading. The Commissioners recognised that a detailed survey of the proposed frontier was necessary before it could be demarcated: as a result of their recommendations, a Delimita-

---

* Williams, attached to the Turkish army since 1841, made a name for himself commanding Turkish troops at the siege of Kars, 1855: for this the British Government awarded him a baronetcy and £1,000 p.a. for life. Farrant had been in Persia since his arrival there with the 1833 Military Mission. Curzon, a kinsman of G. N. Curzon, had scoured the Near East in search of old manuscripts; author of *Monasteries of the Levant*.

tion Commission was established on which Williams again served with a small team which included W. K. Loftus as geologist and H. A. Churchill as assistant surveyor and interpreter.

The Commissioners took two years to work their way northwards from Mohammerah to Ararat. Before getting down to work Williams sent Loftus and Churchill off to examine the great mound of Shush, near Ahwaz, on which travellers had often commented but none had properly explored. Later, when Loftus returned to excavate the site on behalf of the British Museum, he was able positively to identify it with that of the biblical Shushan and classical Susa. Loftus* was also the first traveller to draw attention to the bitumen springs in the neighbourhood of Masjid-e-Suleiman where Reynolds and his oil drillers made their great discovery over half a century later. By the summer of 1850 the Commissioners had reached the hills of Luristan, where they pitched their tents for the summer. While there the British offered hospitality to the first tourists ever to visit that remote region—a party of four Irishmen, two young brothers accompanied by a tutor and servant. Stranger still was the fact that one of the brothers, Arthur Kavanagh, had been born limbless with mere stumps in place of arms and legs yet had taught himself to write and paint by using his mouth and to ride strapped into a special saddle. The spirit which took him to the wilds of Luristan later helped him make a name for himself as an Irish Member of Parliament at Westminster.

The British and Russian mediating Commissioners sought, as best they could, to resolve the endless disagreements between their Persian and Turkish colleagues. The Crimean and Anglo-Persian Wars interrupted their work, which was further delayed when Williams' official report was lost overboard at Gravesend when being brought home for further study. Not surprisingly the detailed frontier maps which the British and Russian cartographers separately drew up differed so widely from each other that it was not until 1869 that they somehow managed to reconcile their differences and produce a *carte identique* for presentation to the Persians and Turks. However this map, on the scale of one inch to the mile, no more finalised the frontier than the earlier Treaty of Erzerum had done—it merely indicated a broad strip from twenty to forty miles wide within which the frontier was understood to lie. The Persian and Turkish Governments were left to decide between themselves on the actual line. They made little or no attempt to do so and for many more years the frontier remained uncertain and the subject of

* On his return to England Loftus published what was for many years to be the most complete geological report in existence on any part of Persia. He also provided Kew Gardens with a number of botanical specimens.

renewed dispute, verging on war at times, between the two countries.

Once again the British and Russians felt constrained to step in and offer their mediation. A new Delimitation Commission, composed of the same four Powers, was therefore established in 1913. The British Commissioner, A. C. Wratislaw, had been Consul-General in Tabriz for a number of years; his deputy, Arnold Wilson, had the great advantage of speaking Persian and Arabic and being familiar with much of the terrain and many of the local tribes. For this reason his views carried much weight with all four Commissions. Each Commission travelled as a self-contained unit. The British were the largest party, about one hundred and fifty strong, with their own doctor, Indian surveyors, a thirty-man *sowar* escort and numerous Indian servants. On one occasion, when some of the British officers were out shooting for the pot, they were attacked by Kurds who severely wounded one of them. Apart from this no serious incident occurred, though neither the Persian nor Turkish Government's authority carried much weight among the semi-independent Lurs and Kurds through whose country the Commissioners were travelling. This time the Persian and Turkish Commissioners were under instructions to reach agreement on the spot, failing which they were to refer any differences to the British and Russian representatives for settlement within forty-eight hours. The procedure worked well and by October 1914, shortly after the outbreak of the Great War, the frontier had been agreed and marked with pillars over its whole length from Mohammerah to Mount Ararat where the Empires of Shah, Czar and Sultan met.*

Persia's eastern frontier was of more direct concern to the British, lying as it did on India's threshold. Running from the north-eastern corner of Khorasan in the north to the Makran coast in the south it marched with Afghanistan, Sistan and Baluchistan over each of which Persia had at times ruled in the past but which, by the mid-nineteenth century, were virtually independent territories, each under one or more rulers. The Persians, after their losses in the Russian wars, looked for territorial compensation among these eastern lands, sandy wastes though much of them were. Historic claims were revived. But as they pressed eastwards they found the British, who had themselves been steadily pushing the outer defences of their Indian Empire westwards, standing in their way. Afghanistan and Baluchistan† had become outposts of

---

* Nevertheless this frontier, particularly in its southern reaches, remained in dispute for many years between Persia and Iraq until they reached agreement on their differences in 1975.

† By the middle of the century eastern Baluchistan had become a British-Indian protectorate. The Persian Government, which laid claim to all of Baluchistan, exercised

Henry Layard in Bakhtiari costume with a Bakhtiari servant. From A. H. Layard's *Early Adventures in Persia, Susiana and Babylonia*.

Suspension bridge on the 'Lynch' road between Ahwaz and Isfahan, *circa* 1900. From V. Chirol, *op. cit.*

Road-making, under British army supervision, on the Asadabad Pass, near Hamadan, March 1918. By courtesy of the Imperial War Museum.

Transporting Persia's first oil pipe line: Khuzistan, 1911. By courtesy of The British Petroleum Co. Ltd.

The South Persia Rifles. British and Persian officers and Persian NCOs of the 1st Sultan Ahmad Shah Regiment, Bandar Abbas, April 1916.

British and Indian troops of DUNSTERFORCE on the march near Manjil, 1918.

By courtesy of the Imperial War Museum.

DUNSTERFORCE, 1918. Drilling Persian levies near Hamadan.

Drilling Assyrian levies near Hamadan. By courtesy of the Imperial War Museum.

Empire to be protected against Persian encroachment, not for fear of Persia but of Russian infiltration that might follow. As and when confrontation occurred the British intervened and, because they were the stronger Power, more often than not decided how the frontier should run. In doing so they inevitably paid less attention to Persian than to their own and Indian interests and left a legacy of resentment behind. Such, briefly and perhaps over-simply, is the background to a very complicated series of Anglo-Persian frontier negotiations which took place between 1870 and 1905. In each case the British were the driving force behind five separate boundary commissions on which the Persians and other interested parties were also represented but carried relatively little weight.*

The first confrontation was in Afghanistan. When the British forced the Persians to withdraw their army from Herati territory in 1857 they obtained from the Shah a formal abandonment of his Afghan claims as well as an undertaking to refer to the British any future differences with the Afghans before resorting to arms: at the same time the Persians recognised the Hari river as their northern boundary with Afghanistan. Later, as will be recounted, the British intervened again, but this time without arms or landings on Kharg Island, to settle differences between the two countries over their frontier further south where each claimed sovereignty over the province of Sistan.

Further south still, on the Makran coast of Baluchistan, trouble had been brewing for some time between the British and the Persians. When, in the early 1860s, the idea of an Indo-European telegraph line was first mooted the Persians had refused to allow the line to run overland down the coast from Bandar Abbas or Jask to Gwadur for fear that a British presence in the area might prejudice their own claims and ambitions. The British were therefore obliged to resort to submarine cable for this section of the line but were, nonetheless, anxious that the frontier should be clearly defined so that they could deal effectively with local chiefs through whose territories the line ran overland between Gwadur and Karachi. A further factor was the treaty relationship which by then existed between the British and the Khan of Kalat, the principal ruler in this part of Baluchistan: the British wanted a frontier drawn so as to protect his territories from further Persian encroachment. Following a strong British protest in 1870 about Persian activities in Makran it was

---

limited authority through the Governor of Bampur over the western half of this large, undefined region.

* Baluchistan (Makran) Boundary Commission 1870-1: Sistan Arbitration Commission 1872: Perso-Afghan Arbitration Commission 1888: Perso-Baluch Boundary Commission 1896: second Sistan Arbitration Commission 1903-5.

The English Amongst the Persians

decided, at the Shah's suggestion, to establish a Boundary Commission to demarcate the frontier. The Khan of Kalat, as well as the British and Persians, was to be represented on it.

The Sistan question came to a head about the same time. At first the British had been inclined to stand aside and let the Persians and Afghans settle their own differences over this inland delta province watered by the Helmand river. But second thoughts about its strategic importance for India caused the British to change their minds when it looked as if the two countries would go to war in pursuit of their claims. The British Government therefore invoked the 1857 Treaty and with some difficulty persuaded both sides to accept their arbitration.

Major-General Frederic Goldsmid, then Director-General in London of the Indo-European Telegraph Department, was chosen by the British Government in 1870 to be their commissioner on both the Makran and Sistan boundary commissions. He knew the Makran coast better than any other British official and was an obvious choice, though at fifty-two he was no longer young for a task which necessitated much rough travelling in a region where the climate was as hot and enervating as almost anywhere in the world.

It would be tedious to describe in detail the difficulties, physical and political, that Goldsmid and his few assistants* had to face in the course of their Makran and Sistan missions. In this age of comfortable jet travel it is difficult to visualise the hardships and monotony of travel in eastern Persia barely a century ago. Setting out from London in August 1870 and travelling across Russia and the Caspian Sea Goldsmid reached Tehran early in October. Then, riding all the way, he spent four months reaching Baluchistan, travelling by way of Isfahan and Kerman over endless miles of desert. The days were hot under a pitiless sun, the nights bitterly cold. There were delays and difficulties with the Persian Commissioner. At Bampur, the capital of Persian Baluchistan, consternation was caused by the news that the Kalat Commissioner had arrived on Persian soil in company with a British officer and three hundred men. The Persians, already suspicious of British intentions, became even more wary. As the Persian Commissioner was unwilling to co-operate in any way, Goldsmid, after barely two months in Baluchistan and Makran, decided to return to Tehran and settle things there. He drew up a map showing a frontier line that ran from a point east of Chahbahar on the coast to Jalk, a small oasis of date palms about two hundred and fifty miles inland.

Although the Shah, who granted Goldsmid two audiences, showed no

* They included Majors Beresford Lovett (principal cartographer) and O. B. St. John, Capt. C. B. Euan Smith and Mr W. T. Blandford (geologist and naturalist).

enthusiasm for his proposed line which would place a curb on any further Persian advance eastwards, he accepted Goldsmid's proposal 'simply out of regard for the wishes of Her Britannic Majesty's Government that this question should be brought to a satisfactory conclusion by the definition of a boundary line' (1). Goldsmid had triumphed and when he returned to London in September 1871 to make 'personal report of past occurrences, and receive oral instructions for future guidance' (2) he was rewarded with a knighthood. Six weeks later he was on his way back to Persia to settle the much more difficult Perso-Afghan dispute over Sistan. This time he travelled by ship to India and then to Bandar Abbas where he landed at the end of December 1871. He then rode inland to Bam and across the vast expanse of the *Dasht-e-Lut* to Sistan—another arduous journey which took him over a month.

In Sistan Goldsmid and his small band of assistants had a difficult time as the Persian Commissioner and other officials once again went out of their way to be uncooperative. The Commissioner was particularly tiresome, even refusing to allow Goldsmid to fly the Union Jack over his tent—perhaps from a genuine fear that this might lead to annexation of Persian territory. Although the British found him an amusing and good-natured companion he exasperated them by his unwillingness to accept any responsibility, coupled with a ready willingness to accept bribes and extort money from anyone on whom he could prey. After six weeks of frustration and insult Goldsmid decided to withdraw to Tehran and make his decisions there. In due course, like a Solomon, he gave judgement which was to partition Sistan between the two disputants. As with most compromises, neither side was satisfied. The Persians, who claimed all Sistan, regarded partition as a devious swindle by the British to enrich their vassal state, Afghanistan, at Persian expense. The Afghans were equally unhappy to lose territory which in the recent past had acknowledged their suzerainty. Both sides rejected Goldsmid's award. The British, who considered that the Persians had got the best of the bargain by gaining all the most valuable, revenue-producing part of Sistan, refused to make any changes. In the end both countries had little choice than to accept the British proposals, though it was not until the Shah visited London in 1873 and was subjected to heavy pressure there that he finally gave way.

Some years later the Helmand river inconveniently changed course and by so doing re-opened the Sistan frontier problem in acute form, the Helmand waters being the life-blood of an otherwise arid region. The British were again called in to arbitrate and in 1903 Colonel Henry McMahon, who had made a name for himself some years earlier settling the Afghan-Baluch border, was appointed British Commissioner with instructions to study the use made of the Helmand waters by Persians and Afghans and to fix a new boundary conforming, in the altered circumstances, as closely as possible to the earlier Goldsmid line. The task was far from easy and occupied two and a half years, though McMahon was accompanied by a veritable army of helpers including twelve British officers and over 1,500 Indians ranging from surveyors and *sowars* to servants and syces. A train of 2,000 camels (compared with Goldsmid's ninety in 1872) was needed to transport their supplies and impedimenta. The size of the party was designed, in part, to impress the Persians and Afghans whose churlish treatment of the Goldsmid mission still rankled. McMahon took enormous pains over his difficult task and eventually a new frontier line was agreed and demarcated. But this frontier was no more satisfactory to the Persians and Afghans than Goldsmid's. By leaving Persian Sistan mainly dependent on waters which flowed from Afghanistan the seeds of much future trouble, already sown by Goldsmid, remained to bedevil Perso-Afghan relations for many years.

The only other section of the Perso-Afghan border in dispute lay immediately south of the Hari river. Here too the British were asked to arbitrate. Once again a member of the Indian Political Service was nominated for the task* which was completed without trouble in 1891 when the last of the frontier posts was erected.

Thanks to the British Persia's eastern frontier had now been settled, mapped and demarcated except for a three-hundred-mile gap on the Baluch border between Sistan and Jalk where Goldsmid's 1871 line had ended. At that time this remote sandy waste was of little interest to the British and it was not until 1895 that they felt the need to demarcate the frontier as a precaution against tribal raiding and Persian encroachment. At British request the Persians appointed a commissioner to meet Colonel Thomas Holdich, a frontier expert of the Indian Survey Department who had as his assistant Captain Percy Sykes, then serving as consul in Kerman. Sykes, accompanied by his sister Ella and a train of slow-moving camels, rode from Kerman to the Baluch frontier, a distance of about six hundred miles, in exactly forty days. In her account of the journey, mostly across desert, Miss Sykes, who always rode side-saddle, gives an occasional glimpse of the discomforts she and her brother must have endured on their long trek. Because of the daytime heat they usually travelled in the early hours of the morning, extra tents and stores being sent leap-frogging ahead so as to be ready for them on arrival. Starting before the sun was up, 'My brother and I used to walk in the chilly hours before dawn, but had, however, to

* Colonel Charles Maclean. See p. 82.

mount almost as soon as the sun rose, as it sprang up suddenly into the sky and seemed to flood the country with an intense light and heat, making us thankful for pith hats even at this early hour. We were generally in camp by 8.30 am. at latest, very ready for the breakfast spread in the big *pishkhana* tent, after which we amused ourselves as best we could until our caravan turned up with our camp equipage' (3). In Baluchistan the wind was another problem—'nearly every day, about four o'clock, we were visited by a sandstorm, by no means an agreeable experience if it happened to be a violent one. Nothing heralded the approach of these *shaitans* (devils), as the servants called them; but suddenly the tent might be blown down upon us by a sort of miniature tornado, and oh, the dust! Everything was thickly coated with sand, our faces, books and writing materials covered, hair and inkpots full of it in a second: and when it passed away and the tents were swept out, it was almost impossible to write, so gritty were pens and paper, and so sore were our eyes from the sharp particles of sand' (4).

Although, at the very beginning, there had been a brush between the two commissioners on a point of protocol (the British insisting that the Persian Commissioner should make the first call) both sides had got on well with each other. The Persian New Year was celebrated with a gymkhana organised by the British and in the evening the Persians, who had their own band and fireworks, gave a great dinner—'we all dined with the Persian party in a huge tent, pitched on the bank of the stream. . . . We had an excellent Persian dinner, our servants doing the waiting as usual, and the Itisham-e-Vizireh made a fine speech about the Queen, calling her the "Ruler who dwelt in the shadow of Allah", the band playing our National Anthem in style' (5). A few days later, on 24 March 1896, the Frontier Commission had completed its task, maps had been signed and exchanged, and the last cairns marking the frontier erected by Holdich's sepoys. That same night Holdich gave a farewell dinner when one of the Persians startled everyone by singing the 'Highland Laddie'—taught him, he said, by an English girl in London. Next morning, after effusive farewells all round, Sykes and his sister mounted their horses and set off with Holdich for Quetta, over four hundred miles away across the Baluch desert. They had done their job well and settled within little more than a month the last stretch of Persia's eastern frontier.

This long frontier, demarcated by the British, has remained virtually unchanged ever since. The British got little thanks for their efforts which inevitably left one or other side, sometimes both, dissatisfied. To this day Persian school children are taught that Goldsmid and Holdich deprived Persia of a large slice of Baluchistan. Curzon had perhaps been right when he asked 'whether it is wise policy for the Indian Government to undertake these chivalrous but thankless Commissions, which are apt to be misinterpreted by both parties, and usually leave a legacy of odium behind them' (6). But who else than the British could, at that time, have undertaken the task? And without a fixed frontier line in that turbulent corner of Asia the peace which has endured there ever since would surely have been broken.

11

Some Travellers

ENGLISH LITERATURE IS rich in nineteenth-century travel books about Persia. Many of their authors were birds of passage, military gentlemen and civilians, on their way to or from India for, until the 'overland route' through Egypt was opened in the 1840s, the quickest way home was by ship from Bombay to Bushire and then across Persia to Constantinople. Amusing though many of these early books are they rarely contain more than superficial information about a strange country seen for the first time. More valuable are the accounts of men like James Morier and William Ouseley who went to Persia as members of diplomatic missions, stayed longer, and had both the time and inclination to probe more deeply. Other British travellers who contributed much to the outside world's knowledge of Persia were the officers sent from India, sometimes in disguise, usually more openly, to spy out the land and collect topographical and other information about a country which, it was believed, might one day become a theatre of war. There were yet other travellers who visited Persia out of curiosity or for pleasure. They went as private individuals at their own expense and were relatively few in number, conditions being too rough and hazardous to attract any but the boldest. The earliest of these individualists were Robert Ker Porter and James Baillie Fraser. Others followed; some wrote vivid accounts of their travels and adventures, the most notable being Henry Layard, Edward Browne, George Curzon and Mrs Bishop (Isabella Bird).

Napoleon's threatened invasion of India awakened the British to their abysmal ignorance of the borderlands across which he might march. No one was more aware of this than John Malcolm, who, on his first mission to Persia, had written to his father from Shiraz in 1800 to say that he was devoting 'every leisure hour in researches into the history of this extraordinary country, with which we are but little acquainted' (1). Nine years later, back in Bombay, Malcolm sent one of his officers, Captain W. P. Grant, to explore the Makran coast 'to ascertain', as Grant wrote, 'whether an European army could penetrate into India by the south coast of Persia' (2). Travelling alone without disguise the intrepid Grant landed at Chahbahar and made his way inland as far as Bampur before heading back to the coast which he then followed to Bandar Abbas—a difficult journey across as inhospitable and barren a countryside as exists anywhere in Persia. In 325 B.C. Alexander had retreated from India with part of his army along this daunting route. Few, if any, Europeans had used it since.

Malcolm next sent two other officers, Captain Charles Christie and Lieutenant Henry Pottinger,* both of the Bombay Infantry, to explore the undefined frontier area north of Makran. Both had volunteered for what they knew was a hazardous business in unknown country. Their terms of reference were to ascertain 'the nature and resources of those countries, through which an invading European army might advance towards Hindostan' (3). They left Bombay together disguised as horse buyers for a well-known Hindu horse-dealer. Having landed on the Makran coast they made their way into the interior of Baluchistan, passing through Kalat before separating in March 1810 at Nushki. Christie then travelled north through Sistan to Herat where he spent a month collecting information about the ancient walled city and its surroundings. After leaving Herat Christie made for Isfahan, travelling south-west across the great central desert of Persia to Yazd. In the meantime Pottinger, posing as a pilgrim, wandered through Baluchistan, where he collected a mass of information about the tribes. He then moved south until he struck Grant's Makran route of the previous year, then turned north to reach Isfahan via Kerman and Shiraz. At Isfahan he abandoned his disguise and called on the Governor, who invited him to stay in the Chehel Sutun Palace, an old building dating from Safavid times. Some days later Christie, who had travelled over desert tracks hitherto unknown to Europeans, reached Isfahan. He went to ask the Governor for lodgings and was taken to the Chehel Sutun where, in the dusk, he and Pottinger, both still in Persian dress, at first failed to recognise each other: when they did there was a dramatic reunion, neither of them having had news of the other since parting at Nushki four months before.

* Sir Henry Pottinger, G.C.B. (1789–1856). Commissioned in the E.I.C.'s army 1804: Political Agent, Scinde 1836–40; envoy to China 1841; participated in China War; first Governor of Hong Kong 1843–4; Governor of Cape of Good Hope 1846 and of Madras 1847–54. For Christie see pp. 52–3.

Some Travellers

By this time Malcolm himself had arrived in Persia on his third mission with a number of other officers including Grant of Makran fame: they were all instructed to travel and to collect information about the country. Two of them, Grant and Fotheringham, went to explore Luristan in western Persia where, soon after arrival, they were hurled over a cliff and killed, allegedly for refusing to apostasise. The information collected by Malcolm's team was collated by one of their number, Captain John Macdonald Kinneir, and published in 1813 in his *A Geographical Memoir of the Persian Empire*; though dull reading it remained for many years the main source of geographical information in any language about Persia. Malcolm's own two-volume *History of Persia*, published two years later, complemented it on the historical side. In 1816 Pottinger's *Travels in Beloochistan and Sinde*, a lengthy volume of over 400 pages, was published by John Murray in London. Morier's and William Ouseley's accounts of their journeys appeared between 1812-19. Persia was at last becoming better known.

James Morier, William Ouseley and other members of Sir Gore Ouseley's mission had landed at Bushire with their chief in March 1811. They were under instructions from the Foreign Office to collect information about the country through which they were passing on their way to Tehran. While held up at Shiraz in the summer of 1811 awaiting his wife's *accouchement* Ouseley despatched his brother William, an erudite orientalist,* and other members of his staff to discover what they could about Persia's past and present. Despite the heat and the dangers of travel in areas rarely, if ever, visited by Europeans, they went off in different directions. At that time Persepolis and the nearby rock tombs and bas reliefs of Naqsh-e-Rustam were among the few ancient remains known to western travellers. Persepolis alone had been identified for what it really was, the capital of the Achaemenian kings, though the Persians themselves persisted in calling it the Throne of Jamshid. In the course of their wanderings William Ouseley and his colleagues visited a number of important and hitherto unknown archaeological sites.

One of the party, Major Stone, discovered the great cave near Shapur with its fallen stalactite statue of Shapur I. Robert Gordon, who visited Shush, thought that excavations there would yield a rich harvest—a surmise which a succession of French archaeologists have since proved

---

* Sir William Ouseley (1767-1842). Studied oriental subjects in Paris and Leyden. In 1795 he published a treatise on the various styles of Persian handwriting. His illustrated account in three volumes of his travels in Persia and elsewhere contained much interesting new archaeological material. He brought home a large collection of Persian manuscripts and antiquities including stone fragments from Persepolis.

The English Amongst the Persians

abundantly correct. Gordon himself collected antiquities and wrote enthusiastically to his brother, Lord Aberdeen, about the finds he was shipping home from Persepolis and elsewhere. William Ouseley went east from Shiraz to Sarvistan, Fasa and Darab in the mistaken belief that Fasa was the ancient Pasargadae and that he would find there traces of the tomb of Cyrus the Great, founder of the Achaemenian Empire. Had he but known, James Morier had himself seen Cyrus' tomb over two years previously on his first visit to Persia in the suite of Harford Jones when he had come close to identifying it. On that occasion Morier had sketched the structure which he called by its local name, the Tomb of the Mother of Solomon. His detailed description of it together with the sketch was published in London in 1812. Morier recorded that the site was a place of some sanctity, surrounded by modern tomb-stones and that only females were permitted to enter what 'the people generally regard as the monument of the mother of Solomon'. He went on to speculate (the italics being his own) that 'if *the position of the place* had corresponded with the site of Passargadae as well as the *form of this structure* accords with the description of the tomb of Cyrus near the city, I should have been tempted to assign to the present building so illustrious an origin' (4).

When Morier* returned to the tomb with William Ouseley in 1811 he did not revise his earlier conclusions which Ouseley shared.† Eventually, seven years later, another Englishman, Sir Robert Ker Porter, after a close study of all available classical sources, correctly identified the tomb as that of Cyrus.‡

Ker Porter was a new phenomenon among British travellers to Persia. He went there neither as a member of an official mission, nor on his way home from India, but as a traveller and artist on his own account. Born in Durham in 1777 he had studied painting and drawing in London before securing an appointment in 1804 as 'historical painter' to the Czar of Russia. Obliged to leave Russia during the Napoleonic Wars he joined the British Army in Spain, but returned to Russia in 1811, when he married a Russian Princess. Later he was encouraged by the President of the Russian Academy of Fine Arts to visit Persia in

---

* The author of *Hajji Baba* was the first European traveller to publish an illustrated account of the Sassanian ruins and bas-reliefs at Shapur.

† Earlier European travellers had been inclined to dismiss the building as of doubtful antiquity while Islamic travellers gave it no notice. Ouseley himself believed it was coeval with Persepolis owing to the similarity of what he called their 'arrow-head' inscriptions.

‡ It was here that in October 1971 H.I.M. Muhammad Reza Shah Pahlavi inaugurated the 2500th Anniversary celebrations of the founding of the Persian Empire by Cyrus the Great.

order to make drawings of the sculpture at Persepolis and elsewhere. Leaving St Petersburg at the end of 1817 he spent the next two years in Persia with noteworthy results. The archaeological drawings he made were more detailed and accurate than those of any previous traveller: they provide a valuable record of ruins, many of which have since disappeared. Apart from identifying Cyrus' tomb and that of Darius I at Naqhs-e-Rustam he was the first European to notice the most impressive of all Sassanian bas-reliefs, those cut in the rock face of the grotto known as Taq-e-Bustan outside Kermanshah. Although he did not discover or correctly identify the trilingual rock inscriptions and processional figures at Bisitun some miles from Taq-e-Bustan, he was the first traveller to sketch the figures. Though unable to copy the inscriptions he drew attention to them in his book and, by doing so, probably helped inspire Henry Rawlinson's great work of decipherment twenty years later. Porter was also the first European to visit another Sassanian site, known as Takht-e-Suleiman or Solomon's Throne, built round a spectacular circular lake among the hills far off the beaten track in Kurdistan.

Shortly after Ker Porter left Persia another lone traveller arrived on the scene. He was James Baillie Fraser, born in Edinburgh in 1783 of well-to-do parents. Fraser had acquired a taste for eastern travel after two months in the Himalayas with his brother who was employed by the East India Company. In 1821 he left India in company with Surgeon Andrew Jukes of the East India Company, but Jukes died at Isfahan, leaving Fraser to proceed alone to Tehran. From there in December 1821, accompanied by a Persian interpreter, four Persian servants and a negro attendant brought from India, Fraser, wearing Persian dress, set off for Mashad. He hoped to reach Bokhara but this proved impossible because of unsettled political conditions in Central Asia. Instead he explored the Caspian shores and after visiting Rasht and Ardebil reached Tabriz. He then went through Kurdistan to Baghdad before returning to England where he spent the next few years writing two travel books which gave the British public their first descriptions of the southern Caspian shore. He also wrote a number of romantic novels with Persian backgrounds.

Fraser was back in Persia in 1834, sent by Palmerston on an intelligence-gathering mission. His travels on this occasion provided material for two more lengthy books in which he described little-known areas of Kurdistan and Azarbaijan. Unfortunately, though his books covered new ground, they made little contribution to systematic geography 'owing to the author's lack of all but the most elementary knowledge of physical science' (5). He believed the 'detested' Qajar dynasty was tottering to its fall and blamed Persian rulers for the deplorable character of the people, whose 'prominent features certainly are falsehood and treachery in all their shapes, cunning and versatility, selfishness, avarice and cowardice: there is no deceit, degradation, or crime, to which they will not stoop for gain, and their habits of falsehood are so inveterate, that untruths flow, as it were, spontaneously from their tongue, even where no apparent motive exists' (6).

Some years previously another British traveller* from India had written in similar disparaging vein about the Persians whom he described as 'pleasing and entertaining companions; but not the least reliance is to be placed on their words or most solemn protestations. You should always, therefore, be on your guard against their insidious offers; and to be so, it is necessary to distrust all their declarations. The manners of the Persians are formed, in a great degree, on the principles of Lord Chesterfield; they conceive it their duty to please: and to effect this, they forget all sentiments of honour and good faith. They are excellent companions, but detestable characters.' Pottinger, in his book mentioned above, described Persia as 'the very fountain-head of every species of tyranny, cruelty, meanness, injustice, extortion, and infamy, that can disgrace or pollute human nature' (7).

It is a sad fact that most later British travellers and writers† took an equally jaundiced view of the Persians and thus helped to sow seeds of resentment and misunderstanding between the two countries. Joseph Rabino of the Imperial Bank had good reason, as late as 1898, to complain of the 'astounding ignorance of Persia in England' (9) where, with the single exception of Curzon's *Persia and the Persian Question*, he knew of no book which made any attempt to give an impartial view of Persia and her people. Yet Curzon's estimate of the Persian character was no less offensive to Persian feelings than that of earlier travellers—'The finest domestic virtues,' he wrote, 'co-exist with barbarity and supreme indifference to suffering. Elegance of deportment is compatible with a coarseness amounting to bestiality. The same individual is at different moments haughty and cringing. A creditable acquaintance

---

* E. Scott Waring of the East India Company's Bengal Civil Establishment. He visited Persia between April–September 1802 for reasons of 'ill health and curiosity'. His *A Tour of Sheeraz* was a creditable early attempt to give an account of 'the manners, customs, laws, language, and literature of the Persians'.

† While often recognising the outstanding intellectual qualities of the Persians British writers were all too inclined to treat their moral character as 'a compound of the most odious defects'. Religious prejudice played its part. The Rev. A. A. Isaacs, who never visited Persia, described the Persians as 'plunged in debauchery and the lowest forms of sensual pleasure'. One of the rare voices on the other side was that of Percy Sykes who considered them 'the finest and most gifted race in Western Asia' (8).

Some Travellers

with the standards of civilisation does not prevent gross fanaticism and superstition. Accomplished manners and a more than Parisian polish cover a truly superb faculty for lying and almost scientific imposture' (10).

There were, of course, reasons for this. Differences of language, religion and a whole way of life made for misunderstandings. The Persians, an old and proud race, reacted to displays of arrogance and assumed superiority in the niceties of comportment or the Englishman's refusal to share a wayside room with other travellers. The English were, it was said, all too apt to behave as they did in India.* But if the Persians could be offended, so too could the British. The religious doctrine of *tekiyeh* or dissimulation together with the belief, in the much quoted words of their favourite poet Sa'adi, that 'a falsehood mixed with expediency is better than a truth which stirs up trouble' were little appreciated by the more direct British. Feelings were often wounded by Persian displays of hostility and contempt for the Christian visitor—by the spitting as he passed, the breaking of a glass defiled by his lips or the refusal of a night's lodgings. In 1822, when in Mashad, Fraser was refused admission to a public bath which he had already visited once. He was told that a *mullah* had ordered that no infidel was to be admitted again and that the stone on which he had lain after his first bath was unclean and must be removed. In Isfahan Henry Layard was given his food on a separate tray: years later he recorded that he never altogether got over the sense of humiliation at being treated as unclean and unfit to dip his fingers into the same dish with true believers. In 1895 an English visitor to the Tabriz bazaar found 'the natives so fanatical that it is impossible to obtain a cup of tea or coffee, generally even a drink of water, unless one has one's own cup to drink it out of' (12). Arrogance and contempt for the foreigner were not an exclusive British monopoly.

Among the soldier-travellers in Persia Henry Rawlinson made a unique and scholarly contribution to knowledge. He first went there in 1833 as a young officer of twenty-two with the Military Mission from India. His military duties provided him with the opportunity both to travel widely and to study the cuneiform rock inscriptions near Hamadan and Kermanshah. He made two long cross-country marches with the Kurdish troops he had trained—the first took him from Zohab in Kurdistan to Khuzistan and back to Kermanshah through unknown

---

* The French diplomat, de Gobineau, wrote from Tehran in 1857 that 'les agents anglais se considèrent ici comme ils feraient dans l'Inde ... ce n'est pas ici un moyen de réussir que de témoigner du mépris pour le peuple qui se regarde comme le premier du monde' (11).

The English Amongst the Persians

Luristan: the second, from Tabriz through the heart of Persian Kurdistan to the ruins of Takht-e-Suleiman first visited by Ker Porter, and then north-east to the shores of the Caspian. He described both journeys in long, scholarly papers, in the Journal of the Royal Geographical Society,* which honoured him with their Gold Medal for his first journey. But a far greater achievement was his deciphering of part of the trilingual rock-cut inscriptions at Bisitun: this earned him world-wide fame as the 'father of cuneiform'.

How Rawlinson's interest in the mysteries of the wedge-shaped cuneiform script was first aroused is not known. John Malcolm probably deserves the credit. He had taken Rawlinson under his wing during the long voyage—Rawlinson's first—to India in 1827 and had fascinated the young cadet with stories of Persia. After landing at Bushire Rawlinson marched with the Military Mission past Persepolis where he first saw the cuneiform inscriptions. On his way to Kermanshah a year later he made a careful copy of an inscription cut in an easily accessible rock on Mount Alvand outside Hamadan. Study of this provided him with a working alphabet of Old Persian. His next step was to copy what he could of the trilingual inscriptions, in Old Persian, Elamite and Babylonian, cut high up on the face of the great cliff of Bisitun which towered over the surrounding plain some twenty miles outside Kermanshah. So determined was Rawlinson to discover the secret of the script that he would ride out there whenever free of his military duties. There, without rope or ladder, he time and again risked his life by edging his way over the cliff face so that he could get near enough to copy the inscriptions. He was unable to get close enough to the Babylonian inscriptions but by 1837 had managed to copy most of the other two before being posted elsewhere. Before leaving Kermanshah he succeeded, by brilliant detective work and only limited access to the work of other European scholars then wrestling with the problems of cuneiform, in making a translation of the first two paragraphs of the Old Persian text. He was, however, determined to return to Bisitun to complete his work there. The opportunity came in 1843 when he left the army and, to his delight, was appointed Resident in Baghdad. From there he twice returned to Bisitun, first in 1844 and again in 1847, each time armed with ropes and ladders. But the Babylonian inscription still proved inaccessible until a wild Kurdish boy came to his aid. Enticed by the promise of a handsome reward the boy performed almost

* Vols. IX and X of 1839 and 1841. Colonel W. Monteith's *Journal of a tour through Azarbaijan and the shores of the Caspian* was the first paper on Persia published by the R.G.S. (1833. Vol. III). Thereafter papers on Persia appeared frequently in the Journal: in 1838 alone there were seven.

Some Travellers

impossible feats of climbing, 'hanging on', according to Rawlinson, 'with his toes and fingers to the slightest inequalities on the bare face of the precipice . . . passing over a distance of twenty feet of almost smooth perpendicular rock in a manner which to a looker-on appeared quite miraculous' (13) and then, by driving wooden pegs into fissures in the rock making himself, with rope and ladder, a swinging seat from which, under directions shouted at him by Rawlinson, he was able to take a paper cast or 'squeeze' of the elusive Babylonian inscription. All three inscriptions had now been faithfully copied by Rawlinson's perseverance: it was only a matter of time before he and others were able, by working on these texts with the help of the already deciphered Old Persian, to reveal the secrets of the Elamite and Babylonian language.

During his first year in Baghdad Rawlinson began what was to become a life-long friendship with Henry Layard,* soon to be acclaimed as the excavator of Nimrud and Nineveh, the two great Assyrian cities on the banks of the Tigris. Layard, like Rawlinson, had already spent some time in Persia, though in very different circumstances. His hair-raising adventures there among the Bakhtiari tribesmen read more like fiction than fact.

Bored after six years in a London solicitor's office Layard decided to seek his fortune in Ceylon, where he had relatives and the prospects of a job. In 1839, aged twenty-two, he and a friend, Edward Mitford, left London with the intention of travelling slowly overland to Ceylon and seeing all they could of the countries through which they were to pass. Layard's interest in eastern lands had been stirred by his childhood reading of the *Arabian Nights*. As he grew older he read every book about eastern travel on which he could lay hands. He had met Baillie Fraser whose romantic novels on Persian life he devoured together with the works of Morier, Malcolm, Claudius Rich and others: they filled him, to use his own words, with 'a longing to visit Persia, Babylonia, and the wild tribes of Kurdistan' (14). He started learning the Arabic script and the Persian language at an early age: once the decision had been taken to leave London Layard, though ten years younger than his companion, took the lead in planning a route that would enable them to visit as many historical sites as possible. He got in touch with the Royal Geographical Society and, with the confidence of youth, offered them his services 'in clearing up any doubtful geographical questions connected with the countries in Asia through which we intended to pass' (15). He also persuaded the Society to instruct him in the elements

---

* Sir Henry Layard, G.C.B. (1817–94). Archaeologist and diplomatist. M.P. (L) for Aylesbury 1852–7 and Southwark 1860: Under-Secretary for Foreign Affairs 1852 and 1861–6: Minister to Spain 1869–77 and Ambassador to Turkey 1877–80.

The English Amongst the Persians

of map-making and surveying; a retired sea-captain gave him lessons in the use of the sextant. The Society drew his attention to the account they had recently published of Rawlinson's journey through Kurdistan and Luristan: they also encouraged him to visit some ruins in the Bakhtiari mountains believed (incorrectly) by Rawlinson to be those of the Palace of Shushan mentioned in the Book of Daniel.

With the energy and thoroughness which he retained all his life Layard next sought medical instruction in the symptoms and treatment of the various diseases he was likely to encounter on his journey. He also secured an introduction to Sir John McNeill, the British Minister to Persia, who happened to be in London at the time. McNeill confirmed the practicability of Layard's plans and encouraged him to persevere in them in the hope that 'we might, during our journey, obtain information of use to the British Government, and of value for the elucidation of the geography of a little-known part of Asia'* (16).

Layard and Mitford travelled across Turkey and Syria to Jerusalem, when Layard went off on his own to explore Petra, Jerash and Amman. After this he and Mitford joined a caravan at Aleppo making for Mosul where Layard insisted on remaining two weeks so that he could examine the great mounds of ancient Nineveh. He and Mitford then hired a wooden raft, supported by fifty inflated goat-skins, on which they floated three hundred miles down the Tigris to Baghdad, passing more ancient mounds on the way. In Baghdad, where they spent nearly two months, Layard busied himself learning Persian and reading in the well-stocked Residency library.

Layard and Mitford left Baghdad for Persia at the end of June 1840 undaunted by the weather, which was becoming unbearably hot. They joined a large caravan 'made up of a motley company of Persians—petty traders with their wares, pilgrims with their wives and children, on their return from the holy cities of Kerbela and Kausimain . . . and a few ordinary travellers on their way home. Some rode on horses, mules, or donkeys, generally perched on the top of their baggage; others went on foot. Most of the men were armed. The women were enveloped in "chaders", or ample mantles of silk or cotton—some richly embroidered with gold or silver thread—which envelop the whole person' (17). Layard had grown a beard and wore Persian dress but neither he nor Mitford (who stuck to his western garb) made any attempt to disguise the fact that they were Europeans. As Christians they were treated with contempt and hostility by the more devout of their fellow travellers, who

* McNeill's suggestion was no more than a personal one: there is no evidence that Layard or his companion received any official encouragement from the British Government.

Some Travellers

would not even allow the two Englishmen to rest near them when the caravan halted for the day or drink from the same vessel when, tired and thirsty, villagers brought them water. Women were obliged to pull down their veils and children to run away 'as if we were infected with the plague' (18) whenever Layard or Mitford came near. As they rode through the night—it was too hot to travel by day—they could hear a *mullah* from Mashad cursing them as he chanted.

Outside Kermanshah Layard spent some time sketching the Sassanian bas-reliefs and copying the inscriptions at Taq-e-Bustan. Further on, at Bisitun, he saw the rock inscriptions but found them 'at so great a height from the ground, and so completely inaccessible, that it was impossible to make copies of them' (19). The mystery of these inscriptions and of the Assyrian mounds he had already seen in Mesopotamia increased Layard's reluctance to leave such an absorbing corner of the world until he had seen more. When, owing to difficulties in Hamadan with the Persian authorities who suspected both men as spies, Mitford decided to hurry on to Ceylon, Layard chose to remain behind. Before continuing his journey he wanted to visit Isfahan and then, as he wrote to his mother, to travel across the country 'inhabited by the Bakhtiari and Lurs, the most savage and wild races in Persia', so that he might 'reach Shusan, the "Shusan the Palace" which no European has yet visited' (20). The unknown but very real perils of such a journey in those unsettled times were clearly more an encouragement than deterrent to the adventurous and impetuous Layard.

Layard then went on alone to Isfahan where he managed to meet one of the more important Bakhtiari khans who agreed that they might travel together into the Bakhtiari mountains which lay to the west. Layard was lucky in his timing. Britain and Persia were then almost at war over Herat: British troops had seized Kharg Island. The Bakhtiaris, ever at odds with the Tehran Government, regarded any enemy of that government as a natural ally. They therefore welcomed Layard whom they almost certainly—though incorrectly—assumed to be an agent of the British Government. Layard soon got on good terms with the Bakhtiari khan, who was already familiar with British ways, having served in one of the levies trained by the British Military Mission. In late September Layard, who now adopted Bakhtiari dress and dyed his hair and beard, set off with his new-found friend on a twelve-day journey through the mountains to Qaleh-e-Tul, a fortified castle and residence of Muhammad Taqi Khan, chieftain of the Chahar Lang, one of the two branches into which the great Bakhtiari tribe was divided. There he became the guest of the powerful Bakhtiari khan whom the Persian authorities regarded as a

The English Amongst the Persians

rebel.* Layard quickly won his confidence by providing quinine, which saved the life of the khan's eldest son, aged ten, already given up for lost by the tribal medicine men. Thereafter Layard was treated as a member of the family and allowed to roam at will over the countryside. He travelled far and wide, studying archaeological sites, copying rock-cut inscriptions, taking notes on tribal organisation, exploring the possibilities of trade with India. He was robbed and on more than one occasion his life was in danger from tribesmen who thought he was a spy. Muhammad Taqi Khan† sent him on a highly secret mission to Kharg Island to enquire whether the British there would, in the event of war between Britain and Persia, accept Bakhtiari assistance: in return he wanted British protection from the vengeance of the Shah and recognition as the independent ruler of Khuzistan. Layard, by now a staunch champion of the Bakhtiari cause, got no comfort from the British. They told him that there would probably be no war between England and Persia and that he should not encourage Muhammad Taqi Khan to look to them for support.

After a fortnight on the island Layard returned to Qaleh-e-Tul. Shortly after this the Governor of Isfahan, acting on instructions from Tehran, led a military expedition against Muhammad Taqi Khan to collect arrears of tax. Layard, at great personal risk, identified himself wholeheartedly with his Bakhtiari friends in their struggle against the Governor. When the Governor demanded the surrender of the khan's young son as a hostage Layard travelled with the boy as far as Shushtar. He returned to Qaleh-e-Tul to tell the family about the boy, then rode back to Shushtar in an attempt, which failed, to arrange for his escape. Later he searched, at considerable risk, for Muhammad Taqi Khan who had gone into hiding. When the khan surrendered himself to the Governor of Isfahan Layard joined in a desperate but unsuccessful night raid to rescue him. Next he tried to help arrange for the khan's wife to be given asylum by a distant tribe but was captured and imprisoned by hostile tribesmen before he could complete his mission. He escaped during the night and fled for his life, barely eluding his pursuers. His next move was to return to Shustar to enquire about the khan's fate. He unwisely called on the Governor who was well aware of Layard's association with the Bakhtiaris and angrily burst out, 'You Englishmen are always meddling in matters which do not concern you, and interfering in the affairs of other countries' (21). Layard was ordered not to

* Rawlinson had marched against him in 1836. See p. 57.

† The khan was intriguing with the three exiled princes now back in Baghdad but wanted British support before agreeing to champion their cause against the Shah. See p. 54n.

Some Travellers

leave Shustar without the Governor's permission. Some weeks passed before Layard, with the help of money borrowed from a French friend in Isfahan, was able to escape by crossing the river to Basra in Turkish territory; he eventually reached Baghdad after more hair-raising adventures.

But Layard was not finished with Persia. His curiosity and quest for knowledge were insatiable. In October 1841 he was back in Shustar, making contact with the chief of the Haft Lang, the other great branch of the Bakhtiari tribe: he also visited his old friend, Muhammad Taqi Khan, still a prisoner bound in iron fetters, on his wrists and ankles, attached to a heavy collar round his neck. He then travelled deep into Luristan, determined to see something of the notoriously wild Feili Lurs who had murdered Grant and Fotheringham in 1810. He was at first rudely received by the Vali of Pust-e-Kuh, the Feili chieftain, who enquired 'Why have the British placed ships on the Tigris and Euphrates? . . . the English are about to take possession of our country, and they have sent this person to spy it out and to prepare for their arrival' (22). With some clever flattery Layard managed to overcome the Vali's suspicions and was allowed to leave peacefully. He returned to Baghdad early in 1842 but a few weeks later set out on the last of his Persian adventures—to test with Lieutenant Selby of the Indian Navy the navigability of the Karun river, a subject which greatly interested Layard. He believed that much could be done to develop trade with the rich Bakhtiari lands by making use of their rivers. Selby and Layard, in the steamer *Assyria*, sailed from Mohammerah to Ahwaz and over the rapids there to within seven miles of Shustar before running aground: they managed to refloat the ship and get to within a mile of the town, thus proving that steamers could be sailed far into Persia to a point where tracks led over the mountains to Isfahan. Many years would pass, however, before the Persian authorities could be persuaded to allow the British to exploit this discovery.

Layard had by now abandoned any thought of continuing his journey to Ceylon. For the next few years he concentrated on excavating the great mounds he had noticed close to the Tigris at the beginning of his travels. He never returned to Persia but was not forgotten. When Durand, the British Minister, and his wife visited Qaleh-e-Tul in 1899, nearly sixty years later, they found everyone there still talking about him. Both at the time and for many years to come the Persians were all too ready to regard Layard as a political agent sent by the British Government to stir up trouble among the Bakhtiari against the Shah.*

---

* If the Persian writer, K. M. Sassani, is to be believed Layard spent fifteen years in Persia intriguing to separate Luristan and Kurdistan from Persia!

The English Amongst the Persians

They found it difficult to believe that so young a man should have been adventuring and risking his life on his own account. Yet this is what he did, simply because he enjoyed it.

Though Layard was no agent of the British Government there were others who were. Their purpose was not to intrigue against the Shah's Government but to collect information for those charged with the defence of India. This intelligence-gathering activity falls broadly into two periods. Firstly between 1809 and 1838 when, as mentioned earlier, officers attached to the various military missions travelled widely in quest of information; secondly, from the early 'sixties onwards, when plans for the telegraph to India and alarm over the steady Russian advance in Central Asia caused the authorities in India to send officers to collect topographical information, explore routes and recruit agents to spy on the Russians. This was all part of the Great Game in which Persia was a pawn.

This second group of officers, often trained engineers attached to the Indo-European Telegraph Department or the different boundary commissions, travelled far and wide, usually accompanied by Indian surveyors. Others, when taking leave from India, were encouraged to travel through Persia, particularly along the northern frontier. They recorded in their notebooks such details as the location of wells, the availability of fodder, and the suitability of routes for the transport of guns. Under cover as Assistant Commissioner on the Perso-Afghan Boundary Commission an officer was employed on 'special service' on the Khorasan frontier, where he was expected to report every move of the Russians—a lonely life which drove one man almost to despair.*

Little attempt was made to hide the activities of these men from the Persians, who often provided military escorts for them when travelling in the remoter areas. The Assistant Commissioner on the Khorasan frontier joined the Shah when he toured the frontier. A number of them wrote articles for the Journal of the Royal Geographical Society or books about their travels for all to read. They also wrote long and very detailed secret reports for the Intelligence Branch in India. These, together with information from consuls and other sources, formed the basis of the Survey of India's maps of Persia. They also provided the raw material for massive tomes, known as Gazetteers. Marked 'Secret' or 'For official use only', these Gazetteers were a remarkable series which embraced

---

* Major Charles Stewart who, when applying for leave in 1884, wrote that he dreaded 'passing another year of utter loneliness without speaking to a civilised being'. He later served as Consul at Rasht, Mashad and Tabriz, and wrote *Through Persia in Disguise.*

Some Travellers

much of India and her borderlands.* Designed originally to provide detailed factual information that would be useful to military commanders, their scope was extended by Lord Curzon who, when Viceroy, called for a *Gazetteer of the Persian Gulf* that would also be useful to political officers in the area.

There was at this time one British traveller more interested in the Persians as people than in their country's topography and monuments. He was Edward Granville Browne—the future Professor E. G. Browne of Cambridge—who in due course won the esteem and affection of the Persians as no other Englishman had ever done.

Browne's interest in the East had first been stirred by the 1877-8 war between Turkey and Russia when he was still a schoolboy at Eton. His ambition was to help the Turks by becoming an officer in their army and he started learning Turkish for this purpose. But the war came to an end, so instead of joining the army he went to Cambridge to read medicine. However by now his interest in oriental languages was such that he decided to study them as well—Arabic, Persian and Hindustani in addition to Turkish. He gave early evidence of his genius by securing First Class Honours in the oriental language Tripos and shortly afterwards qualified as a doctor. While working at St Bartholomew's Hospital in 1887 Browne was overjoyed to be offered a Fellowship by his old college, Pembroke. He therefore abandoned medicine in favour of oriental languages and decided to spend a year in Persia—the home of Sufi mysticism in which he had become deeply interested—before taking up the Fellowship which was to keep him in Cambridge for the rest of his life.

Browne was twenty-six when he reached Persia in November 1887, having travelled out from England by the Black Sea route to Trebizond and Tabriz. He moved on to Tehran and then to Isfahan and Shiraz before spending his last few months in Yazd and Kerman. He travelled light, with only one servant, and was always ready to fall in with such company as he met on the way. Already equipped with a rare knowledge of Persian he lost no opportunity as he travelled of probing the inner thoughts of those whom he met. The book he wrote on his return to England, *A Year Amongst the Persians*, is unlike any other travel book about Persia for the insight it gives into Persian thinking. Browne does this by vivid accounts of metaphysical and theological conversations

---

* The *Gazetteer of Persia* was first published about 1870: revised editions were issued from time to time. The *Gazetteer of Kermanshah* (1907) was compiled by H. L. Rabino. J. G. Lorimer's masterpiece, The *Gazetteer of the Persian Gulf, Oman and Central Arabia* (1908 and 1915) ran to nearly 5,000 pages, a mine of historical and geographical information.

The English Amongst the Persians

with a wide variety of Persians—Moslems, Zoroastrians and Babis—of all classes. Dennison Ross, himself a great orientalist, described *A Year Amongst the Persians* as 'one of the world's most fascinating and instructive books of travel. . . . It is, however, more than a mere record of travel and goes beyond the ordinary limits of such works, for apart from its lively and entrancing descriptions of Persia and its people, it is an infallible guide to modern Persian literature and thought, and as such should always find its place on the student's bookshelf beside the author's monumental *Literary History of Persia*' (23).

Browne returned to Cambridge in October 1888. He never went back to Persia, but his year there had filled him with an undying love for the country and its people—'he so loved his Persians', Ross wrote, 'that he forgave everything, and only stayed to praise and admire' (24). To those who criticised the Persians for their many alleged vices Browne replied 'these vices are undeniably common amongst the creatures of the Court, with whom Europeans having official positions in Persia come most in contact, but few who have mixed on intimate terms with all classes of the people, and especially the middle class, will assert that these vices are general, or will deny that where they exist they are largely the outcome of the intolerable system of government' (25).

Persian admiration for Browne was slower in coming, but when it came it was unbounded. At first they disliked—as they still do—his sympathetic interest in the persecuted Babi sect about which he had much to say both in *A Year Amongst the Persians* and in various later publications. Persian awareness that in Browne they had a staunch champion dates from his defence of the Constitutionalists' revolt against Muzaffar ed-Din Shah in 1906. From then onwards Browne, despite his heavy academic work, was tireless both as a lecturer and writer of pamphlets and newspaper articles in defence of the reform movement in Persia. He deplored the Anglo-Russian Convention of 1907 dividing Persia into spheres of influence and bitterly denounced Russian activities in Tehran and Tabriz: he also played a leading part in forming the London Persia Committee* which included influential members of both Houses of Parliament and aimed to promote better Anglo-Persian understanding. Browne's book *The Persian Revolution of 1905–1909*, published in 1910, was an outspoken attempt to explain Persia's problems, caught as she was in Big Power rivalry. Here at last was an Englishman who saw things as Persians saw them. The Persians took Browne to their hearts, less perhaps as a scholar (though he was the

---

* H. F. B. Lynch (1862–1913), a strong supporter of Persian causes, was a co-founder. Son of T. K. Lynch, the founder of Lynch Bros.: M.P. (L) for Ripon 1906–10: author of *Armenia: Travels and Studies*.

Some Travellers

greatest Persian scholar of his time) than as a political friend. When he was sixty a touching illuminated address was sent to him by his Persian admirers, among them three former prime ministers, who expressed their 'gratitude for the labours which you have undertaken for us and for our country, whereby you have made the Persian nation your eternal debtor' (26). In 1966, on the fortieth anniversary of his death, he was still remembered by old friends and admirers who organised a service in Tehran in his memory.

A year after Browne's departure from Persia George Curzon, then a thirty-year-old Member of Parliament for Southport, arrived there. Every inch an aristocrat, he had the finely chiselled features of a Roman patrician and the haughty bearing associated with his class. He had taken the unusual route of crossing the Caspian by ship from Baku to Uzun Ada on the eastern shore: from there he travelled 300 miles on the newly-opened Transcaspian railway to Ashkhabad in Turkoman country before making his way across the border to Kuchan in northern Khorasan. Then, after being denied permission to enter the great natural border fortress of Kalat-e-Naderi, he made for Mashad.

Although commissioned by *The Times* to write a series of twelve articles at £12.10.0. a piece on Persia, Curzon's main purpose was to collect material for a book of his own. To this end, though he rarely left the beaten track, he spent nearly six months travelling from Mashad to Tehran and then south to Bushire by way of Kashan, Isfahan and Shiraz. He then steamed up the Karun from Mohammerah to Shustar before returning home to write *Persia and the Persian Question*. Curzon devoted nearly two years of concentrated effort to this remarkable, detailed study of Qajar Persia.

Curzon's interest in the East had been awakened by a chance lecture he had attended while still a schoolboy at Eton. After leaving Oxford he embarked on a succession of journeys which took him to Egypt, Turkey, India and Russia (including the newly-conquered khanates of Central Asia) as well as the Far East and North America. Long before he reached Persia in September 1889 he ardently believed in the civilising virtues of the British Empire: by the time he left he was convinced that 'the preservation, so far as is still possible, of the integrity of Persia must be registered as a cardinal precept of our Imperial creed' (27). This conviction was to remain with him all his life: so too his belief that Russian ambitions in Persia were a threat to the British position in India, the Empire's most precious possession.

In contrast to the splendour associated with his name, Curzon travelled alone and without a servant. Where he could he used the *chapar* service, riding in all weathers up to sixty miles a day from one dirty *chaparkhaneh* to another. There at the end of a tiring day, in pain from the steel brace that spinal trouble caused him to wear, he would cook his own supper. The preserved foods he had chosen with such meticulous care before leaving London stood him in good stead. He wrote from personal experience when he recommended Crosse and Blackwell's tinned soups as 'quite excellent, and, besides being easily prepared, are almost a meal in themselves. Soup in tablets or powders are good in their own way and economise space, but require more trouble and time in cooking. Sardines, potted meats, chocolate or cocoa, Liebig's beef tea, and tea or coffee, are useful adjuncts, which should be procured in Europe' (28).

Although Curzon's interest in Persia was essentially political he was also captured by the country's beauty and antiquity. His biographer, Harold Nicolson,* believed that his mind, like that of others who have lived and travelled in Persia, was 'for ever haunted by those plains of amber, those peaks of amethyst, the dignity of that crumbled magnificence, that silence of two thousand years' (29). Curzon, the romantic, never quite got Persia out of his system: had he done so he might have pressed less hard for an Anglo-Persian Treaty in 1919 at the end of the Great War and so avoided what Nicolson considered the 'most galling, because the most personal, of his many diplomatic defeats' (30).

Curzon left Persia in January 1890, sailing for three days up the Tigris to Baghdad in one of the Lynch steamers. Among his fellow passengers were the Rev. Robert Bruce of the C.M.S. Mission in Isfahan, Major Herbert Sawyer of the Indian Army and Mrs Isabella Bishop (*née* Bird) from Scotland. The last two had travelled together from Karachi and made an incongruous pair. The Major, aged thirty-eight, was tall and exceptionally handsome: Mrs Bishop, cousin of Mary Bird, the C.M.S. missionary, was short, dumpy and plain, and in her fifty-ninth year. Curzon must have been intrigued to know more about them.

Sawyer was attached to the Intelligence Branch of the Quartermaster's Department in India and was under instructions to make a military reconnaissance of the Zagros Mountains, the home of the Bakhtiari and Lur tribes. British interest in the region had greatly increased since Layard's day, particularly after the opening up of the Karun river. Sawyer had met Mrs Bishop in Simla shortly before leaving on his mission and had agreed that she might travel with him. Apart from doing a good turn by providing a lady with some protection in

---

* Sir Harold Nicolson, K.C.V.O. (1886–1968). Author and critic. He knew Curzon, having served under him at the Paris Peace Conference: he also knew Persia where he was born and served as Counsellor at the British Legation, 1925–7.

Some Travellers

lawless country Sawyer was probably glad of her company, having lost his wife a few months previously.

As for Mrs Bishop, few would have guessed from her age and diminutive stature that she had recently spent several months travelling alone on mule and yak in western Tibet or that she had undertaken a number of other arduous journeys in different parts of the world—Australia and New Zealand, the Sandwich Isles, Hawaii, the Rockies, Malaya, Japan and Egypt. The curious would have been even more surprised to learn that until she was forty Miss Isabella Bird (as she then was) had been a semi-invalid, unable to rise before midday, devoting herself to good works and writing articles for respectable journals. The quest for good health started her late in life on the travels which, once begun, continued until the end of her days. Between travels Isabella returned to the Isle of Mull where she and her sister, to whom she was devoted, shared a cottage. When her sister died Isabella at long last accepted the hand of Dr John Bishop, ten years younger and her suitor for many years. She was then almost fifty. Five years later her beloved John died, leaving Isabella grief-stricken and lonely once again. She sought consolation in foreign travel with the object of visiting Christian mission stations in different parts of the world and in January 1889 sailed for India. First she went to Kashmir where she founded a missionary hospital, the first of several she was to establish in various parts of the East to her husband's and her sister's memory. From Kashmir Isabella rode over high passes into Western Tibet where she spent some time before returning in the autumn to Simla. After meeting Major Sawyer she decided, instead of returning home, to travel with him to Persia. Thus it was that she embarked on the most arduous of all her journeys.

When their steamer reached Baghdad Isabella and Sawyer quickly made arrangements for the first stage of their journey which would take them over the Zagros mountains to Kermanshah and then across the bleak plateau to Tehran over three hundred miles away. Isabella had already engaged a servant in Bushire: she now hired five mules, two of them for riding. Wearing a cork sun-helmet and a warm jacket over her 'American mountain dress' she left Baghdad with the Major on 10 January 1890. At first they rode through rain and mud but winter had set in and soon, as they climbed the Zagros, they encountered intense cold. Camping was impossible: each night after struggling through snow and bitter winds they dossed down in caravansarais crowded with humanity and animals and usually 'deep with the manure of ages' (31) or smoke-filled Kurdish huts 'with a fire of cow-dung in the middle of the floor, and men, mules, horses, asses, cows, and poultry all together' (32). By the time they reached Kermanshah Isabella was ready to admit that she would never have undertaken the journey had she known of 'the long marches, the wretched food, the abominable accommodation, the filthy water, the brutal barbarism of the people' (33). But there was no thought of turning back and they ploughed on through snow and mud. When they reached Tehran poor Isabella was at the end of her tether. Her vivid description of their arrival at the Legation deserves to be quoted in full:

> Just as endurance was on the point of giving way, we turned from the road through a large gateway into the extensive grounds which surround the British Legation, a large building forming three sides of a quadrangle, with a fine stone staircase leading up to the central door. Every window was lighted, light streamed from the open door, splashed carriages were dashing up and setting down people in evening dress, there were crowds of servants about, and it flashed on my dazzled senses that it must be after eight, and that there was a dinner party!
>
> Arriving from the mud of the Kavir and the slush of the streets, after riding ten hours in ceaseless rain on a worn-out horse; caked with mud from head to foot, dripping, exhausted, nearly blind from fatigue, fresh from mud hovels and the congenial barbarism of the desert, and with the rags and travel-stains of a winter journey of forty-six days upon me, light and festivity were over-whelming.
>
> Alighting at a side door, scarcely able to stand, I sat down in a long corridor, and heard from an English steward that 'dinner is waiting'. His voice sounded very far off, and the once familiar announcement came like a memory out of the remote past. Presently a gentleman appeared in evening dress, wearing a star, which conveyed to my fast-failing senses that it was Sir H. Drummond Wolff. It was true that there was a large dinner party, and among the guests the Minister with thoughtful kindness had invited all to whom I had letters of introduction. But it was no longer possible to make any effort, and I was taken up to a room in which the comforts of English civilisation at first made no impression upon me, and removing only the mackintosh cloak, weighted with mud, which had served me so well, I lay down on the hearth-rug before a great coal fire till four o'clock the next morning (34).

Three weeks rest under Drummond Wolff's hospitable roof restored Isabella's strength and spirits and in mid-March she was again on the move. This time, except for an interpreter and a cook, she rode alone to Isfahan, where she had arranged to meet Sawyer for the second leg of their planned journey. Where possible she stayed at the telegraph

Some Travellers

stations along her route. Spring was now in the air and she thoroughly enjoyed the exhilarating freedom of the desert. She stayed nearly a month with the missionaries in Julfa, preparing for her journey across the Bakhtiari mountains with Sawyer. They had agreed that Isabella should make her own arrangements and travel more or less independently while camping each night within the ring of Sawyer's sentries. She hired a horse for herself and four pack mules for her tents and provisions. Meanwhile the handsome Major was a big hit among the Europeans of Julfa causing, in Isabella's words, 'an immense sensation in this minute community, which vegetates in superlative stagnation. His splendid appearance, force of character, wit, brutal frankness, ability, and kind-heartedness, make a great breeze, and I hear his sayings and doings are the one topic' (35).

On 30 April 1890 Isabella and Sawyer rode out of Julfa for the Bakhtiari mountains where they spent the next three months. This time the weather was no problem: much of the journey was over upland meadows dotted with the black goat-hair tents of the Bakhtiaris, set against 'mountains with long, straight summits, mountains snow-covered and snow-slashed, great spires of naked rock, huge ranges buttressed by huge spurs herbage-covered, with outcrops of barren rock' (36). These mountains had to be crossed and provided Isabella with some terrifying moments as, dizzily, she zigzagged her way up and down one rocky cliff-face after another. At times she was forced to dismount and lead her horse: at other times it slithered under her trying to gain a hold on rocks worn smooth by generations of nomads and their flocks. In places the track was so narrow that the horse could not place its two feet alongside each-other: a slip often meant instant death far below.

Isabella, with her well-stocked Burroughs and Wellcome medicine chest, was much in demand as a *hakim* or doctor: sometimes she had to cope with as many as two hundred Bakhtiari men and women in a day, performing minor operations and cleaning sores as well as dispensing pills and powders. She also proved a useful assistant to Sawyer when his Indian surveyor fell ill. They reached Burujird on the far side of the mountains on 9 August, having covered much ground without mishap apart from being robbed. They had managed to remain good friends though Isabella found some of the Major's ways irritating, particularly the over-bearing manner with which he treated the Persians. At Burujird they parted company, Sawyer to return to India, where his maps and report won high praise: Isabella to spend three weeks laid up with fever in Hamadan before another three months of strenuous travel on her own across more high mountain passes through Kurdistan to Lake Van:

The English Amongst the Persians

then on to Erzerum and down the old caravan route to Trebizond where, now in her sixtieth year, she took ship for Constantinople in mid-December.

As soon as she was back in Scotland Isabella prepared her travel journal for publication by John Murray. This appeared in two volumes before the year was out and showed her to be a shrewd observer with strong views of her own. Unlike Layard she was not bewitched by the Bakhtiaris or their nomadic way of life with 'its total lack of privacy, its rough brutality, its dirt, its undisguised greed, its unconcealed jealousies and hatreds, its falseness, its pure selfishness, and its treachery' (37). She distrusted the professed Bakhtiari friendliness for the English and surmised that their favours would always be sold to the highest bidder.* On the other hand she confessed that her early impression of Persian 'effeteness and ruin' was perhaps wrong. Having learnt something of their 'vitality, energy and industry . . . and of the capacities of her prolific soil, I have come to regard her resurrection under certain circumstances as a possibility' (39). Curzon, too, had returned home with some hope for Persia's future. He concluded his 1300-page 2 Vol. book on Persia with a ringing sentence:

> Remote and backward and infirm Persia at present is; but, for all its remoteness and backwardness and present debility, I hope I have shown it to be a country that should excite the liveliest sympathies of Englishmen; with whose Government our own Government should be upon terms of intimate alliance; and in the shaping for which of a future that shall be not unworthy of its splendid past the British nation have it in their power to take a highly honourable lead (40).

---

* Ex-Queen Soraya, herself the daughter of a minor Bakhtiari khan, states in her autobiography that because the A.P.O.C. would not increase the oil royalties paid to the khans 'many Bakhtiari became so hostile to England that in the first World War they were on the side of the Kaiser' (38).

12

World War I and the End of an Era

NOTWITHSTANDING PERSIA'S DECLARATION of neutrality when Turkey entered the Great War on Germany's side in November 1914, British, Russian and Turkish military forces were soon engaged in operations of one sort or another on her soil.* As the war progressed all three Powers became increasingly involved in Persia. When the last British troops were withdrawn in the spring of 1921 nearly 3,600 dead were left behind, most of them Indians. They also left scars; for no country likes to be under foreign occupation, no matter what blessings in terms of law and order the occupier may bring.

In British eyes Persia was, as she had been for more than a century, an outer bastion in the defence of India; additionally her oilfields and the refinery at Abadan were of vital importance for the Royal Navy. For the British, therefore, the protection of those interests was a matter of paramount importance. The Persians saw things very differently. Their sympathies lay heavily with Germany because she was fighting Russia, their old and detested enemy. As Russia's ally, Britain, already widely distrusted because of her 1907 deal with Russia, was also an enemy. The fact that Turkey, a Moslem power, was on Germany's side increased Persian sympathy for the Central Powers. Early German successes on the western and Russian fronts encouraged pro-German sentiment in Persia, not least among the Swedish officers in command of the 7,000-strong Persian Gendarmerie. This force, established in

* When war broke out British troops in Persia consisted of about 180 infantry and *sowar* guards at Bushire in addition to the much smaller Legation, Consular and Telegraph guards elsewhere. Several thousand Russian troops were in virtual occupation of Tabriz, Mashad and other parts of north Persia. Turkish troops entered Persia in November 1914 in order to frustrate Russian plans to invade Turkey from Persian territory. They captured Tabriz from the Russians in January 1915.

171

1911 to preserve law and order in south Persia, became an instrument which was turned against the British in their own sphere of influence.

In these circumstances the opportunities for German intrigue and propaganda were considerable. Some two hundred German agents, liberally provided with funds, wireless sets and hostile tracts, entered the country in early 1915 and found fertile ground on which to whip up anti-British feeling. The British could expect no help from a weak and largely hostile Persian Government which showed no inclination to treat German activities as unneutral. To be understood, British intervention in Persia during the 1914 War must be seen against this background.

From the outset the British Government were determined to defend their vital interests at the head of the Persian Gulf. To this end a small force sailed from India and in November 1914, after landing a party to protect the Abadan refinery, captured Fao and Basra from the Turks. In late January 1915, after Turkish troops and Arab tribesmen from Mesopotamia had invaded Khuzistan as a prelude to marching on Ahwaz and the oilfields, an Indian battalion together with thirty men of the Dorsetshire Regiment sailed up the Karun from Basra to defend Ahwaz and restore morale among the Arab tribes in the area. The Shaikh of Mohammerah, who proved a staunch friend of the British throughout the war, feared for the loyalty of these tribes unless the British acted quickly. Reinforcements followed. Despite these moves, Arabs in Turkish pay succeeded in cutting the oil pipe line in a number of places and putting it out of action for over three months. The Turks advanced to within twenty-four miles of Ahwaz. British-Indian troops, now over 12,000 strong, went into action in March and May 1915. They drove the Turks and their Arab allies out of Khuzistan: for the remainder of the war Khuzistan, with its oilfields and refinery, remained trouble-free, thanks to the presence there of British troops and the support of the Shaikh of Mohammerah and some of the Bakhtiari khans.

Although the Persian Government had acquiesced in the despatch of troops to Ahwaz they objected strongly to high-handed British action at this time in arresting and deporting the German Consul at Bushire. The British also arrested another German, Herr Wassmuss, a former consul at Bushire, together with two Indian nationalists discovered near Shustar but Wassmuss managed to escape and for the rest of the war was a thorn in British flesh.

Wassmuss' exploits deservedly won him fame as the 'German Lawrence'. His first success was to stimulate the Tangistani tribesmen of the coastal strip to attack the Residency at Bushire, the symbol of

World War I and the End of an Era

British power in the Persian Gulf. Although their attacks on 12 and 13 July 1915 were driven off, two British officers were killed in an ambush and British prestige suffered a hard knock. Retribution followed. At the beginning of August British forces, after seizing the port and town of Bushire, took over its administration: the Union Jack replaced the Persian flag. A few days later a punitive expedition destroyed, at the cost of many lives on both sides, the Tangistani headquarters about twenty miles along the coast from Bushire. However, these were no more than Pyrrhic victories. Tangistani hostility and a further attack by them on Bushire in September necessitated the retention there of forces desperately needed elsewhere: also hostile propaganda made much play of the British military occupation of Bushire.*

About this same time parties of Germans,† accompanied by armed Persian followers, were moving across Persia towards Afghanistan and Baluchistan by way of Kerman, Tabas and Birjand—their objective being to incite the tribes against the British and encourage an Afghan invasion of India. To foil these plans the British and Russians decided to seal off Persia's eastern frontier by establishing what became known as the East Persia Cordon. British-Indian forces entered Persian Baluchistan and Sistan: they occupied a line running north from Nushki in British Baluchistan through Birjand to Qain where the Russians took over.‡ To assist in manning the six-hundred-mile British stretch of the cordon the consuls in Mashad and Sistan raised local levies of Hazaras§ and Sistanis who were then trained by British officers and Indian N.C.O.s. The consul in Mashad was also much occupied in rounding up escaped Austrian and German prisoners of war from Transcaspia. For this purpose he made use of friendly Hazaras and his own Indian *sowars*. The prisoners, when caught, were handed over to the Russian consul for return to Russia, despite strong Persian protests about this infringement of their neutrality.

* Bushire was formally returned to Persian control on 18 October 1915 on the appointment of a new Governor.

† One of them, Niedermeyer, succeeded in reaching Kabul in 1915: another, Zugmayer, penetrated British Baluchistan: others stirred up trouble in Makran. They and their colleagues were assisted by Austrian and German prisoners of war escaped from Russia, Turks, deserters from the Indian Army, and locally recruited Persian levies.

‡ The cordon was extended in March 1916 when a small military mission was sent to Makran, where two British officers had been murdered. Brigadier-General R. E. Dyer, later to achieve notoriety at Amritsar, commanded the British sector of the cordon during most of 1916.

§ Shi'i refugees of Mongolian origin from Afghanistan, many of whom had served in the Indian Army. They tended to look to the British for protection.

173

The English Amongst the Persians

The East Persia Cordon could do little to check German activities within Persia. Wassmuss, after his success at Bushire, had gone to Shiraz, where he established fruitful contact with the Governor-General, the powerful Qashqai khans and Swedish officers of the Persian Gendarmerie. As a result of his intrigues and encouragement the British Vice-Consul, an Indian, was shot and killed in a Shiraz street in September 1915. A month later the head consular clerk and one of the *gholams* accompanying him were attacked, the former being wounded and the latter killed. The final humiliation came in early November when the German-inspired 'National Committee for the Protection of Persian Independence' issued an ultimatum calling for the surrender of the British Consul-General, O'Connor, together with all members of the British colony. The Consulate building was surrounded by heavily armed parties of the Gendarmerie and telegraph wires were cut. O'Connor had little choice than to surrender. He and his small community—eleven in all, among them the wife and daughter of the Manager of the Imperial Bank and two other ladies—were rounded up and escorted to the coast. The women were set free in Bushire but the men were kept prisoner for the next seven months at the headquarters of one of the Tangistani chiefs, barely thirty miles from Bushire. They were not badly treated but suffered much from the heat: one of them died in captivity.

German and Turkish successes were such that in the course of 1915 British consuls and communities were obliged to go through the humiliating business of withdrawing from one town after another—from Kermanshah, Hamadan, Sultanabad, Isfahan (where the British Consul had been wounded in an attempt on his life and one of his *sowar* escort killed), Yazd and Kerman. The Germans and their Persian friends occupied the telegraph stations and looted the branches of the Imperial Bank.

By the end of the year the situation had deteriorated so badly that the British, in agreement with the Russians, decided on drastic action whether the Persians liked it or not. Sykes, who had returned home in 1913 and been posted to Chinese Turkestan after seven years at the Mashad Consulate, was instructed to return to Persia as head of a Mission with the object, in Sykes' words, of 'raising a Persian force, 11,000 strong, to take the place of the gendarmerie. . . . The object of the Mission was to create a force for the restoration of law and order in the interests of the Persian and British Governments' (1). He might have added that the restoration of British prestige was also a major objective. Similarly the Russians were to increase the strength of the Persian Cossack Brigade which they officered in the north. Britain and

World War I and the End of an Era

Russia were to equip and maintain these forces for the duration of the war and, by way of a sop, pay the Persian Government an annual subsidy of 200,000 tomans (£65,000). The weak and impoverished Persian Government had no alternative than to accept this Anglo-Russian decision which was greeted by an angry outburst of criticism from Persian Democrats and Nationalists. The fact that the South Persia Rifles, or S.P.R. as the force which Sykes* raised came to be called, might introduce some law and order into south Persia mattered little to Persians who were sick of foreign interference in their country's affairs and, in any case, had no wish for a British victory in the war.

Sykes landed at Bandar Abbas in March 1916, accompanied by six officers, three of them Indian, twenty Indian N.C.O.s and a *sowar* escort. He immediately started recruiting, the promise of regular pay being an attraction to many. In May, accompanied by some of his recruits and a stiffening of British-Indian troops, Sykes led his little army inland by stages to Kerman, Yazd, Isfahan and Shiraz—an arduous but rewarding march of over a thousand miles, mostly over treeless country under a torrid sun. German agents in their path were rounded up or fled: evacuated British communities were able to return and the Imperial Bank to reopen its branches: recruits were enlisted and a depot established at Kerman where Sykes was already well known.

Before leaving Bandar Abbas Sykes had supplied the friendly head of the Khamseh tribal confederation† with arms and ammunition which were used to good purpose in defeating hostile tribesmen and capturing some sixty Germans and Austrians together with a number of Turks and Indian Army deserters.

Sykes reached Shiraz, which became the S.P.R.'s headquarters, in November 1916. Life was not easy for him.‡ He had trouble in trying to absorb the disaffected gendarmerie. The Qashqai and other tribes, who controlled much of Fars, were hostile and working closely with

---

* As far back as 1905 Sykes had advocated the formation of a mounted force in south Persia under British officers as the only way of terminating 'the present state of chronic insecurity' (2). The S.P.R. eventually totalled about 8,000 officers and men of whom approximately 6,000 were Persians and 2,000 British and Indian.

† Qavam ul-Mulk, who had taken *bast* in the Shiraz Consulate in 1911, became as pro-British as his deadly enemies, the Qashqais, became pro-German. Shortly afterwards he fell from his horse and was killed. His son, who succeeded to the title, also supported the British from whom he received a regular subsidy during the war.

‡ Sykes got some support from the new Governor-General in Shiraz, Abdol Hossein *Mirza*, Farman Farma, an old friend from Kerman and grandson of Abbas *Mirza*. Farman Farma was distrusted by many Persians as a protégé of the British who, between 1916–19, paid him a regular subsidy, partly to defray costs of local administration, partly on personal account. He was the father of 36 gifted sons and daughters, many of whom have made a mark in post-Qajar Persia.

The English Amongst the Persians

Wassmuss; they encouraged desertions from the S.P.R. and for the rest of the war denied the British the use of the important Bushire–Shiraz road. The Persian Government, despite heavy pressure from the British Legation, refused to recognise the S.P.R. as a Persian force. Instead, in April 1918, they denounced it as a foreign body and a menace to Persian independence. Their demand for its withdrawal from Persian soil sparked off smouldering anti-British feeling in Fars. In May the chief of the Qashqais issued a proclamation of war, apparently with the backing of the Persian Government, against 'the army of the S.P.R. that is unauthorised by the Persian Government' (3). That same month an S.P.R. garrison outside Shiraz mutinied and murdered their two British officers: in July the larger garrison at Abadeh, on the road to Isfahan, also mutinied, killing one British and two Persian officers. An increasing number of deserters went over to the Qashqais or other hostile tribes: if caught they were summarily executed by the British— on one occasion, at least, without trial. *Mullahs* incited their followers against those serving with the S.P.R., Persian and British alike.

Throughout the summer of 1918 the situation in Fars remained critical for the British, particularly when some 6,000 Qashqais and their allies invested the main core of Sykes' reserve in their Shiraz cantonment. Although Sykes took the offensive it was not until October, after a number of sharp encounters, that he finally broke the back of the Qashqais who were adepts at guerilla warfare. Casualties, though heavy on both sides, were light compared with the hundreds—Persian, British and Indian—who died in a terrible influenza epidemic that swept Persia that autumn and winter.

Following the defeat of the Qashqais and their allies British forces based on Bushire and Shiraz were able to open up the Bushire–Shiraz caravan route. British army engineers then did much to improve the old route: new alignments were cut over the high passes so that, for the first time, in February 1919 a motor vehicle travelled over it. Also, in response to an appeal for help from the Bakhtiari Governor-General of Isfahan, 600 men of the S.P.R. under the command of Colonel W. A. K. Fraser* moved north and joined with a Bakhtiari force in routing a large band of plundering brigands who had caused much trouble in that province.

Meanwhile the Russian Revolution in March 1917 and subsequent

---

* Major-General W. A. K. Fraser, C.B., etc. (1887–1969). First went to Persia with the Central Indian Horse 1911–12: served there again from 1917–21 with the S.P.R.. and twice as Military Attaché in Tehran, 1924–8 and 1941–5. Became a well-known figure in Persia. The American writer, D. N. Wilber, in his *Riza Shah Pahlavi*, confuses him with the late Sir William Fraser (Lord Strathalmond), chairman of the A.P.O.C.

World War I and the End of an Era

collapse of the Russian army had greatly increased British difficulties. The new Soviet Russia was looked upon as a friend by the Persians who now concentrated their hatred of Czarist Russia on the British occupiers of their country.* The withdrawal of Russian forces from north Persia and the advance of the Turks in the Caucasus opened the route to Afghanistan and India. The Germans, who had entered the Ukraine, planned to organise an army for the invasion of India from the thousands of Austrian and German prisoners of war now freed in Transcaspia. The British felt compelled to react by despatching more troops into Persia.

Indian troops took over the Russian sector of the East Persia Cordon, their commander, Major-General Wilfred Malleson, establishing his headquarters in Mashad during the summer of 1918. Earlier, in January 1918, Major-General L. C. Dunsterville, the original of Kipling's 'Stalky', had been sent from Baghdad to make a dash by way of the Caspian for Baku and Tiflis. The objective was to stiffen local resistance among the Georgians and Armenians against the Turks and deny the Baku oilfields to the enemy. Dunsterville and his advance party, in forty-one Ford cars, travelled via Kermanshah, Hamadan and Qazvin.† But they got no further than Enzeli where Persian Jangalis‡ aided by Russian Bolsheviks forced them to retreat. Dunsterville then established his headquarters at Hamadan, moving later to Qazvin. An attempt to reach Tabriz stalled at Mianeh owing to stiff Turkish opposition. Thereafter, with the help of Assyrian and other levies raised locally, Dunsterforce concentrated on watching the Turkish flank in Azarbaijan and northern Kurdistan; and on keeping the road to Baghdad open. In July 1918, after some hesitation, Dunsterville decided to make another attempt to reach Baku. After defeating the Jangalis outside Rasht and relieving the besieged British Consulate there he sailed from Enzeli on 16 August with a small party in a White Russian ship under the command of a British Naval officer.§ But, though he received

---

* The Bolsheviks wooed the Persians by voluntarily surrendering privileges and concessions acquired by Czarist Russia in Persia: they embarrassed the British by publishing the secret Anglo-Russian Agreement of 1915 whereby Britain was to incorporate the Persian Neutral Zone into her sphere of influence after the war.

† This was the only route open. Dunsterville optimistically expected to reach Tiflis in twelve days from Baghdad.

‡ An extreme nationalist group operating in the Caspian forests, or *jangal*, under the leadership of Kuchek Khan. They aimed to rid Persia of all foreign influence.

§ Commodore D. T. Norris who had been sent to Enzeli in August 1918 with a naval party to take control of Caspian shipping. By October 1918 British naval officers commanded five small armed ships, flying the Czarist naval ensign, manned by Russian and British crews. The British Naval Mission was withdrawn in September 1919.

The English Amongst the Persians

reinforcements, Turkish attacks soon forced him to withdraw from Baku with considerable loss of life and face. By late September Dunsterville was back in Qazvin. Though he himself was posted elsewhere British troops—renamed Norperforce—remained, based on Qazvin, until the spring of 1921. Their main function, once the Turks had dropped out of the war, was to prevent Bolshevik* and Jangali forces marching on Tehran from the north. Additionally they were needed, in the revealing words of a War Office telegram from London, 'to support our Minister's policy at Tehran and to induce the Persian Government to subserve British interests' (4).

The presence of large numbers of British and Indian forces on Persian soil at this period aroused strong nationalist feelings. The execution of S.P.R. deserters: the arrest and deportation by the British of political agitators: the summary removal from office of unfriendly officials: and the pressure brought on the Shah to appoint anglophil ministers in Tehran were bitterly resented. Rumours that the British were responsible for the high cost of food and for starving the Persian people were readily believed despite sincere efforts to provide relief from a cruel famine which ravaged the country. Persian pride was hurt and the British blamed (with good reason) for the refusal of the Allies to give the Persians a hearing at the Paris Peace Conference.

Curzon could hardly have chosen a more unfavourable moment in which to launch a cherished scheme for the regeneration of Persia under British tutelage. By 1919 he was in charge of the Foreign Office and thus able to pursue his dream of protecting the approaches to India with a chain of vassal states stretching from the Mediterranean to the Pamirs. He saw Persia as a vital link in this chain and on 9 August 1919, after protracted secret negotiations, an Anglo-Persian Agreement designated as 'making provision for British Assistance in promoting the progress and prosperity of Persia' was signed in Tehran. The agreement gave the British a free hand, to the virtual exclusion of others, in the affairs of Persia. They were to lend such expert advisers as were required, supply munitions and equipment for a national army to be trained by British officers, provide a £2 million loan for necessary reforms, revise the Customs tariff and help survey and build railways. Curzon explained to his Cabinet colleagues that the agreement was necessary in order to prevent Persia, lying as she did between the newly-acquired British Mandate for Mesopotamia and India, from being over-run by the

---

* By early 1920 Bolshevik forces controlled much of the Caspian coast, where they were contained by Persian Cossacks commanded by a Russian officer, Colonel Starosselsky.

World War I and the End of an Era

Bolsheviks or from becoming 'a hotbed of misrule, enemy intrigue, financial chaos, and political disorder' (5).

The Agreement soon came under fire not only in Persia but also in France, America and Russia, where the secrecy with which it had been negotiated and the dominant position it gave the British were much criticised. For the Persians it meant a further tightening of the British stranglehold: in their eyes foreign tutelage and national independence were incompatible. The triumvirate of high-born Persian Ministers* with whom Curzon and Cox, the British Minister in Tehran, had negotiated the Agreement were unrepresentative of their country and widely distrusted as British protégés, particularly when it became generally known that they had been handsomely rewarded by the British Government for their pains.† This aristocratic trio, no less than Curzon and Cox, underrated the post-war mood of nationalism abroad in Persia and the strength of anti-British feeling. Curzon brushed aside warnings from Cox's successor‡ and the Government of India. Despite threats and bullying the Agreement was never taken to the Majles for ratification and eventually, in mid-summer 1921, following Reza Khan's *coup d'état*, was denounced by the Persian Government. British experts and military advisers sent to Persia in anticipation of ratification were given notice to quit and orders issued for the disbanding of the S.P.R. By the end of 1921 not a single British adviser remained in the service of the Persian Government: British influence and prestige had reached their nadir. Since that time Persian writers and journalists have never let their public forget for long the unhappy circumstances surrounding the signature of this ill-starred Agreement. In many Persian minds it ranks, more than half a century later, with the Anglo-Russian Convention of 1907 as a warning signal: *Beware of the British!*

The British Government had already decided, in late 1920, largely on grounds of economy,§ to withdraw Norperforce from Persia by 1 April

---

* Vusuq ed-Dowleh, Prime Minister: Akbar *Mirza*, Sarem ed-Dowleh, Minister of Finance, son of Zill ul-Sultan: Firuz *Mirza*, Nosrat ed-Dowleh, Minister of Foreign Affairs, eldest son of Farman Farma.

† Rumours were confirmed in November 1920 when a Foreign Office Minister admitted in the House of Commons that an advance payment had been made from the £2 million Persian loan. The amount involved was 400,000 tomans (£131,000), paid out in August and September 1919. The three Ministers were also given written assurances of asylum in the British Empire should necessity arise.

‡ Herman Norman, who replaced Cox in June 1920, quickly summed up the situation but his warnings fell on deaf ears.

§ By the end of 1918 British expenditure in Persia was at the rate of £30 million p.a. In addition to the cost of their own forces they were subsidising the Persian Government and Cossack Brigade and paying the Shah 15,000 tomans (nearly £5,000) monthly so long as he supported Vusuq ed-Dowleh as Prime Minister.

The English Amongst the Persians

1921. Before this happened dramatic events, that were to change the face of Persia, took place in Qazvin and Tehran. The British were to some extent involved, but not to the degree often imagined.

Major-General Sir Edmund Ironside* had taken over command of Norperforce on 4 October 1920 from Brigadier Hugh Bateman-Champain†: some months earlier the force had beaten a hasty and ignominious retreat from the Caspian area in the face of Russian Bolshevik landings there and were badly demoralised in consequence. Ironside's task was to restore morale, hold off the Bolsheviks and prepare for eventual withdrawal. His force at that time numbered about 6,000 officers and men: an Indian detachment was stationed at Zanjan on the Tabriz road while most of the British troops were deployed to guard the Manjil Pass on the Qazvin–Rasht road: the remainder were held in reserve at Qazvin.

Shortly after Ironside's arrival the Persian Cossacks, about three thousand strong, under Russian and Persian officers, were driven out of Mazanderan by Bolshevik forces and retired to a camp at Agha Baba close to Qazvin where, by agreement with the Persian authorities, they were to be refitted under Ironside's supervision. Ironside, a tall, impressive professional soldier, did not belie his reputation as a man of action and quick decisions. Believing, with good reason, that the Russian officers were demoralised, anti-British and an easy prey for Bolshevik propaganda, he decided they must all go. With the help of Norman, the British Minister in Tehran, a very reluctant Shah was persuaded to agree to their dismissal.‡ In doing this Ironside and Norman acted on their own initiative without authority from London, much to the annoyance of Curzon, who was watching every move in Persia.

The Shah appointed an ineffective political figure, Sardar Humayun, to command the Cossacks in place of their dismissed Russian commander. At the same time Ironside appointed Lt. Colonel Henry Smyth§ of the Cheshire Regiment to control the administration and

---

* Field Marshal The Lord Ironside, 1st Baron Ironside of Archangel and Ironside, G.C.B. etc. (1880–1959). Commanded Allied Forces, N. Russia 1918–19 and Norperforce 1920–1: Commandant, Staff College, Camberley 1922–6: held various high commands in India and in UK before becoming Governor of Gibraltar 1938–9 and C.I.G.S. 1939–40.

† A son of the first Director of the Indo-European Telegraph Department in Tehran.

‡ Ironside anticipated any attempt by the Russian officers and NCOs to rally behind their commander and resist dismissal by separating them from their troops and then arresting them.

§ A member of the British Military Mission sent, under the terms of the 1919 Agreement, to help organise a national army.

finances of the Cossacks during the process of reorganisation. When he visited them in their camp on 2 November 1920 Ironside announced that he had no intention of replacing the Russians by British officers. He made enquiries about their Persian officers and noted in his diary that evening that 'Reza Khan, the commander of the Tabriz *atryad* is certainly one of the best. Smyth recommends him as the practical head of the show, acting under the political commander, who was appointed from Tehran'.* On 14 January when Ironside again visited the Cossacks he recorded:

> I have been down to the Persian Cossacks and had a look at them. Smyth has got them in much better order. Payment has been regular and the men are now clothed and housed. . . . The Commander of the Cossacks is a useless little creature and the real life and soul of the Show is Reza Khan, a Colonel, the man that I liked so much before. Smyth says he is a good man and I have told him to give Humayun leave to visit his estate.†

By sending Sardar Humayun on leave Ironside put Reza Khan in effective command. He now began to worry about Norperforce's withdrawal once the unusually heavy snows had melted and also about the future of the Cossacks. Withdrawal was bound to be a risky operation owing to the chaotic state of the country and a possible breakdown of law and order once the British troops had gone. The road would then be open for the Bolsheviks to move down from the north: the Cossacks might mutiny against their officers and 'rush over to Tehran and make a revolution'.† Ironside came to the conclusion that the safest thing would be to give the Cossacks their head while British forces were still in command of the situation. His decision was undoubtedly influenced by his confidence in Reza Khan and the rapid progress towards efficiency the Cossacks were making under his leadership.‡

Ironside saw Reza Khan again on 31 January in company with Smyth but recorded nothing of their conversation other than that Reza Khan 'wishes to get on with some work and frets at not being in anything'.†

---

* Mr Ardeshir Reporter (q.v.) had met Reza Khan in 1917 and been much impressed by his patriotism: he states in his unpublished memoirs that he first introduced Reza Khan to Ironside.

† From the personal Diaries of the late Field Marshal The Lord Ironside. © The Lord Ironside.

‡ He wrote in his diary on 14 January 1921 'Personally, I am of opinion that we ought to let these people go before I disappear. . . . In fact, a military dictatorship would solve our troubles and let us out of the country without any trouble at all.' †

The next and, as it turned out, final meeting was on 12 February when Ironside noted in his diary:

> I have interviewed Reza Khan and have put him definitely in charge of the Persian Cossacks. He is a man and the straightest I have met yet. I have told him that I propose to let him go from my control gradually and that he must make preparations with Colonel Smyth to meet the Rasht rebels when the Manjil column goes. I had a long talk with Reza in the presence of Smyth. I wondered if I ought to have anything in writing, but I decided in the end that writing would be no good. If Reza wants to play false he will and he will merely say that any promises he made were made under duress and that he needn't fulfil them. I made two things clear to Reza when I agreed to let him go:—
> (i) That he must make no attempt to shoot me up behind as he goes or as I go. That would lead to his annihilation and good to nobody except the Revolutionary Party.
> (ii) That the Shah must on no account be deposed. Reza promised glibly enough and I shook hands with him. I have told Smyth to let go gradually.*

Two days later Ironside was unexpectedly summoned to Baghdad to take up a new appointment. Before leaving he motored into Tehran for a farewell audience with the Shah whom he tried, unsuccessfully, to persuade to make better use of Reza Khan. Then on 18 February he left Persia for good, flying from Qazvin in a small two-seater plane whose oil-pipe froze up and crashed in deep snow near Hamadan, luckily with no more than a shaking for its two occupants. That same evening Reza Khan alerted his troops for the march on Tehran. By 20 February they had reached Mehrabad on the outskirts of the capital. There representatives of the Shah and two members of the British Legation sent by the British Minister tried to dissuade him from entering Tehran. But Reza Khan was not to be diverted. He told his visitors that he was tired of weak governments and was determined to establish a strong one that would be ready to oppose the Bolshevik advance which he believed would follow British withdrawal. At the same time he professed loyalty to the Shah but made it clear that he would get rid of the evil counsellors surrounding the throne.

Reza Khan and his Cossacks entered Tehran shortly after midnight on 21 February. They encountered little opposition and the *coup* was all

---

* From the personal Diaries of the late Field Marshal The Lord Ironside. © The Lord Ironside.

World War I and the End of an Era

but bloodless. The British Minister had an audience with the Shah that same morning when, speaking apparently without instructions from London, he advised him that his only possible course was to enter into relations with the leaders of the *coup* and acquiesce in their demands. Four days later the Shah issued a proclamation stating that he was entirely in agreement with the views of the army and appointing Sayyed Zia ed-Din Tabatabai as Prime Minister. Reza Khan was confirmed as head of the armed forces with the title of Sardar-e-Sepah.

Ironside, now in Baghdad, on hearing of the *coup* noted in his diary on 23 February 'Reza Khan has carried out a coup d'etat in Tehran, but true to his promise to me he has declared his loyalty to the Shah ... I fancy that all the people think I engineered the coup d'etat. I suppose I did strictly speaking'.* Smyth is also on record as having told a friend that, 'he had organised the Cossack coup in Tehran ... with the knowledge of the British Legation in Tehran' (6). Another source quotes Smyth as saying, 'I was asked for military advice, and as an Instructor I had to give it' (7). A French teacher who was in Tehran noted in his diary on the day of the *coup* that a Persian officer told him that everyone believed that it was '*un coup d'état monté par le souverain et ses amis les Anglais*' (8). The Frenchman himself thought this. The fact that Sayyid Zia ed-Din, the new Prime Minister, was a well-known anglophil journalist gave substance to this belief as did the knowledge that Smyth and other British officers had been attached to the Cossacks after the dismissal of their Russian officers. Also Firuz *Mirza*, the former Foreign Minister who had negotiated with Curzon and had later become as anglophobe as he had previously been anglophil, joined with a number of others in denouncing the *coup* as a British plot. Not surprisingly, therefore, many Persians assumed that the British had engineered it as a last desperate effort to bring Curzon's Agreement into force.

There is, in fact, no evidence to show that the British Government or Legation were involved in planning Reza Khan's *coup*. It is possible that embarrassing records were later destroyed but this seems unlikely: the strong probability is that Ironside acted on his own initiative as he had done over the Russian officers. He was seriously worried about Norperforce's withdrawal and believed that a strong military dictatorship alone would save Persia from a Bolshevik revolution. Others besides himself were worried by such a possibility. Smyth played second fiddle to Ironside but was in touch with Sayyed Zia and two young Persian officers who were involved with Reza Khan in planning the *coup*. Ironside did not consult the British Minister, whom he regarded as a weak-

---

* From the personal Diaries of the late Field Marshal The Lord Ironside. © The Lord Ironside.

ling, before drafting orders on 14 February for Smyth and Reza Khan releasing the latter from his control. Reza Khan interpreted this as the green light for his march on Tehran. Ironside did, however, tell Norman of what he had done when he paid a farewell call the following day.*
Whether any other members of the Legation were kept in the picture by Ironside or Smyth is uncertain but the soldier's traditional distrust of the diplomat makes this unlikely. Sayyed Zia may well have mentioned something to members of the Legation's Oriental Secretariat. There is, however, nothing on record to suggest that the Foreign Office in London were aware of what was afoot or that the planning of the *coup* was anything but an all-Persian affair. Had the British Government been behind it they would hardly have been so slow and negative in responding to appeals from Norman urging support for Sayyed Zia and the new régime. The British—or rather Ironside's—role had been to provide the conditions and encouragement which made Reza Khan's move possible.

Shortly after the *coup* Reza Khan was appointed Minister of War and, in 1923, Prime Minister. In October 1925 the Majles deposed Ahmad Shah, then abroad, and declared the Qajar dynasty ended†: on 13 December they proclaimed Reza Khan as the new Shah of Persia: and on 25 April 1926 Reza Shah crowned himself Reza Shah Pahlavi, Shahanshah of Persia, in the Gulestan Palace.‡

So ended the Qajar period. And with it the British lost, one by one, the various privileges and concessions that had given them such a special position in Persian eyes during much of that period. Capitulations and consular courts; *sowar* escorts and seigneurial rights at Gulhek; British telegrams, stamps and bank notes; a British quarantine service; naval bases on Persian islands; the Residency at Bushire; the oil company in Khuzistan: and, last of all, British paramountcy in the Persian Gulf—

---

* Diary entries on 14 Feb and 15 Feb respectively read: 'Better a coup d'etat for us than anything else. I'll bounce old Norman' and 'I told him [Norman] about Reza and he was very fearful that the Shah would be done in. I told him I believed in Reza . . . I had to let the Cossacks go sometime or other.' (From the personal Diaries of the late Field Marshal The Lord Ironside. © The Lord Ironside.)

† Before this Reza Khan had sent a personal envoy to England to ask Ironside to release him from his promise not to depose Ahmad Shah.

‡ Mrs Harold Nicolson (Vita Sackville-West), the wife of the Counsellor in the British Legation, describes the coronation in *Passenger to Tehran*. She also mentions that, when preparing for the great day, 'there was no point, however humble, on which they [the Persians] would not consult their English friends'.

World War I and the End of an Era

all had to go before the Persians would feel able to live in their own country amongst the English on terms of equality. Even so the memory and aura of past history remained to haunt many Persians who, to this day, are inclined—for reasons which this book has tried to explain—to look more askance at the British than at other foreigners.

Appendix I

The Qajar Shahs

Agha Muhammad	1787–97
Fath Ali	1798–1834
Muhammad	1834–48
Nasir ed-Din	1848–96
Muzaffar ed-Din	1896–1907
Muhammad Ali	1907–9
Sultan Ahmad	1909–25

Appendix II

British Envoys to the Court of Persia during the Qajar Period

1809–11	Sir HARFORD JONES, Bt. (afterwards JONES BRYDGES) Envoy
1811–14	Sir GORE OUSELEY, Bt. Ambassador Extraordinary and Plenipotentiary
1814–15	JAMES J. MORIER Minister Plenipotentiary *ad. int.*
1815–26	Captain HENRY WILLOCK (afterwards Sir) Chargé d'Affaires
1826–30	Colonel JOHN KINNEIR MACDONALD (afterwards Sir) Envoy from the East India Company
1830–5	Captain JOHN N. R. CAMPBELL (afterwards Sir) 1830–4 Chargé d'Affaires: 1834–5 Consul-General and Plenipotentiary
1836–42	Doctor JOHN MCNEILL (afterwards Sir) Envoy Extraordinary and Minister Plenipotentiary
1842–53	Lt Colonel JUSTIN SHEIL (afterwards Sir) 1842–4 Chargé d'Affaires: 1844–53 Envoy Extraordinary and Minister Plenipotentiary*
1853–55	W. TAYLOUR THOMSON (afterwards Sir) Chargé d'Affaires
1855–9	The Hon. CHARLES A. MURRAY (afterwards Sir)
1859–60	Major General Sir HENRY C. RAWLINSON
1860–72	CHARLES ALISON
1872–9	W. TAYLOUR THOMSON (afterwards Sir)
1879–87	RONALD F. THOMSON (afterwards Sir)
1887–90	Rt. Hon. Sir HENRY DRUMMOND WOLFF
1891–4	SIR FRANK C. LASCELLES
1894–1900	Sir MORTIMER M. DURAND
1900–5	Sir ARTHUR N. HARDINGE
1906–8	Sir CECIL SPRING-RICE
1908–12	Sir GEORGE BARCLAY

* Thereafter, throughout the Qajar period, the British envoys were all accredited as Envoys Extraordinary and Ministers Plenipotentiary except Cox who was appointed "Changé d' Affaires and Special Commissioner". The Legation became an Embassy and the Minister an Ambassador from 1944 onwards.

Appendix II

1912–15	Sir WALTER TOWNLEY
1915–18	CHARLES M. MARLING (afterwards Sir)
1918–20	Sir PERCY COX
1920–1	HERMAN C. NORMAN
1921–6	Sir PERCY LORAINE

Special Missions

1798–9	MEHDI ALI KHAN Envoy from the East India Company
1800–1	Captain JOHN MALCOLM (afterwards Major-General Sir) Envoy from the East India Company
1808	Brigadier-General JOHN MALCOLM Envoy from the East India Company. Was not received by the Shah
1810	Major-General JOHN MALCOLM (afterwards Sir) Envoy from the East India Company
1814	HENRY ELLIS (afterwards Sir) Plenipotentiary. Had joint full powers with Ouseley and Morier to negotiate modifications to the Anglo-Persian Treaty of 1809
1835–6	Rt. Hon. HENRY ELLIS (afterwards Sir) Ambassador on a Special Mission of condolence and congratulation of accession of Muhammad Shah
1903	Viscount DOWNE Special envoy to invest the Shah with the Order of the Garter

Appendix III

British Residents at Bushire during the Qajar Period

1789 circa	Mr CHARLES WATKINS
1795 circa	Mr NICOLAS HANKEY SMITH
1798–1803	MEHDI ALI KHAN (Acting)
1803–4	Mr J. H. LOVETT
1804	Mr SAMUEL MANESTY (Self-appointed)*
1804–7	Lieutenant WILLIAM BRUCE (Acting)
1807–8	Mr NICOLAS HANKEY SMITH
1808	Captain C. PASLEY
1809–11	Mr NICOLAS HANKEY SMITH
1811–22	Lieutenant WILLIAM BRUCE (dismissed in 1822)
1822–3	Captain JOHN MCLEOD (died en poste 1823)
1827	Colonel STANNUS
1827	Captain WILSON
1831	Mr A. D. BLANE
——	Captain S. HENNELL (Acting)
1837	Major MORISON
1838	Captain S. HENNELL
1841	Captain MACKENZIE (Acting)
——	Colonel S. HENNELL
1852–6	Lieutenant ARNOLD B. KEMBALL (afterwards Sir ARNOLD BURROWES)
1856–62	Captain FELIX JONES
1863–72	Lieutenant-Colonel LEWIS PELLY (afterwards Sir)
1872–91	Lieutenant-Colonel EDWARD C. ROSS (afterwards Sir)
1876–7	Lieutenant-Colonel W. F. PRIDEAUX (Acting)
1886	Lieutenant-Colonel S. B. MILES (Acting)
1891–3	Lieutenant-Colonel C. A. TALBOT

* Manesty was the East India Company's representative at Basra. Without authority from London or Calcutta he assumed charge of the Bushire Residency in place of Lovett who was ill. Describing himself as Ambassador for the Government of India he was granted an audience by the Shah. The Government of India censured him because of this.

Appendix III

1893–4	{ Major J. HAYES SADLER (Acting) { Mr J. A. CRAWFORD (Acting)
1894–7	Colonel F. A. WILSON
1897–1900	Lieutenant-Colonel M. J. MEADE
1900–4	Lieutenant-Colonel C. A. KEMBALL
1904–13	Major PERCY Z. COX (afterwards Sir)
1914–15	Lieutenant-Colonel S. G. KNOX
1915–18*	Sir PERCY COX
1918–20	Lieutenant-Colonel ARNOLD T. WILSON (Acting: afterwards Sir)
1920–4	Lieutenant-Colonel A. P. TREVOR

* Cox was also Chief Political Officer with British forces in Mesopotamia.

Appendix IV

British Consular Posts in Persia 1921

CONSULATE-GENERALS
Tehran*
Bushire*
Isfahan
Mashad

CONSULATES
Bandar Abbas
Kerman
Kermanshah
Mohammerah (Khoramshahr)
Nusratabad (Zabol)
Shiraz
Tabriz

VICE-CONSULATES
Ahwaz
Birjand
Hamadan
Qasr-e-Shirin
Qazvin
Rasht
Sultanabad (Arak)
Yazd

CONSULAR AGENTS
Burujird
Kerend
Maragheh
Zanjan

* The Minister in Tehran and Political Resident in Bushire both held *exequaturs* as Consuls-General.

REFERENCES

Abbreviations

B.I.P.S.J.   Journal of the British Institute of Persian Studies.
F.O.   Foreign Office.
I.J.M.E.S.   International Journal of Middle Eastern Studies.
I.O.   India Office Library and Records. (British Library).
P.R.O.   Public Record Office.
R.C.A.S.J.   Journal of the Royal Central Asian Society (now Asian Affairs).
R.G.S.J.   Journal of the Royal Geographical Society.
S.O.A.S.B.   Bulletin of the School of Oriental and African Studies.

PREFACE
1. R. W. Cottam, *Nationalism in Iran*, p. 217.
2. H.I.M. Muhammad Reza Shah Pahlavi, *Mission for my Country*, p. 87.
3. F. Kazemzadeh, *Russia and Britain in Persia, 1864–1914*, p. 502.
4. P.R.O. FO/416/12. Persia. Annual Report 1922.

CHAPTER 1. THE BRITISH INTEREST IN PERSIA
1. Quoted by J. W. Kaye: *The Life and Correspondence of Major-General Sir John Malcolm*, i, p. 90.
2. C. U. Aitchison, *A Collection of Treaties, Engagements, etc.* Vol. 13, p. 48.
3. ibid., p. 54.
4. Kentchurch MSS. 9574 and 9576. Morier to Jones, 27 January 1810 and 11 March 1810.
5. I.O. G/29/30A. Minto to Malcolm, 26 October 1809.
6. Kentchurch MSS. 8583. Wellesley to Jones, 7 April 1810.
7. Quoted by J. W. Kaye, op. cit., i, p. 397.
8. P.R.O. FO/539/1. Clanricarde to Nesselrode, 10 November 1838.
9. *Documents on British Foreign Policy 1919–39.* 1st Series, Vol. IV, p. 1121.

CHAPTER 2. THE DIPLOMATIC SCENE
1. P.R.O. FO/60: 4. Instructions to Ouseley, 13 July 1810.
2. Kentchurch MSS. 8584C. Wellesley to the Persian Prime Minister, 1810.
3. P.R.O. FO/60: 4. op. cit.

4. P.R.O. FO/60: 4. Foreign Office to Ouseley, 10 July 1810.
5. P.R.O. FO/60: 4. Ouseley to Wellesley, 30 April 1810.
6. P.R.O. FO/60: 21. Canning to Wynn, 19 December 1822.
7. P.R.O. FO/60. ibid.
8. J. E. Alexander, *Travels from India to England*, p. 77.
9. G. Fowler, *Three Years in Persia*, i, pp. 85–6.
10. Quoted by F. McNeill in *Memoir of Sir John McNeill*, pp. 168–9.
11. I.O. L/P and S/9: 94. Ouseley Memorandum 1832.
12. H. Rawlinson, *England and Russia in the East*, p. 97.
13. *Documents on British Foreign Policy*, op. cit., p. 1175.
14. Quoted by F. McNeill, op. cit., p. 139.
15. B. Schwartz (ed.), *Letters from Persia*, p. 74.
16. P.R.O. FO/539/7. Murray to Clarendon, 22 February 1856.
17. C. U. Aitchison, op. cit., pp. 85–6.
18. G. N. Curzon, *Persia and the Persian Question*, ii, p. 606.
19. P.R.O. FO/60: 280. Eastwick to Russell, 5 August 1862.
20. ibid., Russell to Alison, 9 July 1863.
21. P.R.O. FO/60: 395. Alison to Clarendon, 8 May 1866.
22. ibid., Alison to Stanley, 26 July 1867.
23. Mrs Bishop, *Journeys in Persia and Kurdistan*, i, p. 188.
24. Salisbury MSS. Wolff to Salisbury, 2 October 1888.
25. G. Gwynn (ed.), *The Letters and Friendships of Sir Cecil Spring-Rice*, ii, p. 103.
26. F. Rosen, *Oriental Memories of a German Diplomat*, p. 126.
27. Hardinge of Penshurst, *Old Diplomacy*, p. 62.
28. Rumbold MSS. 1895 Diary.

CHAPTER 3. FORMALITIES AND FRICTIONS
1. I.O. Factory Records/G/29/22. Malcolm to Edmonstone, 31 July 1801.
2. C. Stuart, *Journal of a Residence in Northern Persia*, pp. 166–7.
3. W. Ouseley, *Travels in various countries in the East*, iii, p. 124.
4. J. E. Alexander, op. cit., p. 154.
5. Murray MSS. GD 261/21.
6. Quoted by F. McNeill, op. cit., p. 149.
7. M. and Mme. Freygan, *Letters from the Caucasus*, p. 308.
8. H. J. Brydges, *An Account of the Transactions of His Majesty's Mission to the Court of Persia, etc*, p. 12.
9. P.R.O. FO/60: 4. Ouseley to Wellesley, 30 April 1810.
10. J. E. Alexander, op. cit., p. 213.
11. Murray MSS. GD 261/10.
12. P.R.O. FO/60/128. Palmerston to Sheil, 30 June 1847.
13. P.R.O. FO/248/186. Russell to Alison, 24 April 1860.
14. E. R. Durand, *An Autumn Tour in Western Persia*, p. 17.
15. Kentchurch MSS. 8870. Jones to Canning, 29 March 1809.
16. A. Hardinge, *A Diplomatist in the East*, pp. 283–4.
17. F. O'Connor, *Things Mortal*, p. 128.
18. C. U. Aitchison, op. cit., p. 67.

References

19. E. B. Eastwick, *Journal of a Diplomat's Three Year Residence in Persia*, ii, pp. 312–13.
20. Quoted by A. D. Hytier, *Les Dépêches diplomatiques du Comte de Gobineau en Perse*, p. 114.
21. P.R.O. FO/416/1. Durand to Salisbury, 12 February 1899.
22. P.R.O. FO/416/35. Marling to Grey, 26 February 1908.
23. P.R.O. FO/60/384. Palmerston to Alison, 1863.
24. P.R.O. FO/539/7. Murray to Clarendon, 22 January 1856.
25. P.R.O. FO/449/2. Sheil to Stevens, 7 September 1852.

CHAPTER 4. WARS AND WARRIORS
1. Kentchurch MSS. 8440. Malcolm to Pasley, 10 May 1808.
2. ibid. 8584B. Wellesley to Mirza Abul Hassan, 6 March 1810.
3. R. Ker Porter, *Travels in Georgia, Persia, etc.*, ii, p. 572.
4. Kentchurch MSS. 9012. Abbas *Mirza* to Jones, 15 March 1812.
5. Aberdeen MSS. British Library ADD. 43209. Fols. 54–58b. Gordon to Aberdeen, 28 February 1812.
6. ibid.
7. P.R.O. FO/248/35. Moira to Morier, 3 June 1815.
8. I.O. L/P and S/9/91. Campbell to Political and Secret Department, Calcutta, 28 July 1830.
9. P.R.O. FO/248/73. Passmore to Campbell, 14 September 1835.
10. Kentchurch MSS. 9777. Willock to Palmerston, 1 December 1838.
11. C. U. Aitchison, op. cit., p. 77.
12. B. English, *John Company's Last War*, p. 139.

CHAPTER 5. UNCROWNED KING OF THE PERSIAN GULF
1. Grattan Geary, *Through Asiatic Turkey*, i, p. 56.
2. J. B. Kelly, *Britain and the Persian Gulf*, p. 199.
3. Quoted by J. B. Kelly, op. cit., p. 200.
4. Arnold T. Wilson, *S.W. Persia, etc.*, p. 10.
5. I.O. L/P and S/9/80. Government of Bombay to Keir, 29 January 1820.
6. James B. Fraser, *Narrative of a Journey into Khorasan*, p. 33.
7. H. J. Brydges, *An Account of the transactions of his Majesty's Mission, etc.*, p. 138.
8. I.O. L/P and S/20/C248C. Government of Bombay to Resident Bushire, 1828.
9. Parliamentary Debates 4th series, 121 (1903), 1348.
10. P.R.O. FO/371/2077. Cox to Government of India, 7 December 1913.
11. Private letter from Herbert Cave.
12. Benjamin B. Moore. *From Moscow to the Persian Gulf*, p. 441.
13. T. S. Anderson, *My Wanderings in Persia*, p. 35.
14. G. N. Curzon, *Persia and the Persian Question*, ii, pp. 236, 398, 451.
15. I.O. L/P and S/20/C248B. Instructions from Naval Headquarters, Bombay 1871.

The English Amongst the Persians

CHAPTER 6. CONSULS, KHANS AND COMMUNITIES
1. J. H. Stocqueler, *Fifteen Months Pilgrimage*, etc., ii, p. 16.
2. P.R.O. FO/60/38. Campbell to Backhouse, 12 March 1835.
3. ibid.
4. James Morier, *A Journey through Persia*, etc., p. 43.
5. P.R.O. FO/539/6. Murray to Sadr Azam, 6 November 1855.
6. Mrs Bishop, *Journeys in Persia and Kurdistan*, i, p. 101.
7. C. J. Wills, *In the Land of the Lion and Sun*, p. 419.
8. P.R.O. FO/539/32. Nicolson to Iddesleigh, 8 December 1886.
9. P.R.O. FO/539/80. Durand to Salisbury, 12 December 1899.
10. P.R.O. FO/449/1. Palmerston to Bonham, 31 May 1837.
11. P.R.O. FO/60/156. Shiel to Hammond, 26 December 1850.
12. P.R.O. FO/60/193. Minute by Shiel, 12 July 1854.
13. P.R.O. FO/539/6. Shah to his Foreign Minister, 22 November 1855.
14. P.R.O. FO/60/167. Minute by Addington, 3 May 1851..
15. Salisbury MSS. Drummond Wolff to Salisbury, 4 August 1888.
16. E. Richmond (ed.), *The Earlier Letters of Gertrude Bell*, p. 267.
17. S. Gwynn (ed.), op. cit., i, p. 288.
18. G. N. Curzon, op. cit., i, p. 172.
19. I.O. L/P and S/10/85. Hardinge to Foreign Office, 9 September 1905.
20. J. C. Hurewitz, *Diplomacy in the Near and Middle East*, i, p. 244.
21. I.O. Administration Report of the Persian Gulf Residency, 1905-6.
22. Quoted by G. R. Garthwaite. The Bakhtiari Khans, the Govt: of Iran and the British Govt: Townley to Grey, 10 July 1912. I.J.M.E.S., 1972
23. I.O. L/P and S/10/652.
24. P.R.O. FO/371/2076. Townley to Grey, 3 August 1914.
25. Mrs Bishop, op. cit., i, p. 245.
26. Rumbold MSS.
27. A. H. Savage-Landor, *Across Coveted Lands*, i, p. 85.
28. Murray MSS. GD261/6.
29. Claudius Rich, *Narrative of a Residence in Koordistan*, ii, p. 225.
30. E. Richmond (ed.), op. cit., p. 335.

CHAPTER 7. THE WORLD OF BUSINESS
1. Benjamin Schwartz (ed.), Charles and Edward Burgess, *Letters from Persia (1828-55)*, p. 33.
2. ibid., p. 58.
3. ibid., p. 57.
4. Lady Sheil, *Glimpses of Life and Manners in Persia*, p. 200.
5. P.R.O. FO/60/142, W. F. Mills to F.O., 10 August 1848.
6. H. J. Whigham, *The Persian Problem*, p. 290.
7. G. N. Curzon, op. cit., ii, p. 524.
8. Arthur Arnold, *Through Persia by Caravan*, ii, p. 41.
9. J. G. Lorimer, *Gazetteer of the Persian Gulf*, i, p. 1715.
10. G. N. Curzon, op. cit., i, p. 480.

References

11. Archives of the British Bank of the Middle East.
12. G. N. Curzon, op. cit., i, p. 477.
13. P.R.O. FO/251/57. Paton to Tehran Legation, 29 August 1891.
14. E. G. Browne, *The Persian Revolution*, p. 52.
15. ibid., p. 57.
16. P.R.O. FO/60/731. Hardinge to Lansdowne, 30 May 1901.
17. I.O. Hamilton Papers. Curzon to Hamilton, 31 July 1901.
18. Arnold T. Wilson, op. cit., p. 55.
19. Hassan Arfa, *Under Five Shahs*, p. 90.
20. P.R.O. FO/60/193. Memorandum by Sheil, 27 July 1853.
21. P.R.O. FO/60/158. Sheil to Persian Prime Minister, 8 January 1851.
22. P.R.O. FO/60/734. Hardinge to Lansdowne, 1 October 1904.
23. Salisbury MSS. Salisbury to Lascelles, 6 October 1891.

CHAPTER 8. MISSIONARIES AND DOCTORS
1. J. W. Kaye, *Lives of Indian Officers*, ii, p. 65.
2. F. McNeill, op. cit., p. 63.
3. P. Gordon, *Fragment of the Journal of a tour through Persia in 1830*, p. 85.
4. ibid., p. 91.
5. ibid., p. 108.
6. G. Keppel, *Personal Narrative of a Journey from India to England*, i, p. 260.
7. Joseph Wolff, *Narrative of a Mission to Bokhara*, i, p. 192.
8. Church Missionary Society Archives. Bruce to C.M.S. London Committee, 21 March 1876.
9. Justin Perkins, *A Residence of Eight Years in Persia, etc.*, p. 220.
10. Rumbold MSS. Rumbold to his father, 17 March 1897.
11. M. E. Hume-Griffith, *Behind the Veil in Persia and Turkish Arabia*, p. 140.
12. J. Morier, *A Journey through Persia, Armenia and Asia Minor*, p. 229.
13. Kentchurch Papers 9016. Lindesay-Bethune to Harford Jones, 17 March 1812.
14. P.R.O. FO/60/38. Record of a conversation between Palmerston and McNeill, 18 December 1835.
15. Arnold T. Wilson, op. cit., p. 28.
16. R. Wilbraham, *Travels in the Transcaucasian Provinces of Russia*, p. 69.

CHAPTER 9. THE ELECTRIC TELEGRAPH AND OTHER INNOVATIONS
1. Quoted by W. K. Dickson in *The Life of Major-General Sir Robert Murdoch Smith*, p. 215.
2. P.R.O. FO/60/299. J. R. Dickson to Hammond, 8 February 1866.
3. F. J. Goldsmid, *Telegraph and Travel*, p. 273.
4. P.R.O. FO/60/299. J. R. Dickson to Hammond, 8 February 1866.
5. G. N. Curzon, op. cit., ii, p. 613.
6. G. N. Curzon, ibid., ii, p. 616.
7. H. Ballantine, *Midnight Marches through Persia*, p. 68.

Chapter 10. Frontier Makers

1. P.R.O. FO/60/391. Persian Minister for Foreign Affairs to Alison, 4 September 1871.
2. F. J. Goldsmid (ed.), *Eastern Persia*, p. xxviii.
3. Ella C. Sykes, *Through Persia on a Side-Saddle*, p. 230.
4. ibid., p. 231.
5. ibid., p. 242.
6. G. N. Curzon, op. cit., i, p. 233.

Chapter 11. Some Travellers

1. Quoted by J. W. Kaye, *The Life and Correspondence of Major-General Sir John Malcolm*, i, p. 124.
2. I.O. Political and Secret Library C 244.
3. H. Pottinger, *Travels in Beloochistan and Sinde*, p. 4.
4. James Morier, op. cit., p. 145.
5. Dictionary of National Biography.
6. James B. Fraser, *Narrative of a Journey into Khorasan in the Years 1821 and 1822*, p. 174.
7. E. Scott Waring, *A Tour to Sheeraz*, p. 103. H. Pottinger, op. cit., p. 212.
8. John Kitto, *The People of Persia*, p. 46. Rev. A. A. Isaacs, *Biography of the Rev. Henry Aaron Stern*, p. 43. P. M. Sykes, *Ten Thousand Miles in Persia*, p. 457.
9. Quoted by F. Kazemzadeh, op. cit., p. 316.
10. G. N. Curzon, op. cit., i, p. 15.
11. Quoted by A. D. Hytier, op. cit., p. 89.
12. Walter B. Harris, *From Batum to Baghdad*, p. 115.
13. Quoted by E. A. Wallis Budge, *The Rise and Progress of Assyriology*, p. 35.
14–19. A. H. Layard, *Early Adventures in Persia, Susiana and Babylonia*, i, pp. 8–10; ii, pp. 205, 227, 242.
20. A. H. Layard, *Autobiography and Letters*, ii, p. 5.
21. A. H. Layard, op. cit. ii, p. 138.
22. ibid., ii, p. 321.
23. Introduction to 1926 edition of E. G. Browne's *A Year Amongst the Persians*, p. vii.
24. ibid., p. xxi.
25. E. G. Browne, *The Persian Revolution of 1905–1909*, p. xv.
26. Quoted by A. J. Arberry, *Oriental Essays*, p. 189.
27. G. N. Curzon, op. cit., ii, p. 605.
28. ibid., i, p. 56.
29. Harold Nicolson, *Curzon: The Last Phase 1919–1925*, p. 121.
30. ibid., p. 120.
31. Mrs Bishop, op. cit., i, p. 82.
32. Quoted by A. M. Stoddart, *The Life of Isabella Bird*, p. 222.
33. ibid., p. 221.
34. Mrs Bishop, op. cit., i, pp. 180–1.

References

35. Quoted by A. M. Stoddart, op. cit., p. 227.
36–37. Mrs Bishop, op. cit., ii, pp. 45, 73.
38. *The Autobiography of H.I.H. Princess Soraya*, p. 29.
39. Mrs Bishop, op. cit., ii, p. 259.
40. G. N. Curzon, op. cit., ii, p. 634.

CHAPTER 12. WORLD WAR I AND THE END OF AN ERA
1. P. M. Sykes, *A History of Persia*, 2nd edn., ii, p. 452.
2. P.R.O. FO/60/698. Sykes to Hardinge, 27 February 1905.
3. P. M. Sykes, op. cit., ii, p. 502.
4. Quoted by F. J. Moberly in *The Campaign in Mesopotamia*, iv, p. 187.
5. *Documents on British Foreign Policy* 1919–39, 1st series, Vol. IV, p. 1121.
6. Quoted by D. N. Wilber, *Riza Shah Pahlavi*, p. 48.
7. W. G. Grey, *Recent Persian History*, R.C.A.S.J., January 1926.
8. E. Lesueur, *Les Anglais en Perse*, p. 153.

BIBLIOGRAPHY

I. Manuscript

A. *Official Documents*
At the Public Record Office: the following F.O. Series: 60 (most productive of all); 248; 249; 251; 371; 416; 449; 450; 539; and 880. Also Works/10/34 for information about the Tehran and Gulhek buildings.
At the British Library, India Office Library and Records the following series: Factory Records G29; L/P and S/9; L/P and S/10; L/P and S/18; L/P and S/20.

B. *The private papers of:*
The fourth Earl of Aberdeen (British Library).
Sir Harford Jones Brydges (Kentchurch Papers, County Library, Hereford).
The fourth Earl of Clarendon (Bodleian Library).
The first Marquess of Dalhousie (National Record Office of Scotland).
The first Baron Ironside (The Lord Ironside).
The Hon. Sir Charles Murray (National Record Office of Scotland).
Sir Henry Rawlinson (Royal Asiatic Society).
Sir Horace Rumbold (Bodleian Library).
The third Marquess of Salisbury (Hatfield House).
Sir Robert Murdoch Smith (National Library of Scotland).
Sir Percy Sykes (St Antony's College)

C. *The archives of the Church Missionary Society.*

II. Published Documents and Official Publications
Aitchison, C. U. *A Collection of Treaties, Engagements and Sanads relating to India & neighbouring countries.* Vol. 13. Calcutta 1933.
Butler, Rohan (ed). *Documents on British Foreign Policy 1919-39.* 1st Series. Vols. 4 and 13.
Foreign Office Lists.
Hurewitz, J. C. *Diplomacy in the Near and Middle East.* New York 1956.
India Office Lists.
Lorimer, J. G. *Gazetteer of the Persian Gulf, Oman and Central Arabia.* 4 parts. Calcutta 1915.

Persia. Handbook, prepared by the Foreign Office, 1919.
Persia. Geographical Handbook, Naval Intelligence Division, 1945.

III. BOOKS AND ARTICLES

N.B. Those books and articles with interest limited to one chapter are listed separately at the end of this section.

A. *Autobiographies, Memoirs and Travel books*
Alexander, James E. *Travels from India to England.* London 1827.
Arfa, Hassan. *Under Five Shahs.* London 1964.
Arnold, Arthur. *Through Persia by Caravan.* 2 vols. London 1877.
Baker, Valentine. *Clouds in the East.* London 1876.
Ballantine, Henry. *Midnight Marches through Persia.* Boston 1879.
Bassett, James. *Persia. Land of the Imams.* London 1887.
Binning, R. B. M. *A Journal of Two Years Travel in Persia, Ceylon, etc.* 2 vols. London 1857.
Bishop, Mrs J. F. (Isabella Bird). *Journeys in Persia and Kurdistan.* 2 vols. London 1891.
Bradley-Birt, F. B. *Through Persia from the Gulf to the Caspian.* London 1909.
Browne, E. G. *A Year Amongst the Persians.* London 1893.
Burnes, Alexander. *Travels into Bokhara.* 2 vols. London 1835.
Collins, E. T. *In the Kingdom of the Shah.* London 1896.
Collins, Henry M. *From Pigeon Post to Wireless* London 1935.
Drouville, G. *Voyage en Perse fait en 1812 et 1813.* 2 vols. 2nd ed. Paris 1825.
Durand, E. R. *An Autumn Tour in Western Persia.* London 1902.
Brydges, Harford Jones. *An Account of the Transactions of His Majesty's Mission to the Court of Persia in the Years 1807–11.* London 1834.
Eastwick, E. B. *Journal of a Diplomate's Three Years' Residence in Persia.* 2 vols. London 1864.
Feuvrier, J. B. *Trois Ans à le Cour de Perse.* Paris 1906.
Fowler, George. *Three Years in Persia.* 2 vols. London 1841.
Francklin, William. *Observations made on a Tour from Bengal to Persia in the Years 1786–7.* Calcutta 1788.
Fraser, James B. *Narrative of a Journey into Khorasan in the Years 1821 and 1822.* London 1825.
Fraser, James B. *Travels and Adventures in the Persian Provinces on the Southern Banks of the Caspian Sea.* London 1826.
Fraser, James B. *A Winter's Journey from Constantinople to Tehran.* 2 vols. London 1838.
Fraser, James B. *Narrative of the Residence of the Persian Princes in London in 1835 and 1836.* 2 vols. London 1838.
Fraser, James B. *Travels in Kurdistan, Mesopotamia, etc.* London 1840.
Freygan, Mr and Mrs. *Letters from the Caucasus and Georgia* (trans). London 1823.
Geary, Grattan. *Through Asiatic Turkey.* 2 vols. London 1878.
Goldsmid, Frederic J. *Telegraph and Travel.* London 1874.
Gordon, Thomas E. *Persia Revisited 1895.* London 1896.
Gordon, Thomas E. *A Varied Life.* London 1906.

Bibliography

Gwynn, Stephen (ed). *The Letters and Friendships of Sir Cecil Spring-Rice.* 2 vols. London 1929.
Hardinge, Arthur H. *A Diplomatist in the East.* London 1928.
Hardinge of Penshurst, Lord. *Old Diplomacy.* London 1947.
Harris, Walter B. *From Batum to Baghdad.* London 1896.
Hedin, Sven. *Overland to India.* 2 vols. London 1910.
Heude, William. *A Voyage up the Persian Gulf and a Journey overland from India to England in 1817.* London 1819.
Holmes, W. R. *Sketches on the Shores of the Caspian.* London 1845.
Hughes, A. W. *The Country of Balochistan.* London 1877.
Johnson, John. *A Journey from India to England in the year 1817.* London 1818.
Keppel, G. *Personal Narrative of a Journey from India to London.* 2 vols. London 1834.
Layard, A. H. *Early Adventures in Persia, Susiana and Babylonia.* 2 vols. London 1887.
Layard, A. H. *Autobiography and Letters.* 2 vols. London 1903.
Malcolm, John. *Sketches of Persia.* 2 vols. London 1827.
Malcolm, Napier. *Five Years in a Persian Town.* London 1905.
Marsh, H. C. *A Ride through Islam.* London 1877.
Mitford, E. L. *A Land March from England to Ceylon.* 2 vols. London 1884.
Money, R. C. *Journal of a Tour in Persia during the Years 1824 and 1825.* London 1828.
Morier, James. *A Journey through Persia, Armenia and Asia Minor.* London 1812.
Morier, James. *A Second Journey through Persia, Armenia and Asia Minor.* London 1818.
Mounsey, A. H. *A Journey through the Caucasus and the Interior of Persia.* London 1874.
Nevill, Ralph. *Unconventional Memories.* London 1923.
O'Donovan, Edmond. *The Merv Oasis.* 2 vols. London 1882.
O'Connor, Frederick. *On the Frontier and Beyond.* London 1931.
O'Connor, Frederick. *Things Mortal.* London 1940.
Ouseley, William. *Travels in Various Countries of the East, more particularly Persia etc.* 3 vols. London 1819.
Pahlavi, H.I.M. Muhammad Reza Shah. *Mission for My Country.* London 1961.
Perkins, Justin. *A Residence of Eight Years in Persia among the Nestorian Christians.* Andover 1843.
Porter, Robert Ker. *Travels in Georgia, Persia, Armenia, Ancient Babylonia, 1817 20.* 2 vols. London 1821.
Pottinger, Henry. *Travels in Belochistan and Sinde.* London 1816.
Rich, Claudius. *Narrative of a Residence in Koordistan.* 2 vols. London 1856.
Richmond, Elsa (ed). *The Earlier Letters of Gertrude Bell.* London 1937.
Rosen, Friedrich. *Oriental Memoirs of a German Diplomat.* London 1930.
Sackville-West, V. *Passenger to Tehran.* London 1926.
Savage-Landor, A. H. *Across Coveted Lands.* 2 vols. London 1902.
Sheil, Lady. *Glimpses of Life and Manners in Persia.* London 1856.
Southgate, Horatio. *Narrative of a Tour through Armenia, Kurdistan, Persia & Mesopotamia.* 2 vols. London 1840.
Sparroj, Wilfred. *Persian Children of the Royal Family.* London 1902.
Stack, Edward. *Six Months in Persia.* 2 vols. London 1882.
Stocqueler, J. H. *Fifteen Months Pilgrimage through untrodden tracts of Khuzistan and Persia.* 2 vols. London 1832.

Stocqueler, J. H. *The Memoirs of a Journalist*. London 1873.
Stuart, Charles. *Journal of a Residence in Northern Persia and the adjacent provinces of Turkey*. London 1854.
Sykes, Ella C. *Through Persia on a Side-Saddle*. London 1898.
Sykes, Percy M. *Ten Thousand Miles in Persia*. London 1902.
Ussher, John. *A Journey from London to Persepolis*. London 1865.
Vambery, Arminus. *Travels in Central Asia*. London 1864.
Vigne, G. T. *Travels in Kashmir, Ledak etc*. 2 vols. London 1842.
Wagner, Moritz. *Travels in Persia, Georgia and Koordistan* (trans.). 2 vols. London 1856.
Waring, E. Scott. *A Tour to Sheeraz*. London 1807.
Wilbraham, R. *Travels in the Transcaucasian Provinces of Russia*. London 1839.
Windt, H. de. *A Ride to India*. London 1891.
Wills, C. J. *In the Land of the Lion and Sun*. London 1891.
Wills, C. J. *Persia As It Is*. London 1886.
Wilson, Arnold T. *S.W. Persia. Letters and Diaries of a Young Political Officer 1907–14*. Oxford 1941.
Wolff, Henry Drummond. *Rambling Recollections*. 2 vols. London 1908.
Wolff, Joseph. *Narrative of a Mission to Bokhara*. 2 vols. London 1845; *Travels and Adventures*. 2 vols. London 1860–1.
Wratislaw, A. C. *A Consul in the East*. London 1924.

B. *Biographies*
Dickson, W. K. *The Life of Major-General Sir Robert Murdoch Smith*. Edinburgh 1901.
Gilbert, Martin. *Sir Horace Rumbold. Portrait of a Diplomat*. London 1973.
Gilmour, David. *Curzon*. London 1994.
Graves, Philip. *The Life of Sir Percy Cox*. London 1941.
Kaye, J. W. *The Life and Correspondence of Major-General Sir John Malcolm*. 2 vols. London 1856.
Kaye, J. W. *Lives of Indian Officers*. 3 vols. London 1880–3.
McNeill, F. *Memoir of the Rt. Hon. Sir John McNeill and his second wife*. London 1910.
McKenzie Johnston, H. *Ottoman and Persian Odysseys*. London 1998.
Marlow, John. *Late Victorian. The Life of Sir Arnold Talbot Wilson*. London 1967.
Maxwell, Herbert. *The Hon. Sir Charles Murray*. London 1898.
Nicolson, Harold. *Sir Arthur Nicolson, Bt. First Lord Carnock*. London 1920.
Nicolson, Harold. *Curzon: The Last Phase*. London 1934.
Rawlinson, George. *A Memoir of Major-General Sir Henry Creswicke Rawlinson*. London 1898.
Ronaldshaw, Earl of. *The Life of Lord Curzon*. 3 vols. London 1928–9.
Sykes, Percy M. *Henry M. Durand 1850–1924*. London 1926.
Waterfield, Gordon. *Professional Diplomat. Sir Percy Loraine*. London 1973.

C. *History and Politics* (written during the Qajar period)
Browne, E. G. *The Persian Revolution of 1905–9*. Cambridge 1910.
Browne, E. G. *The Press and Poetry of Modern Iran*. Cambridge 1914.
Chirol, Valentine. *The Middle East Question*. London 1903.
Curzon, George N. *Persia and the Persian Question*. 2 vols. London 1892.

Fraser, James B. *A Historical and Descriptive Account of Persia.* Edinburgh 1834.
Hytier, A. D. *Les Dépêches diplomatiques du Comte de Gobineau en Perse.* Paris 1959.
Kaye, J. W. *History of the War in Afghanistan.* 3 vols. London 1878.
Kinneir, J. Macdonald. *A Geographical Memoir of the Persian Empire.* London 1813.
Kitto, John. *The People of Persia.* London 1849.
Malcolm, John. *History of Persia.* 2 vols. London 1815.
Markham, C. R. *A General Sketch of the History of Persia.* London 1874.
Rawlinson, Henry C. *England and Russia in the East.* London 1875.
Shuster, W. Morgan. *The Strangling of Persia.* London 1912.
Sykes, Percy M. *A History of Persia.* 2 vols. 2nd edition. London 1921.
Watson, R. C. *A History of Persia.* London 1866.

D. *History and Politics* (written after the Qajar period).
Amini, Iralj. *Napoleon and Persia.* London 1999.
Avery, Peter. *Modern Iran.* London 1965.
Bhariet, Julian. *Economic Development in Iran 1900–70.* Oxford 1971.
Bullard, Reader. *Britain and the Middle East.* London 1951.
Cottam, R. W. *Nationalism in Iran.* Pittsburgh 1964.
Gabriel, Alfons. *Die Erforshung Persiens.* Vienna 1952.
Gail, Marzieh. *Persia and the Victorians.* London 1951.
Greaves, Rose L. *Persia and the Defence of India 1884–92.* Oxford 1959.
Hoskins, H. L. *British Routes to India.* Philadelphia 1928.
Issawi, Charles (ed). *The Economic History of Iran 1800–1914.* Chicago 1971.
Kazemzadeh, F. *Russia and Britain in Persia 1864–1914.* Yale 1968.
Lambton, A. K. S. *Qajar Persia.* 1985.
Rabino, H. L. *Diplomatic and Consular Officers of Great Britain and Iran.* London 1946.
Searight, Sarah. *The British in the Middle East.* London 1969.
Wilson, Arnold T. *The Persian Gulf.* Oxford 1928.
Wright, Denis. *The Persians amongst the English.* London 1985.

Articles
Greaves, Rose L. British Policy in Persia 1892–1903. S.O.A.S.B. 1965.
Greaves, Rose L. Some Aspects of the Anglo-Russian Convention and its working in Persia, 1902–14. S.O.A.S.B. 1968.
Shadman, S. F. A Review of Anglo-Persian Relations 1798–1815. Proceedings of the Iran Society 1943.
Thornton, A. P. British Policy in Persia, 1858–90. *English Historical Review* 1954–5.

E. *Persian Sources*
H. Arfa, F. Kazemzadeh and S. F. Shadman, listed above, are among the few Persians who have written in English about Anglo-Persian relations during the Qajar period. Unfortunately no translations have yet appeared of works by writers who reflect the more extreme Persian view of British activities during this period. They include:
Mahmoud, Mahmoud. *Tarih-e-Ravabet-e-siyasi Iran ve Inglis dargarn-e-nuzdahom-e-*

miladi. (*The History of Political Relations between Iran and England in the 19th century*). 8 vols. Tehran 1957.
Rain, Ismail. *Huquq-e-Bagiran-e-Inglis dar Iran*. (*The Takers of British bribes in Iran*). Tehran 1969.
Sassani, Khan Malek. *Dast-e-Penhan-e-siyasat-e-Inglis dar Iran*. (*The Secret Hand of British Policy in Iran*). Tehran.

IV. BOOKS AND ARTICLES MAINLY OF INTEREST TO PARTICULAR CHAPTERS

Chapter 1. The British Interest in Persia
Marshman, J. C. *The History of India*. 3 vols. London 1867.
Minto, Countess of (ed). *Lord Minto in India*. London 1880.

Articles, etc.
Lambton, A. K. S. Sir John Malcolm & *The History of Persia*. B.I.P.S.J. 1995.
Majumdar, Anita. Lord Minto's Administration in India. Unpublished doctoral thesis. Oxford University.
Savory, R. M. British and French Diplomacy in Persia 1800 10. B.I.P.S.J. 1972.

Chapter 2. The Diplomatic Scene
Chesney, Francis R. *Narrative of the Euphrates Expedition*. London 1868.
Churchill, R. P. *The Anglo-Russian Convention*. Cedar Rapids 1939.
Oudendyk, William J. *Ways and By-Ways in Diplomacy*. London 1939.
Ouseley, Gore. *Biographical Notes on Persian Poets*. London 1846.

Articles
Allen, J. G. British Policy towards Persia in 1879. R.C.A.S.J. 1935.
Willock, H. D. Notes on the Willock Family. London 1902 (printed privately).
Yapp, M. E. The Control of the Persian Mission 1822–36, University of Birmingham. *Historical Journal* 1959–60.

Chapter 3. Formalities and Frictions
Gobineau, C. S. de. *Correspondance entre le Comte de Gobineau et le Comte de Prokesh-Orten (1854–1876)*. Paris 1933.
Murzban, M. M. *The Parsis in India*. Madras 1917.
Karaka, D. F. *History of the Parsis*. 2 vols. London 1884.

Articles
Lambton, Ann K. S. The Case of Jajji ' Abd al-Karim. *Iran and Islam*. Edinburgh 1971.
Wright, Denis, Sir John Malcolm & the Order of the Sun. B.I.P.S.J. 1979 and 1981.

Chapter 4. Wars and Warriors
Armstrong, T. B. *Journal of Travels in the seat of war during the last two campaigns of Russia and Turkey*. London 1831.
Brock, William. *A Biographical Sketch of Sir Henry Haverlock*. London 1858.
Cook, K. C. B. *The North Staffordshire Regiment*. London 1970.
English, Barbara. *John Company's Last War*. London 1971.

Bibliography

Hunt, G. H. *Outram and Havelock's Persian Campaign*. London 1858.
Kotzebue, M. von. *Narrative of a Journey into Persia in the Suite of the Imperial Russian Embassy in 1817* (trans.). London 1819.
Lambrick, H. T. *John Jacob of Jacobabad*. London 1960.
Lumsden, T. *A Journey from Merut in India to London during the years 1819 and 1820*. London 1822.
Macdonald, Robert. *Personal Narrative of Military Travel in Turkey and Persia*. Edinburgh 1859.
Monteith, William. *Kars and Erzerum*. London 1856.

Articles
Campbell, J. G. The Russo-Persian Frontier 1810. R.C.A.S.J. 1931.
Gibbons, R. Routes in Kirman etc. in the years 1831 and 1832. R.G.S.J. 1841.

Chapter 5. Uncrowned King of the Persian Gulf
Anderson, T. S. *My Wanderings in Persia*. London 1880.
Busch, B. C. *Britain and the Persian Gulf 1894–1914*. California 1967.
Hay, Rupert. *The Persian Gulf States*. Washington 1959.
Kelly, J. B. *Britain and the Persian Gulf 1795–1880*. Oxford 1968.
Moore, Benjamin B. *From Moscow to the Persian Gulf*. New York 1915.
Wright, Denis. *Samuel Manesty & his unauthorised Embassy*. B.I.P.S.J. 1986.

Articles
Burrell, R. M. Britain, Iran and the Persian Gulf. From *The Arabian Peninsula*. D. Hopwood (ed). London 1972.
Fraser, Lovat. Gun-Running in the Persian Gulf. R.C.A.S.J. 1911.
Law, H. D. G. Bushire and the Year of Transition in the Persian Gulf (1922). *Iran Society Journal* Jan. 1954.

Chapter 6. Consuls, Khans and Communities
Kennion, R. L. *By Mountain, Lake and Plain*. London 1911.
Morgan, Gerald. *Nay Elias*. London 1971.
Neligan, A. R. *Hints for Residents and Travellers in Persia*. London 1914.
Pahlavi, H.I.H. Princess Soraya. *Autobiography*. London 1963.
Platt, D. C. M. *The Cinderella Service. British Consuls since 1825*. London 1971.
Pollington, Viscount. *Half Round the Old World*. London 1867.
Warzee, Dorothy de. *Peeps into Persia*. London 1912.
Yate, C. E. *Khurasan and Sistan*. London 1900.

Articles
Garthwaite, G. R. The Bakhtiari Khans, the Government of Iran and the British 1846–1915. I.J.M.E.S. 1972.
Wright, Denis. Memsahibs in Persia. R.C.A.S.J. 1983: Burials & Memorials of the British in Persia. B.I.P.S.J. 1998–1999.

Chapter 7. The World of Business

Ainsworth, W. F. *The River Karun.* London 1890.
Edwards, A. C. *The Persian Carpet.* London 1953.
Jones, Geoffrey. *Ben-King & Empire in Iran.* London 1986.
Keddie, Nikki R. *Religion and Rebellion in Iran. The Tobacco Protest of 1891–92.* London 1966.
Longhurst, Henry. *Adventure in Oil.* London 1959.
Longrigg, Stephen. *Oil in the Middle East.* Oxford 1961.
Schwartz, Benjamin (ed). *Letters from Persia 1828–55.* New York 1942.
Whigham, H. J. *The Persian Problem.* London 1903.

Articles

Diplomaticus. The Imperial Bank of Persia. *Asiatic Quarterly Review* 1889.
Frechtling, L. E. The Reuter Concession in Persia. *Asiatic Review* 1938.
Issawi, C. The Tabriz-Trabzon Trade 1830–1900. I.J.M.E.S. 1970.
Lambton, Ann K. S. Persian Trade under the Early Qajars. From *Islam and the Trade of Asia.* D. S. Richards (ed). Oxford 1970.
Lambton, Ann K. S. The Tobacco Regie. *Studia Islamica* 1965.
Selby, W. B. Account of the Ascent of the Karun and Dizful rivers. R.G.S.J. 1844.
Walter, V. A. A Brief History of the British Bank of the Middle East. *Journal of the Iran Society* 1954.
Wright, Denis. Trebizond and the Persian Transit Trade. R.C.A.S.J. 1944.

Chapter 8. Missionaries and Doctors

Bird, Mary R. S. *Persian Women and their Creed.* London 1899.
Cash, W. Wilson. *Persia Old and New.* London 1929.
Elgood, Cyril. *A Medical History of Persia and the Eastern Caliphate.* Cambridge 1951.
Gordon, Peter. *Fragment of the Journal of a tour through Persia in 1820.* London 1833.
Groves, Anthony. *Journal of a Residence at Baghdad during the Years 1830 and 1831.* London 1832.
Hume-Griffith, M. E. *Behind the Veil in Persia and Turkish Arabia.* London 1909.
Isaacs, A. A. *Biography of the Rev. Henry Aaron Stern.* London 1886.
Lee, Sidney. *King Edward the Seventh.* 2 vols. London 1925.
Maclean, Fitzroy. *A Person from England.* London 1958.
Magnus, Philip. *King Edward the Seventh.* London 1964.
Rice, Clara C. *Mary Bird in Persia.* London 1916.
Ross, Elizabeth N. M. *A Doctor in Bakhtiari Land.* London 1921.
Ryland, J. E. *Memoirs of John Kitto.* London 1856.
Sargent, J. *Memoir of the Rev. Henry Martyn: D.D.* London 1819.
Stern, H. A. *Dawnings of Light in the East.* London 1854.
Waterfield, Robin. *Christians in Persia.* London 1973.
Wilberforce, S. (ed). *Rev. Henry Martyn. D.D. Journals and Letters.* 2 vols. London 1837.

Articles

Dunlop, D. M. The strange case of Dr. Joseph Wolff. R.C.A.S.J. 1947.

Bibliography

Chapter 9. The Electric Telegraph and other Innovations

Articles
Harford, L. W. Overland Cable from Bushire to Baghdad. *Geographical Magazine.* 1970.
Scarce, J. Travels with Telegraph and Tiles in Persia. *Arts and Archaeology Research Papers.* 1973.
Simpson, M. G. The Work of the Indo-European Telegraph Department. *Journal of the Royal Society of Arts.* 1928.
Smith, R. Murdoch. Sketch of the History of Telegraphic Communication between the U.K. and India. *The Scottish Geographical Magazine.* 1889.

Chapter 10. Frontier Makers
Curzon, Robert. *Armenia. A Year at Erzerum on the Frontiers of Russia, Turkey and Persia.* London 1854.
Edmonds, C. J. *Kurds, Turks and Arabs.* Oxford 1957.
Goldsmid, F. J. (ed). *Eastern Persia 1870–72.* London 1876.
Holdich, Thomas. *The Indian Borderland.* London 1901.
Hubbard, G. E. *From the Gulf to Ararat.* London 1917.
Loftus, W. K. *Travels and Researches in Chaldea and Susiana.* London 1857.
McCormick, Donald. *The Incredible Mr. Kavanagh.* London 1960.

Articles
Edmonds, C. J. The Travels of Arthur M. Kavanagh in Kurdistan and Luristan in 1850. R.C.A.S.J. 1949.
Edmonds, C. J. The Iraqi-Persian Frontier 1639–1928. R.C.A.S.J. 1975.

Chapter 11. Some Travellers
Arberry, A. J. *Oriental Essays.* London 1960.
Barr, Pat. *A Curious Life for a Lady. The Story of Isabella Bird.* London 1970.
Blanford, W. T. (ed). *Eastern Persia 1870–72.* London 1876.
Budge, E. A. Wallis. *The Rise and Progress of Assyriology.* London 1925.
Holdich, Thomas. *The Gates of India.* London 1910.
Lloyd, Seton. *Foundations in the Dust.* Oxford 1947.
MacGregor, C. M. *Narrative of a Journey through the Province of Khorassan in 1875.* 2 vols. London 1879.
Middleton, Dorothy. *Victorian Lady Travellers.* London 1965.
Rose, Kenneth. *Superior Person.* London 1969.
Sayce, A. M. *The Archaeology of the Cuneiform Inscriptions.* London 1907.
Stewart, C. E. *Through Persia in Disguise.* London 1911.
Stoddart, Anna M. *The Life of Isabella Bird.* London 1906.
Tate, G. P. *The Frontiers of Baluchistan.* London 1909.
Waterfield, Gordon. *Layard of Nineveh.* London 1963.
Yate, C. E. *Khurasan and Sistan.* London 1900.

Articles
Barnett, R. D. Sir Robert Ker Porter—Regency Artist and Traveller. B.I.P.S.J. 1972.
Davis, H. W. C. The Great Game in Asia. British Academy. Raleigh Lecture 1918.
Javadi, Hassan. E. G. Browne and the Persian Constitutional Movement. B.I.P.S.J. 1976.
Morgan, Gerald. Myth and Reality in the Great Game. R.C.A.S.J. 1973.
Wright, Denis. James Baillie Fraser: Traveller, Writer & Artist. B.I.P.S.J. 1994.

Chapter 12. World War I and the End of an Era
Balfour, J. M. *Recent Happenings in Persia*. London 1922.
Busch, B. C. *Mudros to Lausanne*. New York 1976.
Dickson, W. E. R. *East Persia. A Backwater of the Great War*. London 1924.
Donohoe, M. H. *With the Persian Expedition*. London 1919.
Dunsterville, L. C. *The Adventures of Dunsterforce*. London 1920.
Dyer, R. E. *The Raiders of the Sarhad*. London 1921.
French, F. J. F. *From Whitehall to the Caspian*. London 1920.
Ghani, Cyrus. *Iran & the Rise of Reza Shah*. London 1998.
Hale, F. *From Persian Uplands*. London 1920.
Ironside, Lord (ed). *High Road to Command. The Diaries of Major-General Sir Edmund Ironside 1920–22*. London 1972.
James, F. *Faraway Campaign*. London 1934.
Lenczowski, G. *Russia and the West in Iran 1918–48*. Cornell 1948.
Lesueur, Emile. *Les Anglais en Perse*. Paris 1921.
Moberly, F. J. *The Campaign in Mesopotamia*. 4 vols. London 1923.
Moberly, F. J. *Official History of the War. Operations in Persia 1914–1919*. London.
Olson, W. J. *Anglo-Persian Relations during World War I*. London 1984.
Skrine, Clarmont. *World War in Iran*. London 1962.
Sykes, Christopher. *Wassmuss*. London 1936.
Ullman, R. H. *The Anglo-Soviet Accord*. Princeton 1972.
Wilber, D. N. *Riza Shah Palhavi. The Resurrection and Reconstruction of Iran*. Hicksville 1975.

Articles, etc.
Bullard, Reader. Persia in the two World Wars. R.C.A.S.J. 1963.
Douglas, J. A. The Operations on the Bushire-Shiraz Road 1918–19. R.C.A.S.J. 1923.
Dunsterville, L. C. Military Mission to N.W. Persia. R.C.A.S.J. 1921.
Edmonds, C. J. The Persian Gulf. Prelude to the Zimmerman Telegram. R.C.A.S.J. 1960.
Ellis, C. H. The Transcaspian Episode. R.C.A.S.J. 1959.
Haig, Wolseley. Reminiscences of Persia during the War. Unpublished book (available at St Antony's College, Oxford).
Norris, David. Caspian Naval Expedition 1918–19. R.C.A.S.J. 1923.
Safiri, Floreeda. The South Persia Rifles. Unpublished doctoral thesis. Edinburgh University.

INDEX

Abadan, *see* Anglo-Persian Oil Company
Abbas *Mirza* (Crown Prince), *see* under Qajar
Abbott, Keith, 79, 80, 98
Abbott, William George, 80
Abdol Hossein *Mirza* (Prince), *see* Farman Farma
Aberdeen, Lord, 52, 152
Abol Ghassem Khan, *see* Nasir ul-Mulk
Adcock, Sir Hugh, 125
Adrianople, Treaty of, 95
Afghanistan, 1, 3–5, 7, 14, 143 *et seq.*, 173, 177. *See also* Herat
Aganoor family, 78
Agha Muhammad Shah, *see* under Qajar
Ahmad Shah, *see* under Qajar
Ahwaz, 11, 41, 84, 101, 109, 172
Akbar *Mirza* (Prince), *see* Sarem ed-Dowleh
Alam, Amir Muhammad Ibrahim Khan, *see* Shaukat ul-Mulk
Alison, Charles, 25–8, 37, 46, 90, 129
Anglo-Persian Oil Co. Ltd. (A.P.O.C.), xiii, 10–11, 71, 86, 109–10, 125–6, 128, 171–2; Abadan refinery, 71, 109, 171–2; Persian view of, 111; pipe line, 109–10, 172. *See also* Oil
Anglo-Persian relations, British and Persian attitudes, xiv–v, 10–11, 15–16, 18–20, 30, 107, 111–12, 119, 127, 134, 145, 154–5, 164, 169–70, 178; causes of friction, 32–48, 57–9, 61, 78, 88, 102–3, 106–7, 130–1, 136, 138, 147–8; commercial, 2, 4–5, 10–11, 29, 79–80, 94–112; rupture of relations, xiii, 15, 24, 43, 58–9, 76, 124. *See also* Frontiers of Persia, Persian Gulf, Tribes
Anglo-Persian Treaties etc., of 1801, 3–5, 94; of 1809, 5–10; of 1812, 14; of 1814 (Treaty of Tehran), 16, 18, 20, 58, 139; of 1841 (Commercial Treaty), 76–7, 95; of 1857 (Peace Treaty), 24, 43, 61, 77; on slavery, 70; on frontiers, 140, 144–6; on telegraph, 129, 131–2; of 1919 (Curzon Agreement), 31, 178–9
Anglo-Persian War of 1856–7, 24, 42–3, 58–61, 77, 128
Anglo-Russian Convention of 1907, xiv–v, 30, 48, 164, 171, 179
Anglo-Russian rivalry; xiv, 3, 19, 22, 30, 40, 44, 46, 56–8, 76–7, 82–3, 87–8, 95, 136–7, 143, 162, 165. *See also* India (defence of)
Anglo-Russian Secret Agreement of 1915, 177n
Arabistan, *see* Khuzistan
Archaeological sites, Bisitun, 25, 78, 153, 156–7, 159; Naqsh-e-Rustam, 151, 153; Nineveh, 25, 157; Pasagardae (Cyrus' Tomb), 152; Persepolis, 151, 153, 156; Shapur (cave), 151, 152n; Susa (Shush, Shusan), 141, 151, 158–9; Takht-e-Suleiman, 153, 156; Taq-e-Bustan, 153, 159
Ardebil, 53, 55, 153; carpet, 100n
Armenians, 44–6, 51, 55, 98, 108, 117–19, 123, 131; in Julfa, 89, 115, 118–19, 169. *See also* Aganoor family, Cemeteries
Armstrong, Robert, 51, 54
Aslanduz, battle of, 1812, 53–4
Assyrians (Nestorians), 44, 46, 177. *See also* Missionaries

Babis, *see* Bahais
Badger, Rev. G. P., 121

211

Bahais, 44, 120, 164
Bakhtiari khans and tribe. *See* under Tribes
Baluchistan, 1, 132, 142 *et seq.*, 150-1, 173
Bandar Abbas, 2, 41, 66-7, 136n, 175
Banks, *Banque d'Escomte de Perse*, 105n; Imperial Bank of Persia, 10-11, 89, 104, 106, 173-4; New Oriental Banking Corporation, 104
Basidu (Bassadore), 66
Bast (Sanctuary), 41, 44, 46, 47, 48, 133
Bateman-Champain, Brigadier Hugh, 180
Bateman-Champain, Sir John, 129, 130n
Bell brothers, 124
Bell, Gertrude, 81, 92
Bird, Isabella (Mrs Bishop), 89, 149, 166-70
Bird, Mary, 120-1, 166
Birjand, 87, 173
Blandford, W. T., 144
Bonham, Edward, 79, 97
Brant, James, 79, 95, 124n
British communities in Persia; 88-93, 134, 174-5
British India Steam Navigation Co., 100
British-Indian Post Offices. *See* under Communications
British Mission (Legation), Gulhek, 23, 27-8, 47, 90; Lar Valley camp, 28, 91; Tehran, 13, 26-7, 99
British Navy, 10, 74, 110, 171
Browne, Professor E. G., xv, 107, 149, 163-5
Bruce, Rev. Robert, 118-19, 166
Bruce, Lt. William, 63-4
Brydges, Sir Harford Jones, *see* under Jones
Burgess, Charles, 96-7, 112
Burgess, Edward, 96-8
Burmah Oil Company, 108
Burnes, Lt. Alexander, 101n
Bushire, Anti-British demonstrations, 64, 127; British occupation of, 60, 173; British Residency, 2-3, 19, 73-4, 122; British hospital, 127; port of entry for Tehran, 4. *See also* Persian Gulf

Cadogan, Henry, 92n
Campbell, Dr James, 54-5, 122-3

Campbell, Sir John, 18-19, 21, 36, 76, 89n
Canning, Sir Stratford, 25
Capitulary rights (capitulations), 41-2, 88, 185. *See also* Consuls (consular courts), Protection
Carpet industry, 99-100, 112
Cemeteries, Armenian, 26, 55, 92-3, 98; Protestant, 92n
Chahbahar, 41, 67, 136n, 144, 150. *See also* Baluchistan
Chesney, Colonel Francis, 28, 101n; Euphrates expedition, 28n, 98n
Christians in Persia. *See* under Armenians, Assyrians, Cemeteries, Missionaries
Churchill, H. A., 81, 141; and sons (Harry, George, Sydney), 81
Christie, Capt. Charles, 50, 52-3, 150
Clarendon, Lord, 34, 60, 69
Clarke, Mr, 51
Communications, Postal services, 71, 82, 135-6; Railways, 10, 38, 101-2, 135-7; Roads, 135, 137-8, 176 (*see also* Lynch Bros.); Shipping, 57, 100-1, 135; Trade routes, 83-5, 94-6, 101-2; Telegraph, 10, 89, 128-35, 143 (*see also* Indo-European Telegraph Dept.)
Concessions. *See* under Banks, Communications (roads), Mining, Payments by British, Reuter, Tobacco
Connolly, Captain Arthur, 117n
Consuls and Consulates (British), Ahwaz, 84; Astarabad (Gorgan), 81; Bam, 71; Bandar Abbas, 71; Bushire 64n; Erzerum, 79, 95; Isfahan, 84-6, 89, 101, 174; Kerman, 87, 174; Kermanshah, 84, 174; Mashad, 40, 82-3, 173; Mohammerah (Khoramshahr), 84-5; Rasht, 80, 105n; Shiraz, 45, 87, 174; Sistan (Birjand and Nusratabad), 40, 83, 87, 173; Tabriz, 46-7, 76-7, 79-80, 83; Tehran, 75, 79; Trebizond, xiii, 76, 95-6; Torbat-e-Haideri, 87; Yazd, 87, 174; consular courts, 88-9; consular escorts (*sowars*), 40-1, 88, 173; dispensaries, 126; duties, 75, 83-4, 88; need for, 75-7; in World War I, 174. *See also Bast*, Capitulary rights, Native Agents, Protection

212

Index

Cormick, Dr John, 46, 50, 53-5, 122-3
Cormick, Dr William, 124
Cossacks, *see* Military Escorts, Persian Cossack Brigade
Cotton, Sir Dodmore, 2
Cox, Sir Percy, 25, 31, 71, 179
Curzon, George N., Marquess C. of Kedleston, 11, 20, 25, 27, 82, 89, 100, 149, 181; Anglo-Persian Agreement, 31, 178-9; refuses to land, 34; travels in Persia, 165-6; views on frontier-making, 148, oil, 108, Reuter concession, 102, Telegraph Dept., 133-134, Persians, 154-5, Political Resident, 73-4; *Persia and the Persian Question*, 68, 106, 154, 165, 170
Curzon, Hon. Robert, 140
Cyrus the Great, 37, 39, 152

d'Arcy, Major Joseph, 13, 50-3
d'Arcy, William, 85n, 107-9
Decorations and Orders, 38-9, 72, 124-5. *See also* Lion and Sun
Demavend, Mt., 28, 91
Dickson, Sir Joseph, 124
Dickson, William, 124; father of Major-General W. E. R. Dickson, 124n
Doctors, 21, 117-18, 122, 124-7
Dolmage, Colonel J. de G., 89n
Downe, Lord, 125
Drouville, Major Gaspard, 50, 52
Drummond, Henry, 116
Drummond Wolff, Sir Henry, *see* Wolff
Dunsterville, Major-General L. C., 177-8
Durand, Sir Mortimer, 25, 30, 44, 78, 90, 161
Durand, Lady, 37, 161
Dyer, Brigadier-General R. E., 173n

East India Company (E.I.C.), 2-3, 5, 8, 12, 18-19, 62-3, 75, 77, 94, 122. *See also* India
East Persia Cordon, 173-4, 177
Eastwick, Edward B., 26n, 42
Edwards, Arthur, 2
Elias, Ney, 82
Ellis, Sir Henry, 15, 20, 34, 76
Ethersley, Commodore, 60

Farman Farma, Abdol Hossein *Mirza* (Prince) 175n, 179n
Farrant, Colonel Francis, 22, 56-7, 140
Fath Ali Shah. *See* under Qajar
Finkenstein, Treaty of, 5, 49
Firuz, *Mirza* (Prince), *see* Nosrat ed-Dowleh
Foreign Office, 11, 25, 45-7, 103, 151; control of Tehran Mission, 6, 8, 12, 18-20, 36-7, 63, 83
Fraser, J. Baillie, 149, 153, 155, 157
Fraser, Major-General W. A. K., 176
Frontiers of Persia, British role in delimiting, 139-48

Gardane, General, 5, 6, 38n
Gazetteers, 162-3
Gholams (mounted messengers), 40, 135
Gibbons, Sgt. Richard, 56
Gobineau, Count de, 43, 155n
Goldsmid, Sir Frederic, 131, 144-5
Gordon, Captain Peter, 114-15, 123n
Gordon, Hon. Robert, 13, 52-3, 152
Graham, Sir Ronald, 29
Grant, Captain W. P., 150-1
Gray, Paul & Co., 85, 100, 101n; associated with Gray, Dawes & Co., 83, 100
Grey, Sir Edward, 30
Groves, Anthony, 115
Gulestan, Treaty of, 15, 16, 55, 76, 139
Gulhek, *see* under British Mission (Legation)

Hajji Abd al-Karim, 43
Hajji Baba of Isfahan, *see* under Morier
Hammond, Sgt. William, 56
Hanway, Jonas, 2
Hardinge, Sir Arthur, 29, 40, 108
Hardinge of Penshurst, Lord Charles, 29-30
Hart, Major Isaac, 46, 54, 56, 57n, 85, 96
Hastings, Marquis of, Lord Moira, 53
Havelock, Sir Henry, 60
Hector, Alexander, 98
Hennell, Samuel, 70
Henjam island, *see* under Persian Gulf (Islands)
Herat, 4, 21-2, 36, 55, 58-9, 61, 64,

213

69, 82, 150, 159; war over, 59–61. See also Afghanistan
Hoernle, Dr E. F., 118
Holdich, Sir Thomas, 146–7
Hotz & Son, 99
Humayun, Sardar, 181

Imperial Bank of Persia, see under Banks
Imperial Tobacco Corporation, 107
India, Army, 65–7, 171–3, 175–8, 180; Defence of, xiv, 3–4, 7, 10–11, 19, 30, 56, 71, 81, 136, 142–3, 149–53, 162–3, 165, 171, 173, 177; Govt. of, 3n, 62n; Medical Service, 126–7; Mutiny, 20, 61, 128; Persian dislike of British from India, 20, 30; Political Service, 62, 79, 82–3, 88, 146; Trade with Persia, 4, 87, 94, 105, 126. See also Anglo-Russian rivalry, Bushire, East India Co., Foreign Office, Herat, Military Missions, Persian Gulf
Indo-European Telegraph Co., 11, 130n, 133
Indo-European Telegraph Dept., 11, 27, 40–1, 46, 67, 78, 89–91, 126; negotiations, 129, 131–2; erection of line, 130–3; staff, 133–4
Ironside, Sir Edmund, 38, 180–4
Isaacs, Rev. A. A., 154
Isfahan, 2–3, 101–2, 126, 150, 174. See also Armenians (Julfa), Consuls, Missionaries (C.M.S.)

Jacob, Brigadier-General John, 60
Ja'far Ali Khan, 77
Jangalis, 177
Jews, 44–5, 114–18. See also Missionaries
Jones, Sir Harford, 5–9, 12, 34, 35, 37, 40, 49, 52, 69, 95
Jukes, Dr Andrew, 8, 63, 122–3, 153
Julfa, see under Armenians

Karguzars, 88. See also Capitulary Rights
Karun River, 11, 30, 38, 82, 84, 101–2, 136, 161
Kavanagh, Arthur, 141
Kazemzadeh, Firuz, xv
Keir, Sir William, 64
Ker Porter, Sir Robert, 149, 152, 156
Keswick, William, 104

Khamseh Tribal Confederation, see under Tribes
Khans, see Tribes (Bakhtiari), Oil
Kharg Island, 7, 58–61, 64, 69, 159–60
Khoshab, battle of, 60
Khuzistan, 30, 41, 57, 71, 84, 86, 111, 172
Kinneir, Sir John Macdonald, see under Macdonald
Kitto, Dr John, 115
Kurds, 17, 46, 54, 57, 96, 121–2, 142

Lansdowne, Lord, 71
Lascelles, Sir Frank, 29, 30, 92
Layard, Sir Henry, 25, 85, 149, 155, 157–62
Levant Company, 17, 75
Lindley, Dr Lennox, 125
Lindesay-Bethune, Sir Henry, 50, 52–8, 104n
Lindsay, Lt. Henry, see Lindesay-Bethune
Lingeh, 41, 78; Shaikh of, 65
Lion and Sun, Order of, 17, 18, 38, 54
Loftus, W. K., 141
London Persia Committee, 164
Loraine, Sir Percy, xv, 37
Lorimer, Capt. David L. R., 84
Lorimer, J. G., 163n
Lovett, Major Beresford, 81n, 144n
Lynch Brothers, 11, 100–1, 138; Lynch road, 85–6, 101–2; Lynch, T. K. and H. F. B., 164n

Macdonald, Sir John Kinneir, 18, 21, 35, 45, 151
McDouall, William, 84
Mackenzie, Capt. Charles, 80
Mackenzie, Sir George, 85
MacLean, Canon A. J., 121
MacLean, Major-General Charles, 82, 146
MacLeod, Lt. John, 63
McMahon, Sir Henry, 145–6
McNeill, Sir John, 19, 21–2, 28, 34, 36, 57–8, 76, 114, 123–4, 158
McNeil, Lady, 21, 89n
Majles (National Assembly), 47–8, 179, 184
Makran, see Baluchistan
Malcolm, Sir John, 4–10, 40, 69, 113,

214

Index

156-7; 1st Mission to Persia, 4, 32, 34, 94, 149-50; 2nd Mission, 5-7, 49; 3rd Mission, 8, 18n, 38, 49-50, 150-1
Malkom Khan, 102, 107
Malleson, Sir Wilfred, 177
Manesty, Samuel, 63
Martyn, Rev. Henry, 14, 113-14
Mashad, *see* under Consuls
Masjid-e-Suleiman (M.I.S.), 10, 84, 109, 141. *See also* Oil
Masud *Mirza* (Prince), *see* Zill ul-Sultan
Medical and Quarantine Services, 118, 120, 122-7
Mehdi Ali Khan, 4
Military escorts, British, 4, 32-3, 39-40, 73, 82, 146; Russian, 40. *See also* Consuls, *Gholams*
Military Missions, British, 3, 13-14, 17, 22, 49-58, 85, 96, 117n, 155, 178, 181n; withdrawal, 40, 58-9, 89, 179; Military Supplies (British), 7, 49-53, 57; French Mission, 5, 49
Mining, 10, 55, 103-4, 107-8
Minto, Lord, 6
Mir Ali Naqi Khan, 42
Mirza Abul Hasan, 7, 13
Mirza Hashem Khan, 23-4, 42
Missionaries, 113-22; Archbishop of Canterbury's Assyrian Mission, 121-2; Church Missionary Society (C.M.S.), 118-22; London Society for Promoting Christianity among the Jews, 55, 114, 116-18; French and American, 114, 119, 121
Mitford, Edward, 157-9
Mohammerah (Khoramshahr), 60, 84-5, 109, 140
Mohammerah, Shaikh Ghazal of, 43, 71-2, 85-6, 109, 111, 126, 172
Montefiore, Sir Moses, 45
Monteith, Colonel William, 50, 53-5, 139-40, 156n
Morier, James, 6, 7, 13, 15, 17, 23, 122, 149, 151-2; *Hajji Baba of Isfahan*, 7, 17
Moscovy Company, 2
Muhammad Taqi Khan, *see* Tribes (Bakhtiari)
Murdoch Smith, Sir Robert, 93, 130, 134-5

Murray, Sir Charles, 23-4, 34, 36, 42, 60, 91
Muzaffar ed-Din Shah (*Mirza*), *see* under Qajar

Napoleon Bonaparte, 4, 6, 15, 53, 149
Nasir ed-Din Shah (*Mirza*), *see* under Qajar
Nasir ul-Mulk, Abol Ghassem Khan, 81n
Nationalism, 31, 106-7, 110, 127, 133, 136, 174-8
Native Agents or News Writers, 77-9. *See also* Consuls
Nau Ruz (New Year), 36, 39, 147
Neligan, Dr A. R., 125
Nestorians, *see* Assyrians, Missionaries
Nicolson, Arthur, Lord Carnock, 29
Nicolson, Sir Harold, 166n; Lady Nicolson, 184
Nisbet, Alexander, 57n, 115n
Norman, Herman, 31, 179n, 180, 184
Norperforce, 178-81
Norris, Commodore D. T., 177
Nosrat ed-Dowleh, Firuz *Mirza* (Prince), 20, 179n

O'Connor, Sir Frederick, 41, 174
Odling, Dr Thomas, 125n
Oil, 84-5, 104, 107-9. *See also* Anglo-Persian Oil Co. Ltd.
Oriental Carpet Manufacturers Ltd. (O.C.M.), 100. *See also* Carpet industry
Ouseley, Sir Gore, 8, 12-15, 19, 26, 33, 35, 37, 40, 50-1, 75, 113, 151
Ouseley, Lady, 13-14, 89n, 151
Ouseley, Sir William, 13, 149, 151-2
Outram, Sir James, 60-1

Pahlavi, H.I.M. Muhammad Reza Shah, xiv, 152n
Pahlavi, H.I.M. Reza Shah (Reza Khan), xiv, 72, 87, 127, 134n, 137n, 179, 181-4
Palmerston, Lord, 24, 46, 59, 153
Paris Peace Conference of 1919, 11, 178
Parsees, *see* Zoroastrians
Pasley, Capt. Charles, 49
Passmore, Colonel, 56-7
Payments by British, for concessions, 102-3, 106-8; to individuals, 35-6,

215

132, 175n, 179, 180n; to tribes, 86, 132, 170; subsidies and other payments to Persian Government, 7, 14–16, 19, 49–50, 87, 175, 180n
Persian Bank Mining Rights Corporation Ltd., *see* Mining
Persian Carpet Manufacturing Co., 99
Persian Cossack Brigade, 48, 174, 178n, 180–4
Persian Gulf, British interests, 2–3, 62–74, 171–2; disputes over islands, 65–9; gun-running, 70–1; naval forces, 65–6, 69, 73–4; naval landings, 40–1, 58, 60, 67; Piracy, 63–6; Political Resident, 4, 19–20, 41, 62–4, 68–74, 94; Post offices, 135–6; Slavery, 69–70; Treaties with shaikhs, 62–3, 65, 70. *See also* Bushire
Persian Gulf Trading Co., 100
Persian Press, 97–8, 133
Persian Railway Syndicate, 11, 137. *See also* Communications
Persian Road and Transport Co., 138. *See also* Lynch Bros.
Persian studies and antiquities, 13, 18n, 134–5, 151–3, 155–6, 159, 163–4. *See also* Archaeological Sites
Persian Zoroastrian Amelioration Society of Bombay, 44. *See also* Zoroastrians
Perso-Russian relations, 19, 81–2, 95, 103, 107, 136–7; Attacks by Russia, 5, 7, 14, 16; British as intermediaries, 15–16; Cossack escorts, 40; Russian Consulates, 71n, 76, 82, 87–8; Railway Agreement, 137; World War I, 171, 177–8. *See also* Persian Cossack Brigade, Gulestan and Turkmanchai Treaties
Pierson, Capt. William, 27, 130
Plymouth Brethren, 115n
Polo, 90
Pottinger, Lt. Eldred, 58
Pottinger, Sir Henry, 150, 151
Preece, John, 85
Presents, 4, 6, 32, 34–8, 49
Protection by British, 27n, 41–5, 72, 75, 78, 88–9, 99. *See also* Bast, Capitulatory rights, Consuls and Consulates

Qajar dynasty, xiv, 3n, 153–4, 184
Qajar, Abbas *Mirza* (Crown Prince), 16, 49, 50–7, 95–6, 104, 124
Qajar, Agha Muhammad Shah; 3n, 12n
Qajar, Ahmad Shah, 66, 125, 182–4
Qajar, Fath Ali Shah, 4, 7, 12, 14, 16, 18, 19, 32–3, 49, 56, 69, 76, 114, 124
Qajar, Muhammad Ali Shah, 48
Qajar, Muhammad Shah (*Mirza*), 19–20, 27, 55n, 56–7
Qajar, Muzaffar ed-Din Shah, 125, 164
Qajar, Nasir ed-Din Shah (*Mirza*), 23, 39n, 44–5, 59, 91n, 97, 102–3, 107, 124, 129, 135, 144
Qashqai, *see* under Tribes
Qasimi Arabs and Shaikhs, 64–5, 68
Qavam ul-Mulk, 175n
Qishm island, *see* under Persian Gulf (islands)

Rabino, Joseph Rabino di Borgomale, 105; father of H. L. Rabino, 105n
Railways, *see* Communications
Ralli & Angelasto, 98–9
Rawlinson, Sir Henry, 22–3, 25, 36, 56–7, 78, 85, 155; deciphers cuneiform script, 153, 155–7
Religious minorities, *see* Armenians, Assyrians, Bahais, Jews, Zoroastrians
Reporter, Ardeshir, 45, 181
Reuter, Baron Julius de; 102–6, 136.
Reynolds, G. B., 109–10, 141
Reza Khan, Reza Shah, *see* under Pahlavi
Riach, Dr James, 123–4
Rich, Claudius, 92, 157
Ross, Sir E. Dennison, 164
Ross, Dr Elizabeth, 119
Royal Geographical Society, 56, 68, 156–7
Rumbold, Sir Horace, 29–30, 90
Russian Revolution of 1917, 177; Bolsheviks in Persia, 180–1, 183

St. John, Major O. B., 81n, 130n, 144n
Sadleir, Lt. G. Forster, 50
Safavid, Shah Abbas I, 2, 3, 94, 118n
Safavid, Tahmasp Shah, 2
Salisbury, Lord, 111
Sanctuary, *see* Bast
Sarem ed-Dowleh, Akbar *Mirza* (Prince), 179n
Sassoon and Co., David, 100n, 104

Index

Sawyer, Major Herbert, 166–9
Schindler, General A. Houtum, 106
Schroder and Co., 104
Scott, Charles, 91
Selby, Lt. W. B., 101n, 161
Shah Abbas, *see* under Safavid
Shahs of Persia, *see* under Pahlavi, Qajar, Safavid
Shaukat ul-Mulk, Amir Muhammad Ibrahim Khan Alam, 88
Shee, Captain Benjamin, 55
Sheil, Sir Justin, 22–3, 36, 46, 56–7, 80, 89n, 111, 117
Sheil, Lady, 22, 89n, 97–8
Shiraz, 2–3, 33, 41, 45, 63, 73, 113–15, 118, 174–6. *See also* under Consuls
Shirley brothers, 2
Siemens and Co., *see* Indo-European Telegraph Co.
Sistan, 142 *et seq.*, 150, 173. *See also* Consuls
Smart, Sir Walter, 41
Smith, Capt. C. B. Euan, 144
Smyth, Colonel Henry, 181–4
South Persia Rifles, 87n, 174–6, 178–9
Sowars (mounted escorts), *see* Consuls (Consular escorts), Military Escorts
Spring-Rice, Sir Cecil, 29, 30, 81n
Stalker, General, 60
Stern, Rev. Aaron, 117–18
Stevens, Charles, 100
Stevens, Francis, 79, 80
Stevens, George, 79–80, 98
Stevens, Hildebrand, 100
Stevens, Richard White, 46, 79–80, 98
Stewart, Col. Charles E., 81n, 162n
Stileman, Bishop C. H., 121; Memorial School, 120n
Stocqueler, J. H., 85
Stoddart, Colonel Charles, 56–7, 117n
Stone, Major, 13, 50, 53, 151
Strick and Co., 100n
Subsidies, *see* Payments by British
Sutherland, Major James, 52n
Sykes, Christopher, 44
Sykes, Ella, 87, 146–7
Sykes, Sir Percy M., 87, 90, 146–7, 154n, 174–6

Tabatabai, Sayyed Zia ed-Din, 183–4

Tabriz, 16n; *bast* at, 47; HQ of Military Mission, 50; arsenal, 51. *See also* Consuls
Tahmasp, Shah, *see* under Safavid
Talbot, Major Gerald, 106–7
Tangistanis, *see* under Tribes
Taqizadeh, Hasan, 48
Taylor, Miss, 115
Tehran, as capital, 3; European community, 88n, 89–92; Great *bast*, 47–8; Seat of British Mission, 13. *See also* British Mission, Consuls, Treaties
Thomson, Sir Ronald, 25, 28–9, 38
Thomson, Sir William Taylour, 23, 25, 28–9, 43
Tilsit, Treaty of, 6
Tobacco Concession (Regie), 10, 106–7
Todd, Major d'Arcy, 56–7
Trebizond, xiii–iv, 22, 57, 76, 79, 95–6, 101, 170
Tribes, Bakhtiari, 43–4, 57, 84–7, 101, 109, 111, 126, 159–60, 166, 169–70, 170n, 172, 176; Khamseh, 175; Luri, 84–5, 151, 161, 166; Qashqai, 131, 174–6; Shaqaqis, 57; Tangistani, 40, 172–4; Turkoman, 80–1. *See also* Kurds
Turkmanchai, Treaty of, 16, 21, 39, 41, 45, 55, 76, 95, 139

Urumiyah or Urmia (now Rezaieh), 45–6, 100, 121–2. *See also* Missionaries

Vicars, Murray, 117
Vansittart, Lord Robert, 29
Vusuq ed-Dowleh, 179n

Waring, E. Scott, 154
Wassmuss, Herr, 172, 174
Watts, Richard, 2
Wellesley, Arthur, Duke of Wellington, 3n, 6
Wellesley, Lord Richard, Earl of Mornington, 3, 50
Wilbraham, Capt. Richard, 57
Wild, J. W., 27
Williams, Sir Fenwick, 140–1
Wilson, Sir Arnold T., 41, 64, 84, 86, 109, 126, 137, 142
Willock, Sir Henry, 15–18, 21, 50, 54, 59, 65, 89n
Willock, Major George, 17–18, 50, 52, 54
Wills, Dr C. J., 78

Wolff, Sir Henry Drummond, 29–30, 39, 103, 106, 108, 136, 168
Wolff, Dr Joesph, 29, 116–17
Wratislaw, A. C., 142

Young, Dr M. Y., 125

Zia ed-Dın, Sayyed, *see* under Tabatabaı
Ziegler and Co., 99, 100
Zill ul-Sultan, Masud *Mirza* (Prince), 38, 43, 179n
Zoroastrians (Parsees, *guebres*), 44–5

THE THREE SODBURYS – AN INTRODUCTION

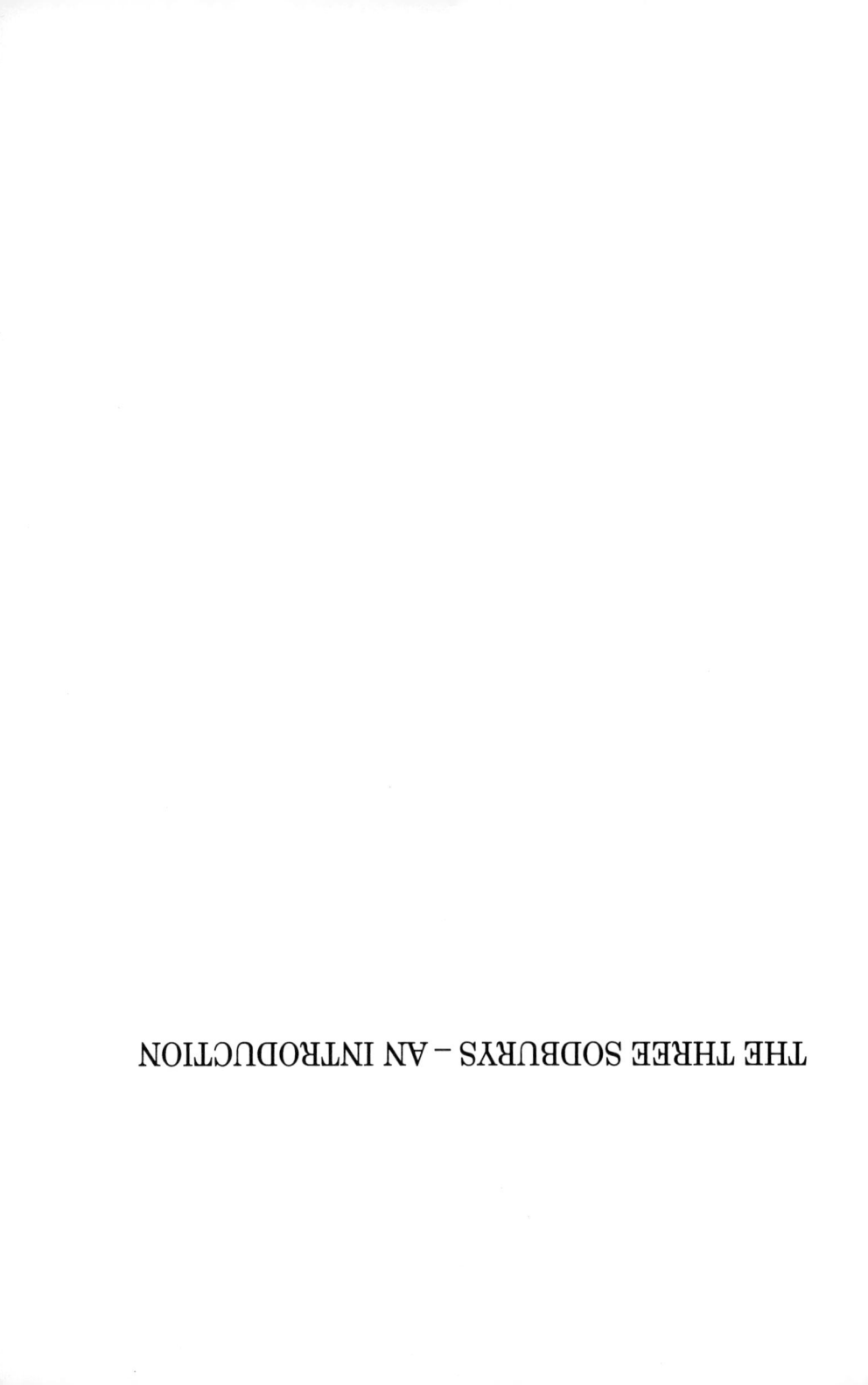